The Congress Founds the Navy, 1787–1798

THE CONGRESS FOUNDS THE NAVY 1787-1798

Marshall Smelser

University of Notre Dame Press · 1959

UNIVERSITY OF NOTRE DAME PRESS
NOTRE DAME, INDIANA

Library of Congress Catalog Card Number 58-14181

Preface

Naval historians have usually given little attention to the political shaping of national naval policy, and political historians (a more numerous species) have generally presented only the final decisions of naval policy without much investigation of the policy-making process. The result of these approaches to the study of American naval history has been the writing of a good deal of apolitical narrative, with emphasis on strategy, operations, technology, heroism—even patriotic slogans—but with very little on what the nation expected of the Navy and how the judgments on its mission were arrived at.

Because these methods have been followed a number of gallant naval officers have been elevated to the rank of fathers of the Navy, among them Jones, Truxtun, Barry, and some of their illustrious contemporaries. These gentlemen were fathers of naval customs and tactical practices but they were not the founders of the Navy. The United States Navy, like other navies, was not founded by sailors but by politicians, and the story of its founding must deal with politics. The Congress of the United States is authorized by the Constitution "to provide and maintain a navy." The making of naval policy is not merely ministerial but is political and therefore inevitably partisan. In the Federalist period the naval decisions were arrived at by the same methods which were used in making any other legislative judgments, and there seems no good reason for considering naval policy as a kind of public concern different from tariffs, public lands, Indian problems, banking, national debt, or any of the other great questions which engaged the attention of the country. On every one of these questions there were at one time or other at least two opposing views, the Federalist and the Republican. And the question of whether to provide and maintain a navy, as this study will try to show, was approached in the same partisan political spirit.

The fountain of policy was the Congress. Whether the members spoke their inmost convictions during their long debates on naval or other questions is a problem which falls outside the limits of historical method. As a knowledgeable group of successful men they no doubt said what they thought they ought to say in order to harmonize with the composite attitude of their constituents. Therefore, I believe, the historian of naval policy must use the Congress as his point of departure and reckon his course made good from there. He must use the *Annals of the Congress* as his Bowditch, and take what cross-bearings he can from private papers, executive reports, and newspapers, whenever a light or a headland looms through the political haze. The work is nearly all dead-reckoning; you never get a reliable celestial fix until naval policy is tested in a war.

The only book on the subject which is written according to these principles is that of Harold and Margaret Sprout, *The Rise of American Naval Policy, 1776–1918* (Princeton, 1939, rev. ed. 1946). Anyone who has read their book will see how large is my debt to them. As the explorers they logged all of the landfalls. My contribution has been to steer the same headings and to survey every rock, shoal, islet, and shore line they sighted, and to describe the results on a detailed chart.

I have had more assistance than anyone could deserve. The United States Naval Academy Committee for Naval History Fellowships supported the research for nine months from privately subscribed funds at its disposal, as their Forrestal Fellowship. The University of Notre Dame gave me a year's leave and augmented the Fellowship with its own subsidy. Rear Admiral W. R. Smedberg, III, U.S.N., Superintendent of the United States Naval Academy, took me into his faculty and made my working conditions superb. The Reverend Philip S. Moore, C.S.C., Vice President of the University of Notre Dame, in charge of Academic Affairs, and the Reverend Thomas T. McAvoy, C.S.C., Head of the Department of History, gave me every encouragement, moral and material.

The staffs of the Library of Congress, the United States Naval Academy Library, the University of Notre Dame Library, the Saint John's College Library, the Maryland State Library, and the National Archives exerted themselves beyond the call of duty. At Annapolis, Senior Professors William Shields and William Jeffreys, Professor and Librarian Vernon D. Tate, Professors E. B. Potter, Douglas Lacey, Wilson L. Heflin, Robert Daly, H. O. Werner, and Robert M. Langdon shared their facilities and their learning in many ways which eased my work. Dr. Percy Powell of the Division of Manuscripts of the Library of Congress was always helpful and sympathetic. In the National

Archives Dr. Buford Rowland and Mr. Harold W. Ryan (a college class-mate) made every visit a pleasure.

Dr. Walter Muir Whitehill, Captain Robert B. Madden, U.S.N., Professor Manning J. Dauer, Dr. James Morton Smith, Dr. John Hemphill, Mr. M. S. Anderson, and Dr. L. H. Butterfield deserve my gratitude for specific acts of assistance.

Thanks are due to the editors of the United States Naval Institute *Proceedings,* to the American Military Institute, publisher of *Military Affairs,* and to the editors of the *Maryland Historical Magazine,* for permission to reprint chapters I and IV, and Appendix A, which previously appeared in those periodicals in slightly different form. All direct quotations of John Adams, from the Adams Papers, are made with the permission of the Adams Manuscript Trust.

Captain Alan Nibbs, U.S.N., accepted me as a pampered passenger in his happy ship, the Department of English, History, and Government of the United States Naval Academy, and provided me with space and many services. I am profoundly grateful to his entire group. Some are officers by Act of Congress. Others are scholars by acts of university corporations. All are ladies and gentlemen by Act of God.

MARSHALL SMELSER

Annapolis, Maryland
Notre Dame, Indiana

Contents

Prologue

Through the spring of 1798 there were rumors and reports of French privateers off shore, at distances from two hundred miles out, right up to the high tide level. The American coast must have been a magnet for privateers as the rich early-season cargoes came from Europe, converging on half a dozen easily watched seaports.[1]

The ship *Nonpareil* was taken off Florida on 24 April by a Frenchman from Guadeloupe. All of the crew but five men were taken out and a new crew of two prize masters and fourteen men was put on board. Silas S. Webb, the *Nonpareil*'s supercargo, was one of the five left in her. He said the members of the prize crew were "very ignorant, except one of the prize masters, (who was an American)" and the only navigator of the lot.

Sturdy Silas soon devised an admirable scheme. After bribing the American navigator, Webb secretly emptied several of the water casks, and then announced a water-shortage. He advised his captors to steer for St. Augustine, in Spanish Florida, the nearest port where a prize-winning Frenchman would be welcomed by a sympathetic ally.

Writing later from Wilmington, North Carolina, the ingenious supercargo told his owners he had intended to take the ship into Savannah, "but falling to the northward I brought my ship in here, still making the wise believe it was St. Augustine, till I had got them snug into the river. I shall give you further accounts per next post, and ship new crew and proceed on to New York along shore." [2]

Unhappily, too few owners commanded the services of such sterling aides as Silas S. Webb. On 1 May a privateer took the trader *Favorite* two days out of Charleston, South Carolina.[3] Hardly had word of this capture been received when an American ship, bound north from Honduras, lay becalmed, close in to Edisto Island, off South Carolina. Her captain and several of his men rowed ashore and bought ten dollars worth of provisions. Gossiping with the farm wife they learned the militia were away to attend their monthly muster, and they told the good woman of the rumored presence of three privateers off the Carolina coast. Then they rowed back to their drifting ship, and with the first fair breeze sailed over the horizon of history. This story rolled northward up the coast, gathering new features with every retelling, until it reached Philadelphia in the middle of May, and ran like this: the fierce desperadoes of three French privateers, taking advantage of the absence of the militia, had swarmed ashore on Edisto Island and terrorized the undefended inhabitants, while picking up naval intelligence and poultry.[4] The mythical invasion of American soil promptly became forensic ammunition for the navy-minded members of the Congress.

On the eighth a privateer took a ship, one day out of New York. Three of the captive crew later swore the privateer's crew included twenty-seven American citizens. The captain tried to enlist the newcomers, but they resisted his cajoleries, and were set on shore. The Philadelphia *Gazette of the United States* proudly announced the intention of the three resistant sailors to join the infant United States Navy,[5] which at the moment had not a ship afloat.

But the frigate *United States* was nearing completion, as were other vessels being hastily finished, purchased, and converted for the public use. Secretary of War James McHenry and Governor John Jay had come to an agreement that the state of New York would lend some heavy guns to the federal government to be used to arm the frigate. Captain John Barry, commanding officer of the *United States,* himself went to Governor's Island to prove the guns, after which they were to be shipped from New York to Philadelphia by water.[6]

A coaster sailed up to Philadelphia's water front on the eighteenth, with the guns on board. As usual, the ship's master was quizzed for shipping news. He had some. His answer produced something rare in eighteenth century journalism, a head-lined story: [7]

> FRENCH PIRATE
>
> The captain of the vessel which brot the Cannon for the Frigate from New-York, who arrived here on Friday, says, that on his passage he saw a French privateer brig off Egg Harbor, lying too [*sic*] under her top sails.

From this moment the coast between the mouths of the Delaware and Hudson Rivers became the American center for agitating and exasperating privateering news.

On the twenty-third a merchant skipper saw a French schooner, three miles east of Cape May, chasing "a black sided and white bottomed schr. which he supposed was bound to [Philadelphia]; being cut off from the land she tacked and stood to the eastward, the privateer following." [8] The color-scheme was no doubt publicized as an aid to identification by uneasy ship-owners.

On Thursday the twenty-fourth, at five o'clock in the afternoon, the schooner *Liberty,* Captain Joseph Canby, from Norfolk, was stopped by the Frenchman, "Cape Henlopen W.S.W. distant 4 miles." This was in the very vestibule of the United States—Canby even had his Delaware River pilot on board. As the privateer luffed-up and drifted along side it was seen that her numerous men all wore the French republican cockade although the ship flew no colors. At a distance of about sixty feet the raider's commander hailed Canby in broken English, ordering him to come on board with his papers. The reluctant Canby had his gig swung out, but at that instant the privateer's mast-head lookout hailed the deck, in easy, idiomatic English—sail ho! and bigger than this one! Quickly the stranger's captain gave his orders. The privateer's sails filled and she raced away after bigger game.

The alternate prey was probably the *Amiable Matilda,* fifty-two days out of Bordeaux, brought to by the privateer under Cape May that same day. Her master, too, was called on board and was there "some time." He later described the visitor: "She is a Virginia built schooner, mounts only 8 iron guns, and has 95 men." She had taken two prizes since leaving Guadeloupe, had chased the *Jane Burke* of Philadelphia on the twenty-third (black topsides? white bottom?), had looted her and turned her loose.[9] *Amiable Matilda,* fresh from France, was in no danger. The French werc looking for British property—although they were capable of impulsive acts of larceny, without much regard for the nationality of the victims.

Worse might confidently be expected. A newly arrived captain from Guadeloupe brought the rumor that four "other pirates" were coming to the United States from the West Indies.[10] Word of the danger was spread over the seas by outbound mariners. Captain Lee of the ship *Aurora,* sailing from London to Philadelphia, heard the bad news from Captain Truman of the sloop *Mary,* three days out of New Haven. He changed his course, steering around Montauk Point into Long Island sound, and thus into New York, having given the raider or raiders plenty of leeway.[11]

Secure in their knowledge of the naval weakness (naval "imbecility" some contemporaries called it) of the United States, the French took their ease 'longshore contemptuously. On the twenty-seventh the plunderer of Delaware Bay was seen cleaning his ship's bottom on the tidal flats—"careening on the anchoring grounds inside of Cape May" [12] —the faster to chase American merchantmen. About the same time the snow *Thetis* [a type of merchant vessel], bound to New York from New Providence Island, was boarded southeast of New York port. The boarders were tired of the staple seagoing fare of the day, and took a barrel of bread, a turtle, a skein of twine, and some pineapples. "They offered no compensation," [13] but sailed off, no doubt, to enjoy turtle soup, tropical punch, and some fishing. To the visiting French their American work must have been more fun than a yacht club cruise.

To many Americans the Frenchman's hey-day was a cause of anger or dejection. Alexander Hamilton, in New York, angrily prodded his disciple, the Secretary of War: [14]

> I presume you will have heard before this reaches you that a French privateer has made captures at the mouth of our harbour. This is too much humiliation after all that has passed—Our merchants are very indignant—Our Government very prostrate in the view of every man of energy.

That very day Secretary McHenry was rejecting a consignment of grape shot intended for the sloop-of-war *Ganges*. Wrong size.[15]

NOTES TO PROLOGUE

1. Gallatin to Hannah Gallatin, 13 March 1798, Henry Adams, *The Life of Albert Gallatin* (Philadelphia, 1879), 196; King to Pickering, 14 Jan. 1798, Rufus King, *The Life and Correspondence of Rufus King*, ed. C. R. King (New York, 1894–1900), II, 271–272. See also, the Philadelphia *Gazette of the United States*, May 1798.
2. Silas S. Webb to owners, 25 May 1798 (printed in Boston *Gazette*, 9 July 1798), Dudley W. Knox, ed., *Naval Documents Related to the Quasi-war between the United States and France* (Washington, 1935–1938), I, 83. Hereafter cited: Knox, *Quasi-war*.
3. New York *Commercial Advertiser*, 19 May 1798.
4. Philadelphia *Aurora*, 26 May 1798.
5. Philadelphia *Gazette of the United States*, 19 May 1798; New York *Commercial Advertiser*, 17 May 1798, gave the number of renegades as seventeen.
6. McHenry to Jay, 19 March 1798, Knox, *Quasi-war*, I, 44–45, to Barry, 18 April 1798, *ibid.*, I, 55, to Jay, 18 April 1798, United States Navy, Miscellaneous manuscripts, Library of Congress; New York *Argus*, 1 May 1798.
7. New York *Commercial Advertiser*, 22 May 1798.
8. *Ibid.*, 28 May 1798.
9. *Ibid.*; Affidavit of Joseph Canby before Chief clerk, Department of State, 26 May 1798, in New York *Commercial Advertiser*, 29 May 1798; the *Amiable Matilda* encounter, *ibid.*
10. *Ibid.*, 30 May 1798.
11. *Ibid.*
12. *Ibid.*, 31 May 1798.
13. *Ibid.*, 2 June 1798.
14. Hamilton to McHenry, 17 May 1798, Hamilton papers, Library of Congress.
15. McHenry to Harris, 17 May 1798, Knox, *Quasi-war*, I, 76.

I

Whether to Provide and Maintain a Navy

1787–1788

In the ratification controversy of 1787–1788 American political leaders warmly debated all of the powers which were delegated to the central authority in the new United States Constitution. Included in the scrutiny were the powers given to the Congress "to provide and maintain a navy."

The United States was diplomatically and militarily weak, forbidden by Spain to use the Mississippi River which formed the western boundary, barred from valuable carrying trade by the prohibitions of other nations, and unable even to take control of western posts held by British troops on American soil. Seaborne trade could not be guaranteed against piracy. And events were soon to prove the difficulty of enforcing American neutrality during a war involving the major powers of Europe.

Today it is generally accepted that these problems and weaknesses might have been more easily dealt with if the American Confederation had been able "to provide and maintain a navy." [1] Although these particular discomfitures were important to the contemporary debaters of naval policy they discussed other important aspects of the question as well.

The records of the naval controversy are to be found in several places. Part of the story—a relatively small part—is found in the journals and notes of the Constitutional Convention. The discussion was much expanded in the state conventions called to consider the ratification of the Constitution. Simultaneously there was a printing press war of pamphlets and letters-to-editors, of which the letters of Alexander Hamilton, James Madison, and John Jay, now known as the *Federalist Papers,* made up the most voluminous and best remembered part. Since it was the public word which influenced the public mind, an adequate understanding of the debate as it was seen by contemporaries can be gained from a comprehensive view of the speeches, pamphlets, and open letters.

Although the discussion was not organized as a whole, and proceeded according to personal and local judgments of opportunities to score points effectively in different places at different times, it can be considered as one grand national debate because the pamphlet and newspaper exchanges seem to have conveyed all of the principal arguments to all parts of the country before the ratification process was completed—a matter of less than a year. Hence the argument is not necessarily best presented by localities nor in the chronological order of the delivery of effective strokes by either side, but in the interest of brevity, and without essential distortion, the conceptual scheme of a single debate may safely be adopted.

ii

In reviewing the work of the Constitutional Convention one finds no trace of a discussion of naval power apart from the general war power. There was a good deal of debate which was concerned with the danger to popular liberty from a standing army or from the abuse of state militia by the proposed federal government, but no one cited a standing navy as a menace to the liberty of the whole people. On naval power the Convention as a whole acted only to approve the present phrasing of the Constitution.[2] Gouverneur Morris once suggested the creation of executive departments by name, including the office of Secretary of Marine, but his proposal was referred to the Committee of Detail and was not heard of again.[3]

If one considered only the official resolutions of the subsequent ratifying conventions it might be thought that they agreed with the Constitutional Convention in ignoring the navy-to-be. Although several of the conventions recommended amendments to the Constitution which would have altered the provisions governing the army and the militia, not one of the recommendations mentioned matters specifically naval.[4] However in the debates on the floors of the conventions and in the press the ore is richer. The question of the use and abuse of the naval power was argued at length several times, although the orators and pamphleteers devoted more words to the general war power, to the much-feared "standing army," and to the militia, than they did to the navy. After all, they were not primarily debating the naval power of the Congress, or any other specific power or limitation on power. They were debating the Constitution. When the naval power was discussed it came about in this way: the supporters of the Constitution (now called the Federalists) urged that if the Constitution were ratified the possession of the naval power would be one of the good results. Their opponents, the anti-Federalists, argued either that it would be one of the bad results, or, if a navy were desirable, it was not necessary to ratify the Constitution in order to have it.

iii

Considering the circumstances of the debate, the Federalists presented a methodical case: The United States needed naval power for self-defense. Only a union under the new Constitution could provide it. Rejection or postponement of ratification would frustrate the hope of acquiring a naval force. Possession of a navy would allow the United States to influence world affairs in its own interest.

To the Federalists the need of a navy for self-defense was an obvious fact. The United States was secure only by the kindness of foreign nations. Under the old Confederation the United States could not protect its foreign commerce. Without men or money, or a government strong enough to raise either, as a member said in the South Carolina legislature, "we hold the property that we now enjoy at the courtesy of other powers." [5] In this defenseless condition the country ought to dread the outbreak of another war in Europe since the unprotected American coast could not be guaranteed against attack. According to James Wilson (perhaps best remembered for his influential constitutional theorizing in the early 1770s), of the Pennsylvania ratifying convention, there might be safety beyond the Appalachians but there could be none in the coastal plains, and he asked, "With what propriety can we hope our flag will be respected, while we have not a single gun to fire in its defence?" [6] Alexander Hamilton observed that the violation of treaties was a major cause of wars. The United States had treaties with six nations of which five were maritime peoples and thereby able to injure the country.[7]

The anti-Federalists devoted a deal of breath to convince their fellows that the United States was in no danger from across the Atlantic, and hinted at insincerity in the Federalists who alleged the peril. In the Virginia ratifying convention Patrick Henry said he could see no danger, because the United States was at peace with all nations. The principal adversaries, if any, would be Britain, France, and Spain, and he claimed that private intelligence from Thomas Jefferson, the United States Minister to France, supported the opinion that there was no danger from them. In fact the United States was very difficult to attack and could therefore be considered relatively strong.[8] In the same convention, William Grayson ridiculed the need for naval defense by sarcastically citing the North African pirates as the chief naval threat which was to "fill the Chesapeake with mighty fleets . . ."[9] An old soldier in the Massachusetts ratifying convention told his colleagues to take courage in the ability of the commonwealth to defend itself—"they cannot starve us out; they can not bring their ships on the land . . ."[10] In both the Massachusetts and Virginia conventions anti-Federalists said that Federalist talk of foreign naval perils was merely a stratagem to frighten the delegates into ratifying the Constitution.[11]

The pirates and extortioners of North Africa gave a ready-made issue to the Federalists, although they did not exploit it as fully as one would expect. Since the British no longer protected American shipping in the Mediterranean the freedom of that sea would have to be won or bought by the Americans. A Moroccan treaty of 1784 had been fairly well observed, but Algiers, Tunis, and Tripoli continued to despoil American trade. John Adams, although later known as a navy-minded President, thought the purchase of safe-conduct would be the most economical practice, while Thomas Jefferson, not usually thought of as predisposed to favor a navy, said the United States should protect its merchants in the Mediterranean. John Jay, while Secretary for Foreign Affairs under the old Confederation Congress, had the notion that privateers might be serviceable in protecting the trade and the merchant crews,[12] but it is hard to see what profit there would be for the owners of the private fleet. Since the Congress was unwilling or unable to act, he thought it would be well to let the national humiliation sink in, because it might stimulate the establishment of a government which could make the country respectable abroad.[13] The idea of gaining some political advantage from the national shame was not Jay's alone. Rufus King, in 1785, had written to Elbridge Gerry that the Barbary pirates were a real menace but the danger was being exaggerated "for mercantile purposes." The uneasiness so generated could be used to benefit the national government and commerce.[14] Both Jay and King were or became experts on foreign affairs. To judge by their attitude toward Mediterranean piracy one could conclude that the Algerine menace has seemed more weighty with modern writers than with those who were alive at the time of the Barbary aggressions. To a nation which had survived a century and a half of Indian fighting and faced another century of it, perhaps the Algerine menace seemed a little remote.

Federalist references to the Algerines usually occurred in the course of cataloging misfortunes which could be blamed on the weakness of the existing Confederation. John Jay in a pamphlet, Charles Cotesworth Pinckney in the South Carolina legislature, and a delegate in the Massachusetts convention, all mentioned the piracies, but only in passing. Hugh Williamson, in a newspaper letter, was more emphatic.

He said the United States could not resist the weakest enemy, that the Algerines could land on the American coast and enslave the citizens, for "You have not a single sloop of war." [15]

The only anti-Federalist to make a reasoned reply to this argument was Melancthon Smith, a delegate to the New York convention, who answered Jay's pamphlet with one of his own. He said it was easier to say than to prove that our troubles with the Algerines were the result of defects in the Confederation. There were two ways to deal with the Mediterranean pirates, fight them or make a treaty. The existing Congress could do either. It only needed money, and he would be willing to allow *reasonable* powers to raise money.[16]

Thus far the Federalist case was concerned with arguing that the United States needed a navy. But there seem to have been those who agreed on the need for a navy but did not agree that the new Constitution was necessary. To them the Federalists said, in effect, only the new union which will result from the ratification of the Constitution can provide and maintain a navy.

That only the Constitution could make naval defense possible was emphatically argued by James Madison, Alexander Hamilton, and David Ramsay, the historian. In a contribution to the *Federalist Papers* Madison said the union will be the source of maritime strength, and maritime strength will be a chief security against foreign dangers. Certainly the coastal inhabitants should be interested, for they had been left in peace so long only by good luck. Virginia and Maryland ought to feel the most anxiety, and, next to them, New York, with its exposed district of Long Island and its great navigable river. Indeed, New York City was almost a hostage "for ignominious compliances with the dictates of a foreign enemy, or even with the rapacious demands of pirates and barbarians." He suggested the possibility of a new European war, in which event an escape from troubles at sea and on the coast "will be truly miraculous." The present government—"the phantom of a General Government"—would be of no help.[17] On the floor of the Virginia convention he admitted that he did not like the maintenance of armed forces in time of peace but he submitted to necessity: "Weakness will invite insults." A strong government was less likely to be insulted. Therefore, to avoid large armaments, establish the proposed government. "The best way to avoid danger is to be in a capacity to withstand it." [18] This speech of the "Father of the Constitution" was surely consistent with his broad aim to establish a government strong enough to preserve the liberty gained by the Revolution.

In the same series, the *Federalist Papers,* Hamilton also adverted to "this great National object, a Navy." Union would help in several ways to provide and maintain a navy. Every institution grows in proportion to the means concentrated upon it, and the navy would be the product of the resources of all the states. Each part of the country had something advantageous to a navy. In the South there was tar, pitch, turpentine, and better wood than elsewhere. A navy built of southern wood would last longer, a fact important both to naval strength and economy. The middle states and some southern states had iron of good quality. As for seamen, they "must chiefly be drawn from the Northern hive." The need of a navy to protect foreign trade was obvious; trade and the navy "by a kind of reaction, mutually beneficial, promote each other." [19] For those who approved of a navy but not of the Constitution he added another advantage of the proposed government. It could secure the fisheries which were the indispensbale "nursery of seamen" for the navy.[20]

David Ramsay asserted in a pamphlet that protection by a navy would be a local advantage to the southern states. If the union were to be dissolved, creditor nations might try forcibly to collect debts owed by the United States (a thing not since unknown in the western hemisphere), in which case southern exports being most valuable would be most liable to seizures. Southern coasts were also the least strongly defended and were therefore the most likely to be attacked. Under the Confederation there could be neither defense at home nor respect abroad. With no money, no navy, no army, "we lie at the mercy of every invader; our sea-port towns may be laid under contribution, and our country ravaged." But under the new Constitution the South was to be protected by the whole union with a navy to defend the coast. And the gain of respect abroad would probably lead to the negotiation of commercial treaties to open the West Indies and revive the dying maritime trade.[21]

By way of peroration to this part of the case, Hamilton contended that to defeat the ratification of the Constitution would end all hope of having a navy. Several maritime powers were already uneasy about the "adventurous spirit, which distinguishes the commercial character of America." They fear the United States may cut into their carrying trade which supports their merchant marine and is "the foundation of their naval strength." Therefore they will discourage the union, "clipping the wings, by which we might soar to a dangerous greatness." [22]

Edmund Randolph, Governor of Virginia and soon to be Secretary of State of the United States, told the Virginia convention that if the Confederation dissolved and no other union replaced it there would be no navy. "I beg gentlemen to consider these things—our inability to raise and man a navy, and the dreadful consequences of the dissolution of the Union."[23] It was, he continued, the experience of recent warfare that the nation which commanded the sea commanded the land, and "The sea can only be commanded by commercial nations." The United States could become such a commercial nation, but not unless the Constitution was adopted.[24] Alexander Contee Hanson, in a pamphlet published at Annapolis, took up the point of the denial of navies to the states individually in peacetime. It was a positive advantage to the southern states, he said, because they could not hope to rival the "eastern states by sea."[25] Jay, in the *Federalist Papers,* deprecated any idea of state or sectional navies, asking his readers to consider how unimportant British seapower would have been if its shipping regulations were the separate rules of the independent kingdoms of England, Scotland, Wales, and Ireland. Local rivalries would prevent the rise of naval strength, and, worse, the local governments, in alliance with foreign nations, would jealously counterbalance each other.[26]

Would the states, in time, without the Constitution, become strong enough to revive their trade? Oliver Ellsworth of Connecticut, later Chief Justice of the United States, thought it very improbable. Other nations profited by the country's weakness. Their trade strengthens them and produces experienced seamen "to man their ships of war when they wish again to conquer you by arms." It may be added, parenthetically, that Ellsworth and the others who referred to the malice of the maritime powers were not imagining difficulties. It had been said in England that it was not to the British interest to protect the Americans in the Mediterranean, that if the Barbary pirates were suppressed small nations could become important carriers.[27]

Edmund Randolph examined the particular situation of Virginia. He doubted that an independent, sovereign Virginia could survive apart from the other states. Even such powerful nations as France and Great Britain had found it necessary to make alliances. "What divine preeminence is Virginia possessed of above other states? Can Virginia send her navy and thunder to bid defiance to foreign nations?" If she were as isolated as San Marino she might exist as an independent nation, but "the large, capacious Bay of Chesapeake, which is but too excellently adapted for the admission of enemies, renders her very vulnerable." Virginia was very well situated for the promotion of foreign trade but "in a very unhappy position with respect to the access of foes by sea . . ."

Virginia bordered Spain, a natural enemy. France, Great Britain and the Netherlands could conceivably attempt by force to collect debts owed to them or their citizens. Other American states had grounds for quarrels with Virginia—Maryland and the use of the Potomac, Pennsylvania and the back lands—and there were the fishery and currency problems which could generate heat. Therefore an independent Virginia must provide and maintain her own armed forces, including a navy. Because a fleet could not be built in a hurry, the ships must be kept ready in time of peace. This would take money, and Randolph doubted whether Virginia could raise it. (As a matter of fact, a two-ship Virginian Navy had been approved in 1783.) [28]

Patrick Henry rose to reply to Randolph. Assuming, for the purposes of his argument, that the country must be strong in order to protect itself from foreign foes, he denied that the Constitution would make it so. The Constitution was only a piece of paper. "Will the paper on the table prevent the attack of the British navy, or enable us to raise a fleet equal to the British fleet?" Great Britain had the strongest fleet in the world; it could attack anywhere. The paper could not "raise a powerful fleet." [29]

In the course of the ratification controversy there had been some discussion of the possibility of calling a second Constitutional Convention in the hope that it would produce a less controversial document, which would meet the objections to the Constitution then being debated. John Jay undertook to defeat this tendency with an inventory of the dangers of delay. Among the hazards he included the hostility of certain nations which did not wish to see the United States become a naval power, and which would exert influence in this country to assure the failure of another convention.[30] A delegate to the Massachusetts convention also brought forward the idea that European powers were standing off and on, so to speak, awaiting the dissolution of the United States. Thereupon they would send privateers "and entirely destroy our commerce." [31]

Hamilton, in the *Federalist Papers,* took a long-range view of American naval policy, which may be appropriately selected to "close" the constructive case for the Federalists. He foresaw the influence of "the establishment of a Federal navy" in shaping world diplomacy to the future advantage of the United States. United under an effective government, the country would be able to found a navy in the not too distant future. Perhaps it would not be able to compete on equal terms with the sea forces of the great powers but it would be enough to give the United States a respectable weight if thrown into the balance of power on one side or the other; for example, a few American ships of the line, if sent into the West Indies during a war, might tip the balance and give victory to the side they aided. Also it should be remembered that the United States could be very useful as a source of supply to any nation fighting a West Indian war. These considerations would increase the value of both the friendship and the neutrality of the United

States, which might thereby become "the Arbiter of Europe in America."

If the states were not united the rivalries of the parts would check each other in this sort of enterprise. They would then be subject to the depredations of the contenders. By weakness a nation "forfeits even the privilege of being neutral." "Under a vigorous national government . . . a flourishing marine would . . . be the inevitable offspring of moral and physical necessity." [32]

Hamilton's dream was Patrick Henry's nightmare. If the Americans approved of the new government it would be "because we like a great, splendid one. Some way or other we must be a great and mighty empire" with an army, a navy "and a number of things." He mourned the decay of the American spirit—". . . in its youth, the language of America was different: liberty, sir, was then the primary object." Nowadays the Americans were unhappy because "we do not make nations tremble. Would this constitute happiness, or secure liberty?" [33] Henry was consistent throughout the ratification controversy. While other men dreamed of a great America, expanding into the silent forests of the west, with a population counted in nine digits, and rivaling Britain and France on the seas, he comes into focus as one whose greatest hope for his country was that it would one day take its place in the family of nations on a par with the United Provinces of the Netherlands or the Swiss Confederacy.

iv

The anti-Federalists had a case of their own. The Atlantic Ocean was three thousand miles broad and a barrier to aggressors. A navy would be the darling of New England and an instrument to oppress the South. As stated in the Constitution the naval power of the Congress was unlimited and therefore dangerous. The United States could use its men and money better than by sending them to sea. To build a navy would provoke Europe to attack the United States, which might otherwise hope to be left in peace. In short, as Melancthon Smith told the New York convention, it would be "wild and ridiculous" to build a navy even if the country had a treasury full of money.[34]

The idea that the breadth of the Atlantic was sufficient naval defense certainly called forth luminous talents. The doctrine of the Atlantic Moat was James Monroe's, in the Virginia convention. The best rebuttals were those of Alexander Hamilton and John Marshall. Monroe asked rhetorically whether there was any danger to the United States from Europe, and answered himself: "View the distance between us and them: the wide Atlantic—an ocean three thousand miles across—

lies between us." He acknowledged that Spain and Britain held territories contiguous to the United States, but dismissed that danger with the simple assertion that both nations profited from American friendship.[35] John Marshall, on the same floor and day, answered that "the sea makes neighbors to us. Though an immense ocean divides us, we may speedily see them with us." And he went on to the usual catalog of prospective evils: destruction of commerce, Algerine piracies, and general naval helplessness.[36] Hamilton's rebuttal has a curiously modern tone: "The improvements in the art of navigation, have, as to the facility of communication, rendered distant nations, in a great measure, neighbors." [37]

The attempt to arouse sectional feeling against the proposed naval power of the Congress was forcibly made in the South Carolina legislature by Rawlins Lowndes. He was one of several anti-Federalists who thought naval threats were being used to alarm delegates into hasty action. It was his opinion that neither France nor Britain would allow the other to conquer the United States, and, as for the navy, even if it were needed to preserve liberty at home and respect abroad, it would be a northern navy, not a southern one, and the country would belong to the north.[38]

Such sectional feeling was, of course, the chief general obstacle to the ratification of the Constitution. Federalists went to considerable lengths to argue against it, indeed, the whole of the Federalist case for the Constitution is a generalized attack on sectionalism. With regard to naval power sectionalism was attacked vigorously in South Carolina and in New York. In the South Carolina legislature the line was taken that whatever advantage might accrue to the North should be accepted for the good of the whole country. A South Carolina legislator was even willing to accept an American "Navigation Act" to monopolize shipping for Americans (a notion usually abhorrent to southern spokesmen) because it would develop the shipping of New England, "for we had no other resource, in the day of danger than in the naval force of our northern friends." The Americans could not expect to be a great nation until they were strong at sea. If any part were invaded it would be difficult for the Congress to send help any long distance overland. If the United States became a naval power Europe would hesitate to risk forces so far from home, and, it should be remembered, the route of West Indian trade passed close to the United States and could be easily attacked from these shores.[39] On the same subject, Charles Cotesworth Pinckney contended that South Carolina was too weak to be independent. If an invader sent a fleet to the Chesapeake to distract the Virginians and then attacked South Carolina, as Sir Henry Clinton did in 1780, it would be dangerous to the defenders, and if the enemy came with a larger force than Clinton's he would conquer. South Carolina should have a very close union with New England because that section had naval strength. The northerners did not need the South to maintain their independence, but they needed the union for the protection and extension of their seaborne commerce, while the South needed New England for survival. Southerners should allow northerners to have such privileges as will make them wish for union, always remembering that independence had actually damaged the commerce of the North.[40]

David Ramsay's pamphlet summarized the case against a sectional animus toward American naval power. He emphasized the point that if each state tried to have its own navy New England would be the best protected section. It would obviously be better to leave the power to the Congress. "A common navy, paid out of the common treasury, and to be disposed by the united voice of a majority for the common defence of the weaker as well as of the stronger states, is promised, and will result from the federal constitution."[41]

In New York, Jay, Hamilton, and Robert R. Livingston separately made the point that New York was defenseless against attack from the sea. Jay and Livingston added that the neighbors—New Jersey and Connecticut—were unfriendly owing to their resentment of state customs duties they paid in order to bring merchandise through New York port. Jay said the neighboring states suspected New York of delaying the ratification of the Constitution in order to continue the collection of these imposts. This implied that New York would stand alone if the union were dissolved and she were attacked. Hamilton stated this as a specifically naval problem: "Your capital is accessible by land, and by sea is exposed to every daring invader . . ."[42]

James Iredell's pamphlet referred to the sectional feeling in a more general way, and supported the naval power of the Congress by assuming its merit. To those who feared the passage of navigation acts under the new Constitution he suggested that competition for cargoes among American shippers would keep freights at reasonable rates. It would also encourage shipbuilding and the country could move gradually toward "raising a navy in America which, however distant the prospect, ought certainly not to be out of our sight."[43]

Several anti-Federalists pointed to the absence of limits on the naval power of the Congress as reason for rejecting the Constitution (although not on that ground alone).[44] No Federalist answered this specific point but there was a closely related debate on broader ground. In New York it had been suggested that separate lists of objects taxable by the states and by the United States should be written into the Consitution. Alexander Hamilton answered this at length in the *Federalist Papers* and included an analysis of the relation of taxation to seapower: National defense needs are impossible to predict. If the nation intends to be a commercial power it must have the means to defend its commerce. "The support of a navy and of naval wars would involve contingencies that must baffle all the efforts of political arithmetic." A new war could break out in Europe soon and it is not certain that the United States would be unaffected. The passions of war are stronger in human beings than are the sentiments of peace. It would be unrealistic to build national policy on "speculations of lasting tranquillity." (His "hard-boiled" opinion of the nature of man, so well known in other connections, was made plain here.) His auditors were also asked to reflect on the fact that in Britain fourteen out of fifteen shillings of public revenue went to pay the interest on old war debts and the current costs of fleets and armies.[45] In short, his advice was, do not in advance make it impossible for the Congress to finance the unpredictable costs of naval warfare.

The Virginia convention heard the most extended attack on the naval power of the Congress. It was delivered on two days by William Grayson (who died two years later while serving in the United States Senate). His basic argument was that the United States could not afford to have a navy. He began by considering the alleged danger, that the country would be involved, in any war between France and Britain, and argued that the member-nations of the "Armed Neutrality" could protect neutral nations. But, he went on, even if this were not true the profits of a temporary wartime trade would not make up for the expense "of rendering ourselves formidable at sea . . ." or compensate for the danger of the attempt. To have a navy at present would be "impracticable and inexpedient." Both seamen and factory workers must be drawn from surplus population, yet the American population, considered in relation to its land area, was small. "I think, therefore, that all attempts to have a fleet, till our western lands are fully settled, are nugatory and vain. How will you induce your people to go to sea?" Any man would rather be a farmer than a sailor.[46]

It would be dangerous to have a fleet while the Americans were so weak and dispersed. European nations with West Indian holdings would be alarmed by the growth of American strength, and "would crush us in our infancy." Instead of providing a navy the first cares should be to promote agriculture and population, and thus become strong enough to prevent partition. "I think the sailors who would be prevailed on to go to sea would be a real loss to the community," that their departure would cause the "neglect of agriculture and loss of labor." Grayson concluded his first installment: When the United States became strong then it should have a fleet, not "a small one, but . . . one sufficient to meet any of the maritime powers."[47]

A good many other speeches intervened and then, two days later, Grayson rose again (apparently having spent the interval in the study of naval estimates). He reintroduced the subject bluntly: "I conceive that the power of providing and maintaining a navy is at present dangerous . . ." The power would be in the hands of those who stood to gain by oppressing Virginia. It would also arouse European nations against the United States. They would wish to prevent commercial competition, and therefore would bring on war to check the creation of a new naval power. Furthermore, the United States could not afford a navy. The workers could be had in this country at lower rates, but not the materials. A seventy-four gun ship would cost ninety-eight thousand pounds. To man and provision her, and to pay the men would require forty-eight thousand pounds more. The United States must pay more than European nations for seamen because arbitrary governments could compel service at improper pay. These probable costs simply meant that ". . . America cannot do it." Instead of the present unlimited clause, the Constitution should provide that there be no more ships than would be needed to protect commerce. Then Europe would not be annoyed.

How, asked Grayson, would the navy be raised? It would be built and equipped in the North, and the South would be in the power of the North. The South would be asked for its share of the expenses but would not get the "emoluments." A navy was soon to be urged in the North because it would mean money in their pockets, but, even if this were not the case, there was no reason to have a fleet. The United States should remain obscure, grow slowly, and avoid giving provocation to Europe. A navy was talked of "daily" in the North, but to build it would bring on a war with Britain or France. Yet a fleet would not be able to defend the South, which was the most exposed section. He recalled that at a time when the South was most distressed the North had privateers in plenty.[48]

Two men replied to Grayson in the Virginia convention, one of whom merely made the mild observation that the Congress would not be required by the Constitution to provide and maintain a navy, that it was a discretionary power.[49] The other, James Innes, felt more strongly about Grayson's contentions. He repeated Grayson's notion that if the United States remained helpless Europe would do her no harm, but if the country tried to become respectable "they will crush you! Is this the language or consolation of an American?" If the Americans followed this advice they would give up their own interest "to please those supercilious nations" and "with every means of acquiring a powerful fleet, would never have a ship of the line." Grayson's position was disgraceful. As for Innes himself, he wished the United States not only free but "formidable, terrible, and dignified," not dependent for national security on the whims of princes.[50] It seems probable that these remarks were equally addressed to Patrick Henry, who had jeered at dreams of national grandeur on the same floor three weeks earlier.

V

In assessing the naval controversy as a whole, three corollaries seem worth noting. They concern the southern interest in the naval argument, the place in the debate of America's chief political classic, the *Federalist Papers*, and the relation of the debate to American intellectual history.

Southerners, to judge by the time and the words they devoted to the subject, were much more interested in the discussion of the naval power of the Congress than northerners were. There were more speeches, pamphlets, and open letters, which made substantial reference to the naval power, by southerners than by residents of the middle states and New England taken together. Their concerns in the matter were made clear in their remarks. The Federalists among them were economically dependent on the export of raw materials, and they had debts which could conceivably provoke foreign creditors to levy upon them by force. Southern anti-Federalists thought the value of the one and the threat of the other were being exaggerated for authoritarian purposes. Southern Federalists also referred to the peculiar difficulty of overland travel in their section as a tactical military problem, and emphasized the need to move defense forces from one part of the coast to another by water. Thus it was that the section of the nation with the fewest merchant ships and the fewest dockyard facilities was the most talkative on the subject of national naval policy.

If the anti-Federalists had any hope of capturing the mind of posterity they were unlucky in that their rebuttal case could not command genius equal to that of the authors of the *Federalist Papers*. When read in the context of the controversy then raging, this work is seen to be more of a day-to-day cumulative utilitarian rebuttal than the constructive classic of political philosophy we sometimes think it. Although a recent student has demonstrated that the authors did not agree among themselves on the political philosophy expressed in the series, there is no inconsistency in their comments on seapower. Hamilton carried the burden of the naval argument. He wrote four times on significant points (numbers III, XI, XXIV, XXXII), and Madison and

Jay each wrote once (XL and IV, respectively). Usually they addressed themselves to different aspects of the question, but all three developed the argument that only by ratifying the new Constitution could the nation be assured of having a navy. In this, as in other matters, the reader who wishes a quick view of the naval side of the grand constitutional controversy would be best advised to consult the *Federalist Papers,* bearing in mind, of course, that the series was written in the interest of one side only.

In the discussion of seapower, in the whole debate, the lines of argument varied according to the vision of the future of America in the minds of the beholders. The imaginations of the debaters were controlled to some extent by the fact that the United States was planted on a continent (no doubt the discussion would have been quite different if the participants had been an island people). But the controversy was not merely the conflict between the ocean and the continent. The debate revealed not two viewpoints, but three, one favoring the naval power of the Congress, and two opposed.

The Federalists had a dream of the United States as a true nation in the eighteenth century sense, dressed in the panoply and regalia of power, her seaports forested with masts, her trade guarded by a public fleet built of southern timber and manned by northern men, her integrity guarded at the carronade's mouth, her envoys abroad respected as men of some influence in shifting the weights in the balance of power.

The anti-Federalists, on the other hand, were divided. One set of men also prophesied greatness, but a greatness to be achieved by turning their backs on the seas and the older worlds. They hoped to direct the national energies toward the interior where there were trails to blaze, silent rivers to navigate, forests to cut, and raw clearings to plow. They believed that the people, of their own inclination, faced west toward farmland. At some remote day the country might be able to spare men to go to sea but, meanwhile, men's strength and skill were needed more for axmanship than helmsmanship. Although today we are not likely to agree that they faced an "either-or" choice, this was a respectable position, quite in accord with the American character—the true continental dream.

Allied with these westward-looking men there was another, smaller group, opposed to greatness and detesting national power. They might be called the Little Americans, whose ruling doctrine was localism. In the Revolution they had won home rule for their neighborhoods and that was all they cared about. They seem to have envisioned the United States as peopled by fiercely republican freemen, loosely confederated on a long narrow coastal strip, their provincial affairs more engrossing than the transactions of the distant, gaudy monarchies beyond the concentric arcs of the ocean and the sky.

A great generalization of the history of the human intellect holds that the progress of ideas is not from the simple to the complicated but from the vague to the clear. In the controversy over the future of American seapower we see a step in the clarification of an ill-defined idea of American membership in the international community (although not a community based on altruism or benevolence). This idea was contending with a rather more distinct conception of the American people as self-sufficient, and unassociated with the rest of the world.

NOTES FROM PAGES 5 TO 20

1. Harold and Margaret Sprout, *The Rise of American Naval Power, 1776–1918,* rev. ed. (Princeton, 1944), 16–17.
2. Max Farrand, ed., *The Records of the Federal Convention of 1787,* 3v. (New Haven, 1911); Charles Callan Tansill, comp., *Documents Illustrative of the Formation of the Union of the American States* (Washington, 1927).
3. Gouverneur Morris, 20 August 1787, Jonathan Elliot, ed., *The Debates in the Several State Conventions on the Adoption of the Federal Constitution . . .* 4v. 2d ed. (Washington, 1836); a supplemental volume V, *Debates . . . in the Convention . . . at Philadelphia in 1787* (Washington, 1845); the five volumes hereafter cited: Elliot, *Debates.* The Morris reference is, Elliot, *Debates,* V, 446.
4. From 7 Dec. 1787 to 10 Jan. 1791, *ibid.,* I, 318–338.
5. Edward Rutledge, 16 Jan. 1788, *ibid.,* IV, 274–275.
6. James Wilson, 11 Dec. 1787, *ibid.,* II, 526.
7. Alexander Hamilton in Hamilton, James Madison, and John Jay, *The Fœderalist,* ed. Henry B. Dawson (New York, 1873), No. III, 13. I follow the attribution of authorship as given by Douglass Adair in two issues of the *William and Mary Quarterly* in 1944, which may be found concisely summarized in Alpheus T. Mason, "The Federalist—A Split Personality," *American Historical Review,* LVII (April 1952), 631. Throughout the text any reference to the *Federalist Papers* is a reference to Dawson's edition, *The Fœderalist,* a less familiar designation to most modern readers.
8. Patrick Henry, 7, 24 June 1788, Elliot, *Debates,* III, 141, 594–595.
9. William Grayson, 11 June 1788, *ibid.,* III, 277.
10. "Gen. Thompson," 23 Jan. 1788, *ibid.,* II, 80.
11. William Widgery, 25 Jan. 1788, *ibid.,* II, 106; John Tyler, 25 June 1788, *ibid.,* III, 638, 639, 640.
12. Merrill Jensen, *The New Nation, A History of the United States During the Confederation, 1781–1789* (New York, 1950), 212.
13. Samuel Flagg Bemis, *Diplomatic History of the United States,* rev. ed. (New York, 1942), 67–68.
14. Jensen, *The New Nation,* 256.
15. John Jay, "An Address to the People of the State of New York . . . ," in Paul Leicester Ford, ed., *Pamphlets on the Constitution of the United States, Published During Its Discussion by the People* (Brooklyn, 1888), 73. Jay's pamphlet is hereafter cited: Jay, "An Address." Ford's collection (which includes fourteen pamphlets) is hereafter cited: Ford, *Pamphlets.* Jay's was printed about 17 April 1788.

   Charles Cotesworth Pinckney, 17 Jan. 1788, Elliot, *Debates,* IV, 282; Thomas Thacher, 4 Feb. 1788, *ibid.,* II, 143; Hugh Williamson, "Remarks on the New Plan of Government," undated, *State Gazette of North Carolina,* 1788, in Paul Leicester Ford, ed., *Essays on the Constitution of the United States, Published During Its Discussion by the*

People, 1787–1788 (Brooklyn, 1892), 403. This collection (which contains seventeen essays from contemporary newspapers) is hereafter cited: Ford, *Essays.*
16. Melancthon Smith, "An Address to the People of the State of New York," April 1788, Ford, *Pamphlets,* 112–113.
17. James Madison, *The Fœderalist,* No. XL, 283–284.
18. James Madison, 12 June 1788, Elliot, *Debates,* III, 309.
19. Alexander Hamilton, *The Fœderalist,* No. XI, 70.
20. *Ibid.,* 69–70.
21. David Ramsay, "An Address to the Freemen of South Carolina, on the Subject of the Federal Constitution," undated, Ford, *Pamphlets,* 378–379. Hereafter cited: Ramsay, "An Address."
22. Alexander Hamilton, *The Fœderalist,* No. XI, 65.
23. Edmund Randolph, 6 June 1788, Elliot, *Debates,* III, 78–79.
24. *Ibid.*
25. Alexander Contee Hanson, "Remarks on the Proposed Plan of a Federal Government," Annapolis, 1788, in Ford, *Pamphlets,* 251n.
26. John Jay, *The Fœderalist,* No. IV, 20–21.
27. Oliver Ellsworth, "The Letters of a Landholder," *Connecticut Courant,* Nov. 1787–March 1788, in Ford, *Essays,* 141; Gardner Weld Allen, *Our Navy and the Barbary Corsairs* (Boston, 1905), 26–27, citing Lord Sheffield.
28. Edmund Randolph, 6 June 1788, Elliot, *Debates,* III, 71–78; Charles W. Goldsborough, *United States Naval Chronicle,* 2v. (Washington, 1824), I, 35.
29. Patrick Henry, 12 June 1788, Elliot, *Debates,* III, 320.
30. Jay, "An Address," Ford, *Pamphlets,* 82.
31. Thomas Thacher, 4 Feb. 1788, Elliot, *Debates,* II, 146.
32. Hamilton, *The Fœderalist,* No. XI, 67–68.
33. Patrick Henry, 5 June 1788, Elliot, *Debates,* III, 53, 54.
34. Melancthon Smith, 1 July 1788, *ibid.,* II, 381.
35. James Monroe, 10 June 1788, *ibid.,* III, 212–213.
36. John Marshall, 10 June 1788, *ibid.,* III, 235.
37. Hamilton, *The Fœderalist,* No. XXIV, 160.
38. Rawlins Lowndes, 18 Jan. 1788, Elliot, *Debates,* IV, 309–310.
39. Edward Rutledge, 17 Jan. 1788, *ibid.,* IV, 299.
40. Charles Cotesworth Pinckney, 17 Jan. 1788, *ibid.,* IV, 284.
41. Ramsay, "An Address," Ford, *Pamphlets,* 374–375.
42. Robert R. Livingston, 19 June 1788, Alexander Hamilton, 20 June 1788, Elliot, *Debates,* II, 212, 232; Jay, "An Address," Ford, *Pamphlets,* 84.
43. James Iredell, "Answers to Mr. Mason's Objections to the New Constitution," 1788, *ibid.,* 358.
44. *E. g.,* William Grayson, 14 June 1788, Elliot, *Debates,* III, 430.
45. Hamilton, *The Fœderalist,* 4 Jan. 1788, No. XXXII, 210–212.
46. William Grayson, 12 June 1788, Elliot, *Debates,* III, 288–289.
47. *Ibid.*
48. William Grayson, 14 June 1788, *ibid.,* III, 428–430.
49. George Nicholas, 14 June 1788, *ibid.,* III, 430.
50. James Innes, 25 June 1788, *ibid.,* III, 634–635.

II

The Nursery of Seamen

1789–1793

The first four years of the history of the United States under the Constitution were years in which precedents of such great importance were established that most aspects of the national story have been carefully scrutinized. Little attention, however, has been given to naval matters in that period [1] because there was no navy afloat or building, no great battles or commanders to attract writers.[2] Nevertheless there were discernible currents and tendencies of naval thought in the proceedings of the Congress [3] where the problems of the merchant and fishing fleets stimulated talk on naval matters.[4]

No one of consequence in public life doubted that the men of the United States would continue to go down to the sea; George Washington put it typically: no nation can prevent the United States "from becoming a great, a respectable and a commercial Nation, if we shall continue United and faithful to ourselves." [5] But the methods for solving the national maritime problems were debatable.

It will be remembered that the United States Navy had no existence, although the Congress made provision for a navy by adding naval affairs to the purview of the Department of War. For a while there may have been some thought of a separate naval department; during the debates on the establishment of the several executive departments a newspaper writer assumed there would be "a marine board" for "the interest of a navy" and went on to describe the qualifications necessary for membership.[6] But the act establishing the Department of War included a provision that the Secretary carry out the wishes of the President concerning "naval forces, ships, or warlike stores of the United States, or to such other matters respecting military or naval affairs . . ." [7] This Department was launched during a moment of calm, for no debate was recorded, although the House of Representatives, immediately before, had disputed fiercely about the President's removal power in the case of the Secretary of State, and when they disposed of the War power, fell to it again on the subject of the duties of the Secretary of the Treasury.[8] In 1790 Secretary of War Henry Knox carried on some correspondence concerning estimates of the costs of building warships, which were reported to the Congress in 1791.[9] These letters are the only surviving documents on naval affairs in the Department of War during Washington's first term. In 1793 Senator Robert Morris of Pennsylvania was corresponding with a Philadelphia builder on the same subject.[10] That is the entire record of official naval activity of the United States government in the years 1789–1793, but it reflects only a minute fraction of the naval thinking in the same years.

Promptly upon the organization of the House of Representatives in 1789 the question of a federal revenue presented itself. As part of the first revenue bill James Madison introduced and argued for a system of discriminations in the levying of tonnage duties which would establish three classes of ships entering the ports of the United States: ships of the United States to pay a negligible duty, ships of nations which had commercial treaties with the United States to pay more, and ships of nations not in treaty to pay most.[11] Madison was very interested in the effect the bill might have in strengthening the nation. A naval force, he said, was necessary to the defense of the country. If it was expedient to use the vessels of the United States in trade it was expedient to have enough "to form a school for seamen, to lay the foundation of a navy, and to be able to support itself against the interference of foreigners." From other of his remarks it was plain that his bill was directed specifically at Great Britain which had refused to negotiate a commercial treaty with the United States.[12]

When the bill was reported favorably from the Committee of the Whole to the House Madison became even more explicit. He said he would favor free trade except that the country needed naval defense.[13] And two days later: "I do not consider this subject as it respects revenue; my great object is to provide a maritime defence against a maritime danger."[14]

Fisher Ames of Massachusetts and Thomas Fitzsimons of Pennsylvania spoke on Madison's side. Ames's only reservation was that the discrimination between American and foreign ships was not great enough and "may perhaps fall short of procuring us a maritime strength equal to our national security."[15] Fitzsimons argued that a strong naval force would make the country a respected neutral power with all the benefits of a neutral carrying trade in time of war, but added that if the United States did not improve its position immediately "two or three British frigates may prevent us from gathering these benefits hereafter."[16]

The leaders of the opposition to the bill were William L. Smith of South Carolina and James Jackson of Georgia. Their argument was that the new shipping which would be built because of the discriminatory encouragement would be a long time building; their states needed ships *now* and preferred to go on as they had in the past [17]—that is, using British bottoms. Madison replied that in war the necessary "maritime force . . . will be particularly employed in defence of the weaker part." South Carolina and Georgia could not defend themselves by sea but "must depend on the other States for their defence." Since tonnage discriminations would make the United States stronger South Carolina and Georgia had an interest in their enactment.[18]

The discriminations were adopted, and American ships were assured of a practical monopoly of the coasting trade because they were required to pay the duty only once a year instead of at each entry. What was said of tonnage discriminations in the Senate is unknown except that Senator William Maclay of Pennsylvania grumbled "that it would be time enough, half a century hence, to talk of measures for a navy." [19] The argument did not die but persisted in desultory fashion for the next few years.[20] For example, in 1790 James Jackson attacked the entire concept of a beneficial carrying trade "unless it be as a nursery for seamen." Only the nations which needed navies needed to carry trade. Jackson's view was so typical of the eighteenth-century American who faced toward the continent instead of toward the ocean that he deserves extended quotation: "Does our national importance, and even our very security depend . . . on the strength of . . . fleets? . . . No, sir, to the agricultural interest—to the hardy sons of the West—to the American yeomanry we shall appeal, and we shall there find support." [21] But, despite this and similar attacks, the principle was retained.

Since most of the public revenue was to come from customs duties the early Congresses made little attempt to manipulate the tariffs on commodities for naval purposes. However the principle of protection was applied to encourage the home production of hemp. The movers of protection made it plain that their goal was maritime strength.[22] In the Second Congress, on the question of raising the duty on hemp, the members had the diverting and not uncommon experience of hearing debaters at once support and oppose the measure for the same reason, that the country did not yet produce enough hemp for its own shipping.[23] In the First Congress it was also proposed that the coal of Virginia be given some protection against the import of foreign coal (much of which came as ballast) in order to encourage the use of Virginia coal for cooking, for steam power "and as a nursery to train up seamen for a navy." [24] Not that miners were considered a peculiarly meritorious naval reserve, but the British coasting trade in coal was said to be useful as a "nursery of seamen"; therefore an American coasting trade in coal would be the same.[25]

No other protective duties were applied for purely naval reasons. Relying on international law Madison thought it unnecessary to move very far in that direction because in any future war the United States could be more easily supplied with military stores from abroad than it was during the War for Independence. Neutrals would have a legal right to supply the United States in an international war, whereas their right to do so had not been so evident in the case of the late "intestine commotion." [26] Another objection to the enactment of protective duties was that they would encourage smuggling, the prevention of which would strain even a large navy. The experience of pre-Revolutionary smuggling was offered in evidence.[27] Of course any customs law required enforcement, and provision was made in 1790 for the construction and manning of ten revenue cutters which were all on duty by 1791—the first armed sea force of the federal government and the precursor of the United States Coast Guard.[28]

Because lack of money made it impossible to grant large subsidies there was not much the Congress could do to promote the carrying trade outside of American coastal waters. That remained the problem of diplomacy, but there were men who dreamed brave dreams. One writer recommended that the United States found "colonies or even factories" practically everywhere in the world. He urged the importance of the matter "as naturally tending to promote the rapid increase of their naval strength, which would soon render [the United States] too formidable to dread any unprovoked injury, or insult." He admitted it was a little early for the government to be able to finance a world empire but he was sure it could be done by private enterprise.[29] Another said the United States should look to promoting commerce after the British mode, copying Britain in order to compete with her. American shipping would then produce native seamen for defense and make it possible to do without the usual foreign mercenaries.[30] In the Congress the only action taken to assist trans-oceanic trade directly was to give a tariff advantage to tea carried from China in American ships, but only one argued a naval benefit to be derived.[31]

Madison had said he favored free trade but that it was impractical under the circumstances. Others, in the Congress and out, agreed. A writer argued (in a letter from England) that Britain's wealth had accumulated because good government protected property and the fruits of toil, not because of the Navigation Acts. However, he said, the Navigation Acts had been the source of British naval power; in short, the promotion of naval power was the only excuse for commercial restrictions [32]—which had been Madison's view in the first session of the First Congress. Another writer took a different tack—that the Navigation Acts made naval power necessary. Free trade needed no navies, or very small ones. Although trade ought to be free, restrictions were multiplying. The colonial nations practiced the theory that commercial monopoly followed conquest. While every trading needed some armed protection the maritime countries carried the theory to an oppressive excess. "A great navy, they pretend, must be kept up to defend colonies, and seamen must be hired to catch cod-fish, and whales, at three times their worth, to man a navy." It took ten times as many ships to guard a monopoly as it required to guard a free trade. Navies had been the "chief instrument and heaviest charge" of wars. They raised the national debts until even the monopolies could hardly meet the cost. "Free trade only can furnish it" [33]—"it," presumably, meaning the cost of servicing national debts. At the moment of publication there was nothing in the public forum to provoke such a letter-to-the-editor. Perhaps it was the reaction of a tax-paying cod-eater who had advance notice that the Congress would shortly consider legislation to aid the fisheries.

The American fisherman had received little immediate benefit from the establishment of the federal union. His chief market had been the West Indies for cod and Great Britain for whale products. In the West Indies the cod trade operated under restrictions as a precarious privilege. Whale products were banned by Britain in the interest of her own whalers. New England rum, made from West Indian molasses, was also barred from Newfoundland and Nova Scotia, where the Yankees had formerly traded it for fish.[34] The cod and whale fisheries were popularly regarded as a source of naval strength. As one writer put it, "they are our natural, principal, and best nurseries for seamen, and the most certain source and support of our naval strength; an object of the last importance to all commercial countries, and *in which the United States are all equally interested.*" [35]

The defenders of the fishing interest were in action in the debates on the first revenue bill. Their particular fear was that the duty on molasses would be so high as to damage the New England distillers. Fisher Ames pointed out that the molasses trade was essentially linked with the fishery. If molasses were overtaxed it would discourage fishing. "The taking of fish on the Banks is a very momentous concern, it forms a nursery for seamen, and this will be the source from which we are to derive maritime importance." (The point was that fish were traded to the West Indies for molasses.) [36] Two weeks later, Jeremiah Wadsworth of Connecticut echoed the notion of the fisheries as a fleet reserve.[37] Two other Representatives developed the theme. Elbridge Gerry of Massachusetts: "it was well known to be the best nursery for seamen, the United States had no other, and it could never be the intention of gentlemen to leave the navigation of the Union to the mercy of foreign Powers." Benjamin Goodhue, also of Massachusetts: if the fisheries "are given up, how are we to form seamen to man our future navy?" [38]

The New England members succeeded in getting the rum duty lowered from the figures first proposed but, as years passed, it turned out that cheap rum alone would not make the fisheries prosper. The next step was to secure what their opponents called a subsidy but what they called a drawback. The proposal (February 1792) was that the tax on imported salt which was used to preserve the fish should be refunded when the fish were exported.[39] Naturally the supporters of the measure urged that it would be a naval benefit.

The debate on the naval aspect of the salt-refund was almost entirely sectional. All supporters of the bill as a source of naval strength were from the North except one. All of the opponents who spoke against it were southerners. William B. Giles and John Page, both of Virginia, were the floor leaders against the measure. Said Giles: The strength of the United States was a land strength. The contrary opinion was maintained, perhaps, because of British habits of thought. Britain had found the encouragement of the fisheries expensive but necessary. "America, whose consequence, as a nation, does not depend on a navy" ought to learn from the British experince. Page developed the continental viewpoint as opposed to the oceanic: The Congress could equally well give bounties to hunters as a "nursery of soldiers" against Indian threats and to "promote the fur trade." He wondered whether it might not be better for the country if all the sailors were farmers. "A nursery of virtuous families, which will produce soldiers, sailors, husbandmen, and statesmen, must be preferable to a mere nursery of sailors, who generally live single, and often perish at sea. I always look upon the loss of a crew to an infant Republic as the loss almost of a new State." William Vans Murray of Maryland thought the bill could be argued as a naval measure only if its supporters actually had "a system of defence in contemplation." And Hugh Williamson of North Carolina expressed the old fear of military excuses for centralization of power: "The common defense and general welfare, in the hands of a good politician, may supercede [*sic*] every part of our Constitution, and leave us in the hands of time and chance." [40]

Fisher Ames made the principal defense of the measure. He argued that the bill would promote justice, national wealth, and national safety. On the last point he said the maritime trade was getting richer and, being unprotected, it tempted nations to war upon the United States. If it were proper for the militia to protect property on land there could be no objection to protecting property afloat. The corps of fishermen was the best protection: as privateersmen their protection cost nothing yet was "more effectual than the whole revenue expended on a navy." In a war, coasters and other seamen were in great demand but the fishermen were out of work and could be "instantly in action." Their fishing experience made them "expert and hardy"—they fought at Bunker Hill, there were five hundred of them at Trenton, they made a grand record at sea in the War for Independence. "Some gentlemen think of a navy: but what navy could do more? What nation would provoke a people so capable of injuring them? Could fifty ships of the line afford more security?" The American fishermen would be "swordfish to attack the whale." "In point of naval protection, we can scarcely estimate the fishery too highly. It is always ready, always equal to the object; it is almost the only sufficient source of security by sea." [41] Ames's speech lacked only a proof of the apostolic succession from the sword-swinging fisherman of Galilee to Colonel Glover of the Webfoot Regiment of Marblehead.

Benjamin Goodhue repeated the familiar theme: "a copious nursery of hardy seamen." Robert Barnwell of South Carolina, the lone southern supporter of the salt drawback: "it is of some importance to have constantly at hand a nursery of seamen." Elbridge Gerry hinted that Virginian opposition was self-centered because in "a marine war . . . that State is pretty secure from depredations." John Laurance of New York admitted that the country might not need a navy but pointed out that no one "can say that we shall never have a war with any European Power." [42]

The declining cod fishers received their refund of the salt duty. The enactment was celebrated in the press because the fishermen were "a militia by sea" and the act "will hasten the naval strength of America to a very early maturity." [43]

The first two Congresses were thoroughly militia-minded when they anticipated the exercise of their naval power. This attitude reflected thinking in and out of doors, as illustrated in an early draft of President Washington's address to the Congress of April 1789, which included the following:

> As our people have a natural genius for Naval affairs and as our Materials for Navigation are ample; if we give due encouragement to the fisheries and the carrying trade; we shall possess such a nursery of Seamen and such skill in maratime [*sic*] operations as to enable us to create a Navy almost in a moment.[44]

Early in 1790 Secretary of War Henry Knox completed a plan for the proper organization of the militia, which was sent to the Congress on 21 January. He included some thoughts on naval manpower, proposing to exempt from compulsory service "all actual mariners," and he quoted with approval Friedrich von Steuben's earlier recommendation for the Legion of the United States in which occurred the supposition that only two kinds of war would threaten the country, an attack by sea or by Indians. Knox's report went on to say: "The local circumstances of the United States, their numerous seaports, and the protection of their commerce, require a naval arrangement." The states must obtain men "on republican principles, for the marine as well as the land service." However a citizen needed special training to be a soldier, but a sailor's daily work trained him for the navy. Thus his training cost the state nothing. All that was required was "to register all actual seamen, and to render those of a certain age amenable to the public for personal service, if demanded within a given period." [45] The report of the Secretary was referred to a Committee on National Defence in April, but no militia bill was passed by the First Congress.[46]

This Congress revealed its thinking on the status of naval officers in a debate on a proposal to give the naval officer veterans the same emoluments which had been given to officer veterans of the Continental Army. Most of the remarks on the floor concerned the expediency of the measure but a theoretical strain intruded occasionally. Naval officers, it was argued, had been somewhat compensated by prize money. They were paid to do what they had been trained for and what they did best, unlike army officers who were torn from their usual pursuits. They were employed in the naval force at a time when war had disrupted commerce and when they would probably have otherwise been unemployed. On the other side of the question it was observed that when they were captured they were not treated as prisoners of war but as rebels. Support of the motion was intersectional but, inexplicably, opposition was northern.[47] Certainly, in this debate, there was no notion of the naval officer as a professional man in a category separate from the merchant master.

The Second Congress passed a militia bill which exempted pilots and "all mariners actually employed in the sea-service of any citizen or merchant within the United States." [48] No reference was made to Knox's plan for the enrollment of a naval militia—which would have been difficult to administer in the existing state of communications.

In the second session of the Second Congress Hugh Williamson moved to have a committee bring in a bill for the direct purpose of increasing the number of American seamen. He cited cases of the impressment of British seamen serving in the American merchant fleet (but, oddly, made no reference to the impressment of Americans). If all of the seamen under the American flag were Americans no British claim on them could be supported. He also spoke of troubles in the French fleet with mutineers of foreign birth. And finally, "Is it necessary to add, that a powerful body of seamen, at some future day, may save us from the vast expense and danger of a standing army? Upon this single argument of native seamen we might rest the question." Thus the Congress might provide the country "with a safe and strong bulwark against foreign tyranny and invasion." Specifically he proposed a drawback from tonnage taxes if a certain proportion of a given crew were American apprentice seamen. He also wished to see provision made for ill and infirm seamen, by a system of deductions from mariners' wages. His motion was referred to a select committee with himself as chairman, but no more was heard of the matter.[49]

In the first four years of federal history most members of the Congress accepted the idea that the United States would some day have a navy. Administrative responsibility for naval affairs was assigned to an existing executive office (although not called upon). The merchant and fishing fleets, and the shipbuilding industry, were encouraged by tax advantages which were given for the explicit reason (among others) of developing the country's naval strength.

The Congress seemed entirely militia-minded, believing that an unorganized naval militia was immediately available from the merchant marine and the fisheries. In Knox's proposal for the enrollment of a naval militia the injection of the phrase "on republican principles" was the injection of a moral judgment concurred in by practically all Americans. The standing regular force, in peacetime idle and debauched, at all times dangerous to liberty, was the mark of monarchy. The militia, virtuous, responsible, and motivated by a love of liberty, was the armor of republicanism.

In the minds of the members there was a conscious and uncontradicted equation of the naval and the merchant service as the same trade, in all ranks and ratings. Except in Ames's glorification of the fisherman they did not say the country should rely on privateers, but when men believed that the merchant service and fisheries trained for the naval service, that in wartime the officers and men of the navy would be doing much the same sort of work that they did as civilians in peacetime one can only conclude that they had been much more impressed by the operations of privateers than by the public fleets of the world.

Excursus

How a Bill Passed Through the House of Representatives.

Because most of the action described on the following pages took place in the House of Representatives it will be useful to sketch the process of legislation in that House. The following explanation applies generally to the first five Congresses.

(1) A resolution was introduced and debated, sometimes amended. (2) If it met with approval it was referred to a select committee, a standing committee, or, more likely, to the Committee of the Whole House. (The standing committee device was used more frequently in later sessions.) (3) If it had been given to a select or standing committee, the committee reported either in general terms or by bringing in a bill. (4) If the report had been in general terms, and was approved, the authors were instructed to bring in a bill embodying the sense of the report. (5) If the resolution had been referred to the Committee of the Whole, or if a bill had been brought in by order of the House, debate in Committee of the Whole followed. (6) The Committee of the Whole rose and reported the bill—"First Reading"—amended or not, to the House. (7) The House—"Second Reading"—debated the report of the Committee of the Whole and further amended the bill of it wished. Motions which had failed to pass in Committee of the Whole could be and often were renewed, sometimes successfully. At the close of this debate, which was the crucial one, the bill was ordered to "Third Reading," a motion which was sometimes opposed in the hope of killing the bill there and then. (8) On Third Reading the entire debate might be reopened, but the bill usually passed if it had survived the process to this stage.

The Committee of the Whole was used much more than the select or standing committee, thus the spadework usually done by modern legislatures in standing committees or sub-committees was done on the floor. The Committee of the Whole had several advantages, given the circumstances of the 1790s. It assured a very thorough scrutiny of every important measure. It brought the Speaker down to the floor where he was free to exercise his political leadership. Each member was free to speak as often as he wished on any motion (if that be an advantage). But the Committee of the Whole was obviously too cumbersome to survive the increase in the size of the house in later decades and too slow to meet the legislative needs of a complex industrial society. For small bodies, especially voluntary associations, it is the "natural" way of doing business. Most voluntary bodies seem to operate under "Committee rules" without knowing it, characteristically allowing speeches on motions not yet introduced, expressions of opinion by the elected heads, and repetition by members who have already spoken to the point.[50]

NOTES FROM PAGES 22 TO 30

1. Harold and Margaret Sprout, *The Rise of American Naval Power, 1776–1918*, rev. ed. (Princeton, 1944), 26. This is the indispensable book on the history of American naval policy as distinguished from operations and biography.

2. It was common before 1789 and after 1793 for their opponents to charge the Federalists with the intention of establishing a navy as a stage in the gradual and deliberate centralization of national power. Between 1789 and 1793 these allegations were relatively fewer. For a typical phillipic see Henry Banks in the *Virginia Gazette*, reprinted in *Gazette of the United States*, 18 Aug. 1792.
3. The debates of the House of Representatives are, of course, available in *Annals of the Congress, 1789–1824*, 42v. ed. J. Gales and W. W. Seaton (Washington, 1834–1856), but in the absence of any claims court the Second Congress was so burdened with private bills that the reporters skimped the debates. Hereafter cited: *Annals*. For the Senate, regrettably, there is only the "atrabilious and parvanimus," "poisoned and distorted" Senator William Maclay, *Journal*, ed. E. S. Maclay (New York, 1890). The adjectives are those of J. F. Jameson quoted by G. H. Haynes, *The Senate of the United States*, 2v. (Boston, 1938), I, 43n.
4. The following examination of these naval trends does not include the influence of the Barbary pirates in the prehistory of the Navy, which the author will treat in the next chapter.
5. Washington to Sir Edward Newenham, 28 Aug. 1788, George Washington, *Writings*, ed. John C. Fitzpatrick, 39v. (Washington, 1931–1944), XXX, 72. Washington and Thomas Jefferson (and others), even before the Constitution was in effect, expected the establishment of a navy and their thoughts turned to John Paul Jones. They exchanged letters on his future usefulness. Jefferson to Washington, 2 May 1788, Washington papers, v. 240, Library of Congress; Washington to Jefferson, 31 Aug. 1788, Washington, *Writings*, XXX, 81. Jefferson, in the 1780s, strongly favored a navy for the United States; see his long letter on the subject to John Jay, 23 Aug. 1785, *The Papers of Thomas Jefferson*, ed. Julian P. Boyd (Princeton, 1950–), VIII, 426–427.
6. "Americanus," *Gazette of the United States*, 17 June 1789.
7. 1 Cong., 1 Sess., 7 Aug. 1789, *Annals*, II, 2158–2159.
8. 24, 25 June 1789, *Annals*, I, 591–592, 592–607.
9. C. O. Paullin, "Early Naval Administration under the Constitution," *Proceedings, United States Naval Institute*, XXXII (1906), 1002–1003; Franklin Delano Roosevelt, "Our First Frigates, Some Unpublished Facts about Their Construction," *Transactions, Society of Naval Architects and Marine Engineers*, XXII (1914), 139.
10. Ira N. Hollis, *The Frigate Constitution* (Boston, 1931), 35–36.
11. The arguments in the Committee of the Whole, 21 April 1789, are in 1 Cong., 1 Sess., *Annals*, I, 176–191. Report was made to the House on 4 May at which time the hands of the proponents were strengthened by a petition from the shipwrights of Baltimore praying for the encouragement of shipbuilding. *Ibid.*, I, 233.
12. *Ibid.*, I, 189, 205.
13. *Ibid.*, I, 237. That naval defense must be based on a large civilian fleet was a common belief of the century. "The defence of Great Britain, for example, depends very much upon the number of its sailors and shipping. The Act of Navigation, therefore, very properly endeavours to give the sailors and shipping of Great Britain the monopoly of the trade of their own country . . ." Adam Smith, *An Inquiry into the Nature and Causes of the Wealth of Nations* (Chicago, 1952), 197.
14. *Annals*, I, 281.
15. 5 May 1789, *ibid.*, I, 255.
16. 6 May, *ibid.*, I, 278.
17. 5, 7 May, *ibid.*, I, 252, 286–287.
18. 7 May, *ibid.*, I, 286.
19. Maclay, *Journal* (15 June 1789), 76.
20. *Gazette of the United States*, 23 Sept. 1789, 23 May 1792; Hugh Williamson in the House of Representatives, 10 May 1790, 1 Cong., 2 Sess., *Annals*, II, 1560–1561; Madison, 13 May 1790, *ibid.*, II, 1571; John Adams to William Smith (at Boston), 20 May 1790, John Adams, Letterbooks, Adams papers, reel 115, Library of Congress. Merchant tonnage in the twelve months before December 1790 increased almost threefold and the gain has been attributed to the discriminations. Samuel Wood Bryant, *The Sea and the States; A Maritime History of*

the American People (New York, 1947), 115. *Gazette of the United States*, 2 March 1791, praised the First Congress for encouraging shipping: "it is already a young lion, and will afford in a few years such naval strength, as to be a terror to our enemies." A few weeks before, 12 Feb. 1791, this "administration organ" had alleged facts to prove that American shipping was adequate to carry out the southern staples.

21. 10 May 1790, 1 Cong., 2 Sess., *Annals*, II, 1564–1565.
22. 15, 16 April 1789, 1 Cong., 1 Sess., *ibid.*, I, 149–156.
23. Bourne and Williamson, 19 April 1792, 2 Cong., 1 Sess., *ibid.*, 560.
24. Bland, 18 April 1789, 1 Cong., 1 Sess., *ibid.*, I, 170.
25. R. H. Lee, 22 Jan. 1794, 3 Cong., 1 Sess., *ibid.*, 266.
26. Madison, 9 April 1789, 1 Cong., 1 Sess., *ibid.*, I, 113.
27. 24 April 1789, *ibid.*, I, 194.
28. Several states had provided their own revenue services before 1789. James Fenimore Cooper, *History of the Navy of the United States of America*, 2v. (Philadelphia, 1839), I, 260. The standard work on the history of the revenue cutters is Stephen H. Evans, *The United States Coast Guard, 1790–1915* (Annapolis, 1949).
29. E. C., "American essays," *Gazette of the United States*, 6 June 1789.
30. From the *Daily Avertiser*, reprinted in *Gazette of the United States*, 3 April 1790. In the *Gazette*'s equivalent of an editorial column the idea was repeated on the same day, with special reference to the great numbers of British merchant ships in American ports.
31. 18 April 1789, 1 Cong., 1 Sess., *Annals*, I, 168–170.
32. *Gazette of the United States*, 14, 18 May 1791.
33. *Ibid.*, 7 Jan. 1792.
34. The Congress was unable to do much for the whalers who solved their problem themselves, partly by emigration from Nantucket to Nova Scotia, France, and Wales. The British motives for welcoming American whalers who came to settle in Milford Haven in October 1792, were to improve their competitive position in the oil industry and to gain naval strength. The story is told in Edouard A. Stackpole, *The Sea Hunters: The New England Whalemen during Two Centuries, 1635–1835* (Philadelphia, 1953), 94–144.
35. "Extract from 'American essays,'" *Gazette of the United States*, 27 May 1789. A writer in the *Salem Gazette*, copied in *Gazette of the United States*, 24 May 1791, praised John Adams for his work at Paris to secure the American fisheries, "that source of wealth and naval strength."
36. 14 April 1789, 1 Cong., 1 Sess., *Annals*, I, 133–134.
37. 28 April, *ibid.*, I, 214.
38. 12 May, *ibid.*, I, 330, 335.
39. The Senate had a fisheries discussion in 1791 which was reflected in Maclay's diary: The object was to make the fisheries "a nursery for seamen" so as to "have a navy." He heard "distant hints of such things" daily—to give up "republican innocence, and, like all other nations, set apart a portion of our citizens for the purpose of inflicting misery on our fellow-mortals. This practice is felony to posterity." It detached the men and the same proportion of women "remain unmatched." Maclay, *Journal* (4 Feb. 1791), 384.
40. 3, 7 Feb. 1792, 2 Cong., 1 Sess., *Annals*, 364–365, 380, 392–393.
41. *Ibid.*, 369–370, 374.
42. *Ibid.*, 366–367, 375, 377, 385. Concerning Virginia's happy geographical situation, precisely the opposite was alleged in the Virginia ratification convention by Governor Edmund Randolph, as a reason for ratifying the Constitution. The Chesapeake, he said, made Virginia vulnerable to attack by sea. Jonathan Elliot, *The Debates in the Several State Conventions on the Adoption of the Federal Constitution*, 4v., 2d ed. (Washington, 1836), III, 72.
43. *Gazette of the United States*, 9 May 1792. This newspaper, which was the closest thing to an administration paper, was not much interested in naval power in these years, and only slightly interested in foreign commerce. A page by page examination of the issues from its founding in the spring of 1789 to March 1793, shows that it vigorously supported Hamilton's funding system, domestic

manufactures, the Bank of the United States, free public education, and free postal carriage for newspapers. The arguments for the funds, manufacturing and the Bank faithfully reflected Alexander Hamilton's thinking as shown in his published works and in his papers (Hamilton papers, Library of Congress). One can conclude that Hamilton at the time had little active interest in naval questions, despite his eloquent naval theorizing in the *Federalist Papers,* and infrequent, incidental mention in his state papers.

44. Washington, ["Proposed Address to Congress,"] April? 1789, Washington, *Writings,* XXX, 302.
45. 1 Cong., 2 Sess., *Annals,* I, 1076, II, 1544, 2092, 2105–2106.
46. *Ibid.,* II, 1791, 1800, 1828.
47. 24 June 1790, 1 Cong., 2 Sess., *ibid.,* II, 1648–1652. Some of the naval officer veterans were later compensated by private bills.
48. 2 Cong., 1 Sess., *ibid.,* 1393. There is nothing in the *Annals* to encourage the thought but a later generation (1829) regarded seamen as a "privileged class" because militia duty was compulsory for all but sailors, while naval duty was not compulsory for them. This was not considered a Bad Thing. It made the Navy a wholly volunteer service. "They feel as freemen and act as such," which was said to be an advantage to the Navy. Samuel Lorenzo Knapp, *Lectures on American Literature with Remarks on Some Passages of American History* (New York, 1829), 276–277.
49. 19 Nov. 1792, 2 Cong., 2 Sess., *Annals,* 691–695.
50. Two exceptions to the foregoing may be noted. (1) In the Fifth Congress bills sometimes went through First and Second Readings without debate, and only then into Committee of the Whole, for debate. (2) Members distinguished between the Committee of the Whole and the Committee of the Whole on the State of the Union but, in this story, the distinction had no important consequence. Readers who wish to pursue the subject farther should see R. V. Harlow, *The History of Legislative Methods in the Period before 1825* (New Haven, 1917).

III

The Algerine Theme

1783–1793

In the late eighteenth century North Africa was ruled by a group of military dictatorships—Morocco, Algiers, Tunis, and Tripoli. With a very primitive agriculture and almost no commerce, the rulers of these petty states relied upon piracy for material goods which would allow them to live above a meager standard. Captive mariners, held for ransom, were their "cash crop," and the occasional negotiation of a racketeer's treaty of "protection" brought naval stores for the pirate fleet and jingling bribes for the officials. Algiers was the strongest of the principalities. Its subjects were known to contemporaries as "Algerines."

In combat the Algerines were prodigal of manpower. To capture a ship they invariably boarded by steering alongside and dropping their great lateen yards across the victim's rail to use as boarding ways. Oversize crews then swarmed aboard with pistols in their belts and cutlasses in their teeth, leaving their hands free for climbing. A good defense was to rig nettings secured by cutlass-proof chains. Then, as the pirates were spread-eagled to climb the nets, they could be dealt with by charges of buckshot or with lances. But they did not maneuver their ships well and the best defense was to stay out of reach.[1]

Before the War for Independence American ships sailed the Mediterranean protected by passes issued by the British government which negotiated terms of immunity with the pirates from time to time. After the Americans gained their independence they were on their own. The crews of two American merchantmen, twenty-two men in all, had the sobering experience of capture by Algerines in 1785. Taken to Algiers and thrown among slaves from many nations, they were put in heavy chains, dressed in coarse clothes, given a single blanket each, and fed a daily ration of fifteen ounces of bread. Although some captives were sold into private slavery (which made them harder to ransom because harder to find) the Americans were relatively lucky because they became state slaves who worked as ship riggers, 'longshoremen, porters, and draft animals. Some were able to pick up pocket money at odd-hour jobs which they used to rent better quarters or spent in the tavern kept by one of them. They had a poorly fed, verminous life which was occasionally worsened by the arbitrary administration of the bastinado. If a slave were injured or fell ill he could be sent to the hospital maintained as a work of mercy for the prisoners by Spanish priests, from which he might be summarily recalled to labor before his recovery. If one were sentenced to death (which none of the Americans were) it would be inflicted by beheading, impalement, or burning alive.[2] In July of 1790 there were fourteen of the twenty-two still in captivity.[3] Six had died of the plague in 1787 and 1788, and two had been privately ransomed by friends.[4] In November they were reported to be in "deplorable" condtion but still hoping for help from home.[5]

When British protection lapsed, American trade with the Mediterranean countries declined to the vanishing point. The Congress had hoped in 1776 to get an explicitly stated French protectorate of the Mediterranean trade to replace the British guardianship but the Treaty of Amity and Commerce which was made with France in 1778 merely promised "good offices and interposition" with the pirates.[6] The hope of being able to aid the trade was one motive for the ratification of the Constitution.[7] Secretary of State Thomas Jefferson in 1790 secured estimates of what had been lost in the ruin of the Mediterranean trade. Customs house records had been destroyed early in the War for Independence but estimates were that Mediterranean ports had taken about a sixth of the exported wheat and flour, a fourth of dried and pickled fish, and some rice, in a trade which used from eighty to a hundred ships annually and employed twelve hundred seamen. "Our navigation . . . into the Mediterranean," he added, "has not been resumed at all, since the peace." The Algerines had to hunt the ships of their neighbors all over their sea but they could pounce on the Americans at the entrance.[8] Jefferson was right about the overt trade but a very few sharp skippers who knew their way about sold their flour and fish from port to port under cover of forged or fraudulently acquired British passes. From time to time one might even manage to sail in the company of a Dutch, Portuguese, or Spanish man of war.[9]

What the Algerine-American situation amounted to was a state of undeclared war between two remote antagonists. That was the way the Barbary powers saw it. Just as many Indian tribes regarded themselves as at war with all comers except those who had actually negotiated a peace, so the Barbary rulers said they and the Turks were sovereign over their landlocked sea and permitted no one not in treaty to navigate it.[10]

Some people thought there was a more immediate danger than the infrequent snatching of an American ship and crew. Although they had never been seen west of the Azores, the Algerines might come to America. Captain Richard O'Brien, of the captives of 1785, said, a year after his capture, "our country being so far situated from them, they will not attempt to approach our coasts. they [*sic*] have very little Idea of America . . ." But five years later, apparently willing to use shock against what must have seemed apathy, he warned "they would go as far as the Western Islands, and, by being acquainted with the navigation that far, would be induced to go on to the coasts of America; then, honored sirs, what would be the fatal consequences—what would be the alarm!" [11] Hugh Williamson of North Carolina used the same threat in 1788 as an argument for ratifying the Constitution.[12] And the Moroccan "foreign secretary" threatened it in the same year: "His imperial majesty will . . . send his frigates to America, provided with European pilots, and if they make any prizes" the ships would be burned and the crews enchained.[13] Robert Montgomery, at Alicante, Spain, applied to Jefferson in 1791 for an appointment to negotiate peace with Algiers. He supported his application with a verbal alarum: if the Portuguese, who blockaded the Straits of Gibraltar to the Algerines, made peace with the pirates, as Montgomery anticipated, "we must expect to see their Cruizers on the coast and in the Bays of America the summer following or so soon as the Russo-Turkish war is ended . . ." [14] Each of these lookouts had something to gain by this warning hail. Perhaps John Adams was on the right course when he replied to Thomas Brand Hollis who had written the same to him: "You seem to suppose our coast in danger from African pyrates; in this I presume you are deceived by the Artifices of the London insurance offices, for we are in no more danger than the Empire of China is." [15]

The Algerine imbroglio was not a "big story" in the United States in these years. A page by page search of the semi-official *Gazette of the United States* from April 1789, to March 1793, turned up ten references to Algiers, all brief. John Adams's letterbooks for the same years mention the Barbary pirates twice. George Washington's unofficial correspondence in the same period referred to the piracies five times, and two of the letters were on the "Algerine prisoner fraud"—a confidence game practiced in America which swindled the relatives of persons lost at sea by telling them their kin were held at Algiers and could be ransomed.[16] The owner of the ship in which Captain O'Brien was taken was unable to raise the ransom for his crew by private subscriptions.[17] The evidence leaves the impression that the public reaction to the North African depredations was as nothing compared with the feeling aroused by Indian attacks. Death at the hands of Indians-unknown was frequently reported and given about the same treatment in the press as the more shocking of modern traffic fatalities. Nevertheless there was a continuous current of official interest, although the stream was thin.

If the United States was to take any action it might follow one of several alternatives: periodic ransoms on a regularly negotiated scale, prepaid tribute according to treaties which provided immunity from capture (which was the usual European practice), or naval action against the pirates.[18] We are here concerned with contemporary thinking on the naval alternative.

Thomas Jefferson, as Minister to France and as Secretary of State, felt a responsibility for solving the problem and no American spent more ink, breath, or lamp oil on the subject. His favorite solution had the merit of easy understanding: fight them. From 1784 Jefferson's correspondence enlarged on the idea of naval war against the Barbary powers, Algiers in particular. His thinking may be divided into strategic and tactical ideas.

From the beginning he urged the building of a navy and saw the Algerine menace as an opportunity. "We cannot begin in a better cause," he wrote in 1784, "nor against a weaker foe." [19] When he first went to Paris he asked other members of the diplomatic corps what their countries paid to the Algerines but he was shrugged off so he set himself to collect scraps of information as he could. His final reckoning was that the United States could buy peace for one hundred to three hundred thousand dollars, annually. Appalled, he concluded immediately that fighting would be better, particularly since Spain, Portugal, Venice, and Naples were all at war with Algiers and would probably open their ports to American men of war, and some or all might even be willing to form a naval alliance with the United States. For that matter, he thought John Paul Jones could do the job with six frigates—a figure he later scaled down.[20]

There was the possibility of Algiers getting naval help from abroad, and he put it to the French Foreign Minister, Charles Gravier, Comte de Vergennes. Would the British help the pirates? Vergennes "seemed to think it impossible, on account of the scandal it would bring on them." [21] Renewing his argument for a navy, Jefferson addressed John Adams, his opposite number in London. Operations against Algiers would cost forty-five thousand pounds yearly. But, after all, the United States should have a navy in any event. A navy would cost half as much to keep up in peacetime. Ergo, naval operations against Algiers should only be charged off at £22,500 per year. His figure assumed a squadron of 150 guns, with half the squadron "in constant cruise." It would cost £450,000 to build, man, and victual the squadron for six months.[22] Several years later he repeated the notion that the United States should have a navy, whether in war or peace. Even if the country made a peace with Algiers a fleet would be necessary to show the Algerines "that we are in condition to chastise an infraction of the treaty; consequently some marine force must be exhibited in their harbour, from time to time." [23]

Considering that he was at the time a civilian foreign service officer, Jefferson had gone deeply into the tactical problem. From the French he learned that a successful blockade had been maintained at Algiers forty years before, using a ship, two frigates, and a sloop of war on fixed moorings at the harbor mouth. Charles-Henri, Comte d'Estaing advised him that a bombardment of Algiers would bring only temporary relief; it was "like breaking glass windows with guineas." [24] Foreign Minister Vergennes recommended ten vessels for such a blockade; it had been done with less but "vessels of relief would be necessary." [25]

From five statements of the strength of the pirates Jefferson deduced that they usually had nine xebecs of ten to thirty-six guns, and four galleys. In 1790 they had six xebecs and two galleys, but they were building a frigate and expected to get two ships from the Turks. Algerine ships were fast but were too lightly framed to take a broadside. Although their crews were large and brave they were not skilled aloft nor at the guns, hence their reliance on boarding. Two of the ships were state ships. The others belonged to officials. They never acted together but hunted singly during the temperate months of the year.

Another Jeffersonian proposal, which would also require force, was that some Algerines be captured for exchange. Although it was not their usual custom they had "sometimes" exchanged at the rate of two for one Christian. But on other occasions they had refused five or six to one.[26]

All of these facts and speculations were given to the Congress late in 1790. They did not influence the Congress to build a navy but his papers establish Thomas Jefferson as a serious and constructive naval theorist. Throughout these years he continued to explore, as well, every avenue of diplomacy which might lead to the release of the prisoners.[27]

Captain O'Brien, John Paul Jones, and John Adams also were on record. The last thing Captain O'Brien wished was the intensification of his alien-enemy-slave status by some American act of violence. Throughout his ten years of captivity he insisted that ransom was the best policy. If money was an object he urged a partial payment in ships and naval stores.[28]

Commodore Jones, chafing on the beach in France, was said to have proposed to Vergennes to sail in "une croisade" against the "Barbaresques," either as commanding officer or frigate captain. He said the European powers feared to attack the pirates because it might antagonize the Sultan of Turkey, they being his nominal vassals. But he pointed out that the Grand Turk could not help the corsairs against a fleet from one of the nations out of his reach by land, and he added some prophetic words on the inevitable link of France and North Africa. Vergennes died shortly after, and with him died the project.[29] Jones later approached the Dutch, at Jefferson's suggestion, with a proposal for a joint Dutch-American expedition. The Dutch did not encourage him and he thought it best for the United States to act alone. He believed he could handle the Algerines with two frigates and two or three sloops of war.[30]

Although John Adams meditated sympathetically on Jefferson's proposals he disagreed that naval action would be the best alternative. Annual tribute would be cheaper than war, he thought, but he categorically agreed that the United States should have a navy.[31] Adams had decided views on the technique of negotiation, writing that European powers usually sent naval force with their ambassadors, offering the pirates a choice of treaty or battle. It was exactly this sort of thing O'Brien was anxious to avoid: "it is bad policy to use any threats or make any parade with cruisers if we intend suing for a peace . . ."[32] It was a long way from Adams's handsome house in the west end of London to O'Brien's dismal dungeon in Algiers—points of view could properly differ.

The Congress had the Algerine problem before it a number of times but rarely for long. In the five regular sessions of the first two Congresses, from 1789 to 1793, the Mediterranean trade or the pirates, or both, were before one or the other house a little less often than a day in every fourth week of the time spent in session. This record shows no sense of urgency, probably because Portugal was on equally bad terms with Algiers and for years kept a squadron at the Straits of Gibralter which corked the corsairs as though in a bottle. As long as the Portuguese did the world's work in this way, and American shipmasters voluntarily avoided the Mediterranean, the situation was tolerable if humiliating.

Occupied in erecting and animating the government of the United States, the first session of the First Congress gave no time whatever to the Mediterranean predicament. In the second session a stranger volunteered a plan for making peace with Algiers and the American captives petitioned for congressional help. Still the Congress did not act, except to refer the petition to the Secretary of State.[33]

At the beginning of the third session of the First Congress President Washington recommended attention to the "relief and protection" of the Mediterranean commerce. A measure of the relative importance of current problems in the President's mind was the award of six lines of the message to Algerine troubles and thirty-four lines to Indian affairs.[34] The Senate appointed a committee headed by John Langdon of New Hampshire to deal with the question. The House referred it to Secretary of State Jefferson.[35]

All of Jefferson's thinking and his supporting documents (as previously summarized) were sent to the Congress late in December 1790. At this place in the story the train of events enters a tunnel. The Senate always met behind closed doors until 1794 and now the House cleared the galleries, so we know very little about the deliberations. The House apparently decided to do nothing about the Algerines, although the Senate authorized the President to do what he could for the captives providing he did not spend more than forty thousand dollars. It also adopted the memorable and often quoted resolution, "That the trade of the United States to the Mediterranean cannot be protected but by a naval force, and that it will be proper to resort to the same as soon as the state of the public finances will admit." [36]

A month later the sole appropriation for the expense of dealing with Barbary pirates passed the First Congress—an appropriation of twenty thousand dollars for meeting the cost of renewing the Moroccan Treaty. There was nothing for the relief of the Americans at Algiers. Apparently the members were staggered by the total of appropriations in the session for a revulsion shook the Senate, as shown by a simultaneous resolution that large sums of money had been voted "for the protection of the Western frontiers" and any ransoming at Algiers should be put off "until the situation of the Treasury shall more clearly authorize appropriations of money for that purpose." This was the economy of temporary legislative panic. It is hard to believe that a nation, dedicated to the dignity of the individual, which was at the moment easily borrowing many, many millions to pay old debts, could not as easily have borrowed another fifty thousand or so to unchain a dozen of its citizens, even if it did not feel financially secure enough to build a navy.[37]

The only record of the congressional discussion is Senator William Maclay's caustic and sometimes passionate diary. Of Jefferson's report he wrote that it "seemed to breathe resentment, and abounded with martial estimates in a naval way." It would be better to ransom the captives and forget the Mediterranean trade.[38] A few days later he thought "there is a wish to engage us in this distant war with these pirates" in order to increase taxes which one Senator in the debate "called the only bonds of our Union." Ill-advised Indian fighting had been authorized for the same reason.[39] "War is often entered into to answer domestic, not foreign purposes." There was no need for force since Captain O'Brien believed peace could be had in exchange for naval stores. O'Brien blamed the "French, Danes, and, above all, the British" for the bad relations with Algiers.[40] The Indian war had been used to justify a standing army. Now there would be an Algerine war to justify a navy. The captives could have been ransomed for about thirty-five thousand dollars but half a million is wanted for a fleet. "This thing of a fleet has been working among our members all the session. I have heard it break out often." [41] When the country had a standing army and navy, and "a host of revenue officers, farewell freedom in America." [42] "Hamilton's people" tried to get a war with the northern Indians but failed. "Britain at one time seemed their object." (The idea of a Hamiltonian Anglophobia is wonderful nonsense.) "Great efforts were made to get a war with Algiers. That failed." Now they will try a war with France.[43] This last entry at least dates the extinction of any hope among his opponents of using naval force against the pirates.

Maclay was quite harsh with those who abandoned the American slaves in Algiers. On the day the Senate resolved that the Algerine ransoms should be postponed, he mentioned the bill for the Moroccan Treaty and the fact that there was

> not a cent for the poor slaves. Hard was the heart that could do it, and clay-cold was the conduct of the President even in the business. I said and did what I could, but all in vain; and we will not only confine to slavery, but murder with the plagues of that deleterious climate, these unhappy men.[44]

He thought money had been appropriated for the purpose by the old Congress in 1788 (it was actually in 1787) and the appropriation would be sufficient authorization for the President to go ahead.[45] Obviously, the President did not take the same view.

Among these eighteenth century men we have seen that there were those who wished the Americans to turn away from the trans-Atlantic world and overrun and exploit the continent. Others, as shown before by their arguments in the constitutional ratification controversy, did not envision an extensive and populous United States but, instead, hoped to keep the country as it was, convinced that the liberty gained in the Revolution could be preserved in no other way. These latter can be called "provincial isolationists," believers in a little America. Since Maclay saw Indian fighting only as an excuse to create a standing army, and was also willing to keep American shipping out of the Mediterranean, and so vigorously opposed founding a navy, he can probably be classed with the provincial isolationists, and seems to have been their spokesman in the Senate.

There was no serious attempt during the Second Congress to found a navy. References to the Algerine problem were confined to the matter of ransom, brought forward in taking action on petitions. Two privately ransomed men asked that their benefactors be reimbursed, Captain O'Brien thrice reminded the Congress of the captives remaining in Algiers, and Hannah Stevens, of Concord, Massachusetts, asked for help in freeing her husband, Isaac Stevens, master of one of the ships taken in 1785.[46] The Senate seems to have been immediately willing to redeem the prisoners. The brake was in the House, according to a note from Washington to Jefferson early in 1792.[47] In the end, the Second Congress voted fifty thousand dollars for the expense of negotiating with Algiers.[48] This Congress spent much time on army affairs, and Indian relations, and gave very little attention to the Algerines or to founding a navy (except that some commercial legislation was intended to encourage shipping as "a nursery for seamen" for future naval use).

Reading the *Annals* of the first two Congresses one must conclude that the Algerine captives and the Mediterranean trade were among their smallest concerns. The President could write that everything possible, "consistent with justice and policy," would be done for the prisoners [49] but in the Congress, for every word on that subject, they uttered a thousand on Indian troubles. The negative effect of Indian problems on foreign policy was great (and it might be instructive to examine Indian relations as they affected foreign policy in later decades). One Representative, Jeremiah Wadsworth of Connecticut, seems to have expressed the controlling idea when he said: "There had never been a day, from the first settlement of America to the present moment, without our being at war with the Indians, in one place or other." [50]

The Congress was pretty busy with many kinds of claims. It reimbursed soldiers for ransoms paid to Indian captors or for pay-days missed while in captivity, it appropriated for the relief of the widows and orphans of officers who had paid military expenses out of pocket, it paid money for the "relief" of Americans impressed into the British Navy, and it replaced compensation-certificates for veterans who had lost them. The Algerine captives were only a few in a cloud of claimants.

Excepting poor Hannah Stevens of Concord, Thomas Jefferson

seems to have felt the plight of the prisoners most deeply. No doubt his study and thinking influenced his North African policy when he became President. It has been said that John Adams's reaction to American helplessness to deal with Algiers in the 1780s influenced him to favor a better national revenue system and has thereby influenced our constitutional thought.[51]

So far as they concern naval history the early Algerine depredations have sometimes been dismissed with the comment that the country wished to do more than it did but was too weak. The eagerness of the country to do something was certainly not seen in the House of Representatives, the most responsive organ. The student who reexamines the subject may end by agreeing with James Fenimore Cooper who was sceptical of conclusions that "the strongest indignation glowed in every bosom" or "this perfidious conduct produced the strongest indignation" —which were typical of Cooper's contemporaries. He doubted the country was so weak and frustrated as all that, and said he could not "but suspect that in the strife of parties, the struggles of opinion, and the pursuit of gain, the sufferings of the distant captives were overlooked or forgotten." [52] The key word in Cooper's remark is probably the word "distant"—overseas, overlooked. Rival claimants nearly all had the advantage of being in some congressional constituency.

As for doing something in the naval line, the United States appears to have been better able to go to sea in 1791 against a petty power than it had been in the 1770s when the first United States ships steered out to take on the whole British Empire. But as long as the Portuguese were willing to confine the Algerines to the Mediterranean by patrolling its entrance, the American response to the plight of a dozen or so enslaved citizens was weak and irresolute.

NOTES FROM PAGES 35 TO 44

1. William Eaton, Consul at Tunis, 1799, cited in Gardner Weld Allen, *Our Navy and the Barbary Corsairs* (Boston, 1905), 9–10. Moroccan pirates, based on their shallow port of Sallee, cruised the Atlantic in small, light-draft ships. They detained an American ship at Tangier in 1784 but made a treaty in 1785 which was fairly well kept. Samuel Flagg Bemis, *Diplomatic History of the United States*, rev. ed. (New York, 1942), 67–68. Being relatively weaker than the Algerines they were probably more agreeable to negotiation, as having less loot to lose by a self-denying agreement.
2. Allen, *Our Navy and the Barbary Corsairs*, 14–22.
3. Short to Jefferson, 7 July 1790, Charles W. Goldsborough, *United States Naval Chronicle* (Washington, 1824), 43.
4. Stimpson (Russian Consul at Gibraltar) to Washington, *Gazette of the United States*, 3 Nov. 1790, 16 Jan. 1791.
5. D'Andries to Moody, 6 Nov. 1790, *ibid.*, 9 July 1791.
6. C. O. Paullin, *Diplomatic Negotiations of American Naval Officers, 1778–1883* (Baltimore, 1912), 48–49; W. M. Malloy, comp., *Treaties, Conventions, International Acts, Protocols and Agreements*,

1776–1909, 2v. (Washington, 1910), 470–471.

7. For example, John Jay, *An Address to the People of the State of New York . . .* (New York, 1788), in Paul Leicester Ford, ed., *Pamphlets on the Constitution of the United States, Published During Its Discussion by the People, 1787–1788* (Brooklyn, 1888), 73.
8. Jefferson to the Congress, 28 Dec. 1790, *State Papers and Publick Documents of the United States*, 3d ed., 10v. (Boston, 1819), X, 41–45. Hereafter cited: *State Papers and Pub. Docs.*
9. Phineas Bond, "Letters," ed. J. F. Jameson, *Report*, American Historical Association (1896), I, 523–524; Allen, *Our Navy and the Barbary Corsairs*, 15.
10. John Adams to Jefferson, 17 Feb. 1786, quoting the Tripolitan Ambassador to London, in R. W. Irwin, *The Diplomatic Relations of the United States with the Barbary Powers* (Chapel Hill, 1931), 40.
11. O'Brien to Jefferson, 8 June 1786, *Naval Documents Related to the United States Wars with the Barbary Powers*, 6v. (Washington, 1939–1944), I, 2–4; O'Brien to the Congress, 28 April 1791, *American State Papers*, ed. Walter Lowrie and Matthew St. Clair Clarke, 38v. (Washington, 1832–1861), Class I, *Foreign Relations*, I, 129–130. These collections hereafter cited, respectively: *Naval Documents, Barbary Powers*, and, *ASP: Foreign Relations.*
12. Hugh Williamson, "Remarks on the new plan of government," *State Gazette of North Carolina*, in Paul Leicester Ford, ed., *Essays on the Constitution of the United States, Published During Its Discussion by the People* (Brooklyn, 1892), 403.
13. Secretary, Foreign Department, Morocco to Consuls at Tangier, 9 May 1788, *Naval Documents, Barbary Powers*, I, 18.
14. Montgomery to Jefferson, 26 July 1791, *ibid.*, I, 33.
15. Adams to Hollis, 11 June 1790, Adams papers, John Adams, Letterbooks, reel 115, Library of Congress *et al.* Rufus King had thought the danger from the pirates real but exaggerated for business and political purposes. King to Gerry, 1 May 1785, Rufus King, *Life and Correspondence*, 6v., ed. C. R. King (New York, 1894–1900), I, 93. A reasonable man could accept the feasibility of a pirate raid on American shores and an officer of state would have to reflect on it. The North Africans showed a real daring. As late as 1817 Tunisians took Hanse ships in the North sea. Allen, *Our Navy and the Barbary Corsairs*, 12.
16. The Algerine prisoner fraud: Thomson to Washington, 12 Aug. 1788, Whiting to Washington, 25 Oct. 1789, Washington papers, vol. 241, 244, Library of Congress; Washington to Thomson, 21 Aug. 1788, to Barclay (official), 31 Aug. 1788, to Thomson, 18 Sept. 1788, to Whiting, 18 Nov. 1789, George Washington, *Writings*, ed. John C. Fitzpatrick, 39v. (Washington, 1931–1944), XXX, 56–57, 84–85, 95, 458–459. To make the story cohere, logic required that one of the alleged seizures had happened a few miles off Sandy Hook. The fraud was exposed in *Gazette of the United States*, 28 Aug. 1790.
17. Washington to Irvin, 20 July 1789, Washington, *Writings*, 357–358, 357n.
18. Jefferson to the Congress, 28 Dec. 1790, *State Papers and Pub. Docs.*, X, 41–47.
19. Jefferson to Gates, 13 Dec. 1784, Merrill Jensen, *The New Nation: a History of the United States during the Confederation, 1781–1789* (New York, 1950), 212.
20. Jefferson to Monroe, 11 Nov. 1784, Monroe papers, Library of Congress.
21. Jefferson to Jay, 23 May 1786, *State Papers and Pub. Docs.*, X, 50 (sent to the Congress, 28 Dec. 1790).
22. Jefferson to John Adams, 11 July 1786, *Naval Documents, Barbary Powers*, I, 10.
23. Jefferson to the Congress, 28 Dec. 1790, *State Papers and Pub. Docs.*, X, 45.
24. D'Estaing to Jefferson, 17 May 1784, *ibid.*, X, 54–55 (given to the Congress, 28 Dec. 1790).
25. Jefferson to Jay, 23 May 1786, *ibid.*, X, 50 (given to the Congress, 28 Dec. 1790).
26. Jefferson to the Congress, 28 Dec. 1790, *ibid.*, X, 46; Jefferson to Washington, 28 Dec. 1790, *ibid.*, X, 60 (given to the Congress, 30 Dec. 1790). A xebec was a fast, three-masted, lateen-rigged ship with long overhangs. Captain O'Brien

said the private owners did not welcome peace. O'Brien, 28 April 1787, *Naval Documents, Barbary Powers,* I, 16.

27. A French writer said the reaction to Jefferson's report was the purchase of the old American Revolutionary frigate *Alliance* "par les autorites navales." Emile Dupuy, *Etudes d'histoire d'Amerique; Americains et Barbaresques (1776–1824)* (Paris, 1910), 66. The writer has found no corroboration. Some of Jefferson's efforts to use the arts of diplomacy to free the captives are a part of the background of the passage of the Naval Act of 1794. See Chapter IV, hereafter. African-American diplomatic history in this period has been explained in detail in Irwin, *The Diplomatic Relations of the United States with the Barbary Powers,* cited *supra.*

28. For example, O'Brien to the Congress, 26 Dec. 1789, *State Papers and Pub. Docs.,* X, 47 (given to the Congress, 28 Dec. 1790), 28 April 1791, *ASP: Foreign Relations,* I, 129–130 (given to the Congress, 9 Dec. 1791).

29. Dupuy, *Americains et Barbaresques,* 59–62.

30. Allen, *Our Navy and the Barbary Corsairs,* 44.

31. *Ibid.,* 38; John Adams to Jay, 16 Feb. 1786, *State Papers and Pub. Docs.,* X, 52, to Jefferson, 31 July 1786, *Naval Documents, Barbary Powers,* I, 12.

32. John Adams to Jay, 16 Feb. 1786, *State Papers and Pub. Docs.,* X, 52 (given to the Congress, 28 Dec. 1790); O'Brien to Jefferson, 8 June 1786, *Naval Documents, Barbary Powers,* I, 3.

33. 1 Cong., 2 Sess., 18 Jan. 1790, *Annals of the Congress, 1789–1824,* 42 v., ed. J. Gales and W. W. Seaton (Washington, 1834–1856), I, 937, 940. Hereafter cited: *Annals.* (The *Annals* of the First Congress are in two volumes, hereafter distinguished by the usual roman numerals.) 14 May 1790, *ibid.,* II, 1572.

34. 1 Cong., 3 Sess., 8 Dec. 1790, the President to the Congress, *Annals,* II, 1730. Senate and House agreement with the President, *ibid.,* II, 1733, 1799.

35. 1 Cong., 3 Sess., 14, 15 Dec. 1790, *ibid.,* II, 1735, 1803. Langdon was a ship builder who had been active in naval affairs for the Continental Congress during the War for Independence. Lawrence Shaw Mayo, *John Langdon of New Hampshire* (Concord, N.H., 1939), 99–100, 230.

36. 1 Cong., 3 Sess., 30 Dec. 1790–1 Feb. 1791, *Annals,* II, 1740–1741, 1744, 1749, 1753, 1838.

37. 1–3 March 1791, *ibid.,* II, 1774, 1775, 1781. "An act making an appropriation for the purpose mentioned therein," signed 3 March 1791, was a bill appropriating for the expense of the renewal of the Moroccan treaty. The bill may be found at II, 2340. Jefferson was sensitive to the appearance of callousness and explained several times that the United States hoped to ransom at small cost so that American citizens would not appear to be lucrative prizes and be the more sought after. He also insisted that a peace treaty be an integral part of any ransom deal, to protect the merchant seamen generally. See Jefferson to Humphreys, 21 March 1793, and enclosure of a letter to John Paul Jones, 1 June 1792. Jefferson papers, Library of Congress.

38. William Maclay, *Journal,* ed. E. S. Maclay (New York, 1890), (3 Jan. 1791) 364. The Sprouts thought Maclay was speaking the anti-naval sentiment they found in the West. Harold and Margaret Sprout, *The Rise of American Naval Power, 1776–1918,* rev. ed. (Princeton, 1944), 27.

39. Maclay, *Journal* (6 Jan. 1791), 366.

40. *Ibid.* (21 Jan.), 375–376.

41. *Ibid.* (1 Feb.), 383.

42. *Ibid.* (11 Feb.), 389–390.

43. *Ibid.* (26 Feb.), 406–407. This may well be the only allegation after 1789 that Hamilton was an Anglophobe.

44. *Ibid.* (1 Mar.), 408–409.

45. *Ibid.* Maclay had probably heard of a decision of the Continental Congress of 12 Oct. 1787 to use money left over from an appropriation of 1785 "for the Barbary Treaties" (Morocco) to redeem the captives. In September 1788 the Congress approved expenditures for their maintenance. Jay to the Congress, 12 Oct. 1787, Resolution, 12 Sept. 1788, *Journals of the Continental Congress, 1774–1789,* 34v. (Washington, 1904–1937), XXXIV, 523–525. The prisoners did receive a little money for their comfort. The bulk of the treaty-funds-surplus

went to pay the expenses of the legation at Paris. Jefferson papers, 1793, Library of Congress.

46. Coleville and Robertson, 2 Cong., 1 Sess., 4 Nov. 1791, 12 April 1792, *Annals,* 26, 122, see also 559, 599–600, 1386–1387, for disposition, and the appropriation bill passed without regard for them; Captain O'Brien, 10 Nov. 1791, *ibid.,* 29, 613, 673; Hannah Stevens, 17 Jan. 1792, *ibid.,* 74–75.

47. Washington to Jefferson, 10 March 1792, Washington, *Writings,* XXXII, 1; Washington to the Senate, 8 May 1792, *State Papers and Pub. Docs.,* X, 109.

48. 2 Cong., 1 Sess., 8 May 1792, *Annals,* 600, 1387. The story of attempts to negotiate is in Irwin, *The Diplomatic Relations of the United States with the Barbary Powers.*

49. Washington to Jonathan Trumbull, 20 Aug. 1792, Washington, *Writings,* XXXII, 125.

50. Wadsworth of Connecticut, 2 Cong., 2 Sess., 2 Jan. 1793, *Annals,* 773.

51. Irwin, *Diplomatic Relations of the United States with the Barbary Powers,* 52–53, 52n. But see: Adams to Marchant, 2 March 1791, Adams papers, John Adams, Letterbooks, reel 115, Library of Congress *et al.,* in which he said the rivalries of state versus nation, of secretary versus secretary, of the three branches against each other, now existing or soon to arise "give me more serious apprehension, than National Debt, Indian Wars and Algerine depredations."

52. James Fenimore Cooper, *History of the Navy of the United States of America,* 2v., 2d ed. (Philadelphia, 1840), I, 235. The "indignation" statements are, respectively, from John Frost, *The Book of the Navy* (New York, 1842), 72, and Goldsborough, *Naval Chronicle,* 36.

IV

The Naval Act of 1794

Americans watched the growing turmoil of Europe during the early years of the French Revolution with mixed fear and hope. Apart from the moral and political issues of the Revolution there was the question of peace. If the continental war expanded to involve the maritime powers the United States might be entangled. But, if the war did become a naval war, the competing nations might open the West Indian trade to American ships and also allow them a part of the trans-Atlantic long haul.[1] In February 1793 Great Britain and France, at last, were at war, with Spain and the Netherlands joining at the side of Britain. The news, although not unexpected, did not arrive in America until April.[2] From that time until the Congress met in December the chief energies of the executive officers were absorbed in defining and proclaiming American impartiality and in taming the new French Minister, Edmond Charles Genêt, who took a very light view of neutral responsibilities.[3]

To President George Washington and his Secretaries, the United States seemed quite unready for war at a time when peace was very uncertain. The cabinet officers at first suspected that there would be trouble with Spain. Thomas Jefferson recorded this as the unanimous agreement of the Cabinet late in June.[4] However, as months passed, the horizon of threat widened considerably and dangers to the ship of state loomed in the haze of war at every point of bearing. The country had better acquire defenses more concrete than a proclamation. In September Secretary of War Henry Knox handed to the President a memorandum of measures necessary for the defense of the United States. He wished to repair, buy, or manufacture small arms, field artillery, lead, and saltpeter or gunpowder, to move magazines inland, and to repair three forts. He had already acted on some of these matters at the direction of the President, but now submitted them in writing for approval so that he could present estimates to the next Congress.[5] Up to that time nothing had been said about defenses beyond the low-tide mark, although the behavior of the belligerents toward neutral shipping was becoming more and more injurious.

In memoranda used by the President to help him prepare his messages to the new Congress the greatest urgency was given to the task of explaining the neutrality proclamation and to the problem of enforcing it by prohibiting warlike acts within the country or within the "one league limit." None of the authors of these *aides memoires* suggested building a navy. The perennial problem of American captives in Algiers—who had languished in slavery for eight years—was alluded to once, with a marginal note, "Suspended till the close of the year." [6] These memoranda, with Knox's earlier paper, showed the formation of a defense policy: a slow, methodical build-up of defensive strength designed to counter only an invasion of North America.

This was the policy presented to the Congress in the presidential messages. The Congress met on 2 December. On the fourth came a message on Indian troubles, with supporting documents. On the fifth, a message on foreign relations, with special reference to the vexatious behavior of belligerents toward neutrals. On 8 December the Philadelphia press had a new and shocking fact—the Algerine pirates were loose in the Atlantic and were seizing American ships. On the sixteenth the President sent a message on that subject (and the Secretary of State sent over a report on foreign trade which he had kept in the deepfreeze for two years).[7] The Third Congress now had enough work to do to make it the busiest Congress yet convened. One Federalist, or Federalist sympathizer, saw a silver lining. The bad news might make it easier for the country to adopt proper defense measures, the people accepting "regulations and burdens to which they would not submit until the danger became imminent." He expected to see a strengthening of the militia, some new coastal forts and patrols, and "perhaps . . . a small Squadron to check the Algerines." [8]

The material damage suffered by the Americans between April and December 1793 had been to their merchant shipping which was harassed by both sides in the maritime war and by the seagoing extortionists of Algiers. President Washington reported to the Congress that the French had ordered the seizure of neutral ships carrying British property, and the British had limited the grain trade to their ports and the ports of their friends.[9] What he left to his listeners to deduce was that Britain could enforce her rule more easily than the French could enforce theirs. What was unknown in the United States at the moment was that the British had issued a new Order-in-Council the effect of which was to be catastrophic to American shipping in the West Indies.

Anglo-American relations were already strained because some important clauses of the Treaty of 1783 had not been executed. The Nootka Sound controversy had then added the impressment of American seamen into the Royal Navy to the list of American grievances.[10] Some Americans were pained by the restrictions on trading in the British Empire but political leaders disagreed on the remedy.[11] Because of their experience in the War for Independence and their knowledge of the Franco-American Alliance of 1778, the British, early in 1793, expected soon to be at war with the United States.[12] In anticipation, an Order-in-Council of 8 June 1793 (which Washington had spoken of to the Congress) provided that neutral ships carrying provisions to France be detained and purchased.[13] Americans next expected the impressment of their seamen because of the obvious British need, but it was not done immediately,[14] although the Foreign Office would make no promises on the subject to the American Minister.[15] The leaders of the Jeffersonian group which was emerging as the Republican Party, Jefferson, James Madison, and James Monroe, saw British policy toward neutrals as humiliating, and Federalist toleration of it as the elevation of national credit above national honor.[16] Private citizens of the same political persuasion were equally incensed. For examples, Hugh Henry Brackenridge published a proposal to conquer Canada[17] and Joel Barlow suggested borrowing naval power from France.[18] The commercial Federalists, who were the most articulate of their group, found profits enough to offset losses and were peaceful toward Britain,[19] although angry enough at the Jeffersonians.

On the other hand, only the most biased pro-French spectator could say that the French behaved with perfect correctness in the same months. The correspondence of Jefferson while Secretary of State showed that the administration was exasperated and perplexed in its attempts to deal with the French Minister Genêt. His American-based privateers seized British ships, sometimes in American coastal waters, and his Consuls tried to exercise admiralty jurisdiction in the neighborhood of federal district courts.[20] He also encouraged a good many homegrown expansionist projects (nowadays lumped off as Genêt's projects), inciting the Carolinians against Florida, the Kentuckians against the Spanish at the mouth of the Mississippi River, and encouraging the designs of the Vermonters on the Saint Lawrence Valley. His agents also tried unsuccessfully to promote a separatist movement in the trans-Allegheny.[21] Of course all of these enterprises collapsed when he lost his accreditation as Minister.[22]

These general and more or less predictable troubles of a small neutral during a world war were accompanied by a special difficulty, that of dealing with the North African pirates.[23] Throughout most of 1793 David Humphreys was in Spain trying to arrange a conference with the Dey of Algiers. The surviving captives were endangered by the plague and were becoming embittered at the years of delay and apparent neglect.[24] Humphreys was pessimistic of the chance of coming to terms with the Dey within limits earlier prescribed by the Congress.[25] The hard fact was, as the American Consul at Lisbon implied, the pirates wanted loot so ardently that they did not feel they could make peace with all nations [26] but must keep some enemies to prey on. Humphreys found it all the more frustrating to be asked by the British armed forces in the Mediterranean theater to supply them with "all manner of eatables and drinkables. If we had but the free navigation of the Mediterranean," he wrote, "what an extensive market would be open for our produce!" [27]

Humphreys's pessimism was justified. In October 1793 the Portuguese called off their watchdogs after a truce between Algiers and Portugal had been arranged by the British. The Algerines sallied into the Atlantic and fell on American shipping. The news reached the press at Philadelphia, the seat of government, on 12 December.[28] The possibilities of such a truce and the difficulties it would pose had been thought about for years.[29] The effect of the pirate foray on the business community was bad. United States bonds sagged.[30] Business men began talking of a Navy, for "The Algerines will deprive us of all the advantages of the present state of Europe." [31] Although the story had to compete for attention with the enthralling decline and fall of Citizen Genêt (and in Philadelphia with a hotly debated battle of Quakers versus theater licensing) there were letters in the press written in a tone of genuine anger.[32] One exercised correspondent said the government had spent too much money "running a while [*sic*] goose chase after a parcel of Indians" and should have used some of it to build a navy.[33] David Humphreys, deep in the dumps, expected the Algerines to ravage "even the coasts of America," the warning used by navy-minded men as far back as the late 1780s.[34]

While the Americans were deciding what to do [35] the Queen of Portugal personally intervened on their behalf. She ordered that American ships bound to and from Portuguese ports be convoyed in the piracy zone by her men-of-war.[36]

Late in November, when his mission to Algiers was dead, Humphreys wrote what was probably the most influential letter of his life. To Washington he said "a naval force has now (to a certain degree) become indispensable." Convoys would not do. Only by offensive war could the United States "hope to catch some of the Corsairs separately, and perhaps out of the Mediterranean." [37] When this letter arrived in America it encouraged a movement already existing.

American thinking on the proper remedy for the Algerine evil was somewhat complicated by an almost universal belief that Great Britain had made the Portuguese-Algerine truce for the sole purpose of unleashing the pirates on American commerce.[38] It was an admitted fact that the British consul at Algiers had been the negotiator but the British Foreign Office denied any malevolence toward the Americans. The purpose had been only to relieve an ally of the burden of the Straits blockade so that the ships could be used to help Britain in other ways.[39] Since the Algerines were now at peace with the whole world, except the United States and the Hanseatic towns, Americans scoffed. For years they had believed in a British plot to perpetuate the hostility of the pirates against the United States and other small trading nations.[40] (Some Englishmen believed in it too.) [41] To many Americans it seemed that the British used the Indians in the forests and the pirates on the seas to the same end.[42] Denials in the American press were few and brief,[43] although Federalist Congressmen later argued that proof of British malice in these matters was lacking.[44]

The Third Congress acted on more military proposals than any before the "X. Y. Z. Affair" of 1798. In its first session it provided for harbor defenses, arsenals, and magazines; it increased the Army appropriation and added artillery and engineers; it passed new militia regulations; it dealt with the international trade in arms, with galleys, privateering, and dispatch boats; and it made provision for the widows and orphans of officers. Not least, it voted to built a navy.[45]

The first naval decision came out of secret debates in the House of Representatives on the President's messages concerning the Barbary powers. The immediate result was the adoption, on 2 January 1794, of three resolutions, first, to appropriate additional money for diplomatic expenses, second, to provide a naval force adequate to protect American commerce from the "Algerine corsairs," and third, to appoint a committee to report what force would be necessary, to estimate the cost, and to advise on "the ways and means for defraying the same." The only roll-call was on the "ways and means" clause which was approved 46–44.[46] This narrow margin was an omen of controversy. Meanwhile, the Senate waited on the House's action.[47]

The Select Committee, appointed under the third resolution, was stacked with ship-owners. Only one of the nine, Nathaniel Macon, could be called anti-Navy. The party line-up, if the phrase may be used, was Federalists six, Republicans three.[48] In addition to the documents received from the President and the Secretary of State, the Committee had the use of cost estimates prepared by the Secretary of War in 1790, and by Samuel Hodgdon of Philadelphia, for the Secretary, late in 1793.[49] Its report, on 20 January, recommended the construction of four ships of forty-four guns each (eighteen- and nine-pounders) and two ships of twenty guns. The cost was optimistically estimated at six hundred thousand dollars. This sum, it recommended, should be raised from additional customs duties.[50] On 6 February the House resolved to "go into a Committee on the state of the Union" with all mention of the executive documents forbidden, and the debate on the Select Committee's recommendation of a navy was on.[51]

Before reviewing the congressional debate it will be well to notice that there was, of course, an argument out of doors also. General Horatio Gates and Senator James Monroe wrote to friends that the project for a navy was merely a project to centralize power by increasing the patronage and spending of the administration.[52] Robert R. Livingston thought quicker action was needed and he urged the immediate use of privateers [53]—a proposal obviously aimed at Britain. Benjamin Franklin Bache's *General Advertiser* (later *Aurora*) took an unusual line for the fiercest of anti-Federalist newspapers. It printed one incomplete anti-naval essay, "To be continued," and then gave up the attack.[54] Indeed the paper had twice before agreed that a navy was necessary [55] and in printing stories of the captures and cruelties of the corsairs no doubt helped to create a public opinion which made the founding of a navy possible.[56] Noah Webster's *American Minerva,* a typical Federalist paper although rather more objective than most, regularly printed letters which stressed the theme of urgency, with occasional sarcastic needling of the Congress for its procrastination.[57] Both the *Advertiser* and *Minerva* printed a story of an otherwise unrecorded Charleston scheme to buy a frigate for the country with funds raised by public subscription.[58] The correspondence of interested pro-navy men emphasized the interference of the Algerines with the prospects of a prosperous wartime trade. Oliver Wolcott, Sr., wrote an Anglophobic remark when he said a navy, "respectable in the American seas," would make European powers more respectful, because they had property on this side of the water.[59]

To return to the House of Representatives, the debate was a debate of North versus South. Of the eleven speakers in favor of the Report only two came from south of the Potomac. Of nine who spoke against the Report only three came from north of the Potomac. Virginia pitted a quartet against the Report. Massachusetts presented four speakers for it and one against.[60] The northerners who opposed the report represented constituencies which were well inland; the northern supporters came from tidewater or very close to it.

The arguments of the opposition fell into five categories: economic, political, strategic, diplomatic (with special reference to British policy), and humanitarian.

The economic argument hit at the increasing expense of government. When once a navy was established there was no end to it. "We must then have a Secretary of the Navy, and a swarm of other people in office, at a monstrous expense." Most of the debt of Great Britain came from naval spending and the Kingdom of France had been ruined by naval expense. The project was also contrary to the policy of paying the national debt.[61] Tables of trade were produced to illustrate the cost of a navy and the savings effected by it. The conclusion was drawn that the savings were not enough.[62] Since Great Britain and Spain found it wise to bribe the pirates, that must be the better policy.[63]

Politically speaking the founding of a navy was a dangerous matter. A navy was the most expensive engine of defense and it was the expense of government which fastened tyranny on the people by a system of debts which was worse than feudalism because it was impersonal.[64]

The strategic arguments were that the force proposed was necessarily inadequate, the ships could not safely operate in the Mediterranean without assurance of the use of friendly harbors as bases, and their very existence would be more likely to involve the United States in the war than to make for peace. As for the inadequacy of the force, the Algerines had often been at war with nations which had far larger navies, and had hardly noticed it.[65] Concerning the lack of Mediterranean bases it had been said that foul weather was foul for the Algerines as well as for the Americans, but the pirates would be near home while the Americans were three thousand miles away.[66] That a navy would be very likely to provoke war was the sincere contention of the best mind of the opposition, for James Madison wrote to his father "that sending ships of force among the armed powers, would entangle us in the war, if anything wd. do it." [67]

The diplomatic problem was the question of the effect the creation of a navy would have on the policy of Great Britain. If the British had deliberately "unleashed" the corsairs to damage the Americans no peace could be had by dealing directly with Algiers [68] whether by war or diplomacy. Certainly Britain had sufficient motives. Her insurance rates were rising. A neutral America was capturing her carrying trade and luring British seamen into American ships. Therefore Britain would prevent the negotiation of any Algerine-American peace,[69] and would need to take no overt action but merely to aid the pirates "as she did an enemy in another quarter"—the Indians.[70]

The humanitarian point was the opposition's last barb. They assailed the use of force because it would worsen the condition of the Americans enslaved at Algiers.[71]

Simultaneously with the process of creating a navy the House of Representatives was beating down a set of commercial resolutions introduced by Madison to initiate reprisals against Great Britain for her transgressions against the American merchant fleet. The Resolutions were to put into effect the conclusions drawn from the data in Jefferson's report on foreign trade, which had been submitted in December.[72] A good many of the participants in the debate, indoors and out, thought of the commercial resolutions as a proposed substitute for the Naval Bill, a point which will be considered in the next chapter.

The pro-navy forces seem to have expended about four times as much breath on their rebuttal of the opposition as they did on their own constructive case for the Naval Bill.

They were sensitive to the charge that a navy would be an economic drain. A navy would save cargoes and ransoms in the future. Beginning in April 1794 ships westbound across the Atlantic would pay an insurance rate of twenty-five per cent of their value because of the piracy risk, or an extra two million dollars annually. Imported salt would rise a dollar a bushel, perhaps two dollars—the total rise in this one commodity alone being from three to six times the expense of the squadron.[73]

To the claim that a navy would be an instrument of tyranny the reply was that the same could be claimed of any armed force whatsoever,[74] the Congress should not refuse "adequate means to enable the Executive to discharge its Constitutional duties,"[75] and it was not complimenting the intelligence of the Congress to say if it authorized six ships this year it would end by building a hundred.[76]

The supporters urged that the force was adequate, that there was no reason for alarm about naval bases, and that the Naval Bill would not lead the country into a new war. The proposed force was certainly strong enough because the Committee based it on consecutive estimates of the Algerine strength, which pretty well agreed, and the Algerines were unlikely to become stronger.[77] The Portuguese had blocked the entrance to the Mediterranean with three ships, hence six American ships would be plenty, particularly since they would be newer and better than those of the corsairs.[78] It was thought significant that the opposition did not move to enlarge the squadron.[79] As for bases, the pirates were at sea in only seven or eight months of the year. American ships would be welcome in the harbors of France, Spain and Portugal, where they would find ample naval stores.[80] This choice of harbors was a much larger choice than the Algerines had.[81] It was unlikely that the United States would ever be at war with all three of these nations at once.[82] As for getting us into a war, any nation which wished to quarrel with the United States would not need the creation of an American navy for an excuse [83]—for that matter, the country had been at war with Algiers since 1783.[84]

The sponsors of the Naval Bill tried to avoid the admission that Britain uncorked the pirates with malicious intent. They argued the lack of evidence,[85] and the illogic of such an act, which would be more profitable in peacetime.[86] British aid to Algiers need not be feared because the only useful aid would be naval assistance which would cause an Anglo-American war.[87] But Benjamin Goodhue of Massachusetts believed the British used the corsairs against the United States and turned that into an argument that peace could not be bought.[88]

No dependence should be placed on Portuguese protection, because Portugal was an ally of Britain.[89] Even if it were possible to secure Portuguese protection such dependence would be humiliating because it would mean that the United States was tributary to Portugal.[90] It would also mean spending American dollars with no security for performance; how much better to nourish our own industry than Portugal's.[91] The whole project of buying the protection of a foreign nation was irrational. If they were at peace with Algiers no price could be high enough. If at war, no price would be necessary.[92]

The pro-navy men concluded their assault on the opposition arguments by saying that no constructive alternative had been offered.[93]

The constructive case of the proponents was relatively brief. Apparently—and with reason—they thought the facts of the martime crisis would not be improved by ornament. However they equated Indian and pirate defense (if one, why not the other?),[94] and warned that the Algerines, with renegade or European pilots, might ravage the defenseless coast of North America. Surely the prospect of "the plunder of Philadelphia" would tempt them.[95] A navy would prevent the loss of merchant seamen to Algiers or by desertion which could be expected because of lack of protection.[96] As for buying a peace, it would have to be backed by a navy to make it stick, as proved by the British experience.[97] So far the United States had no success in negotiating with the Dey of Algiers; if he saw that the country would not protect its merchants there was even less hope of success.[98]

Pressure for the Bill was steadily built up from outside. On 3 and 5 March the President sent more supporting documents, including what must have been very effective letters from Humphreys ("no choice" but a navy) and Richard O'Brien who had previously opposed the use of force but who now said there was "no alternative." [99] On 5 March the merchants of Baltimore handed in a petition for a "Naval force . . . adequate to the protection of the commerce of the United States against the Algerine corsairs." [100] And two days later came the infuriating news of the British Orders-in-Council of 6 November and 8 January which prohibited all neutral trade with the French West Indies and was followed by the seizure of something under two hundred American ships.[101] Even men famous for Federalism became hotly anti-British.[102] The passion of the moment would have helped to enact any military measure.[103]

A probable aid to passage of the Bill was its last section, which required that construction of the little fleet be stopped if peace were made with Algiers. This was put in by the House, after the Committee Report had scraped through so narrowly [104]—perhaps to mollify the opponents.[105]

The engrossed Bill was brought in on 10 March. After an unsuccessful motion to recommit, spokesmen for each side summarized the argument—with especial warmth on the negative side, when "the bad consequences connected" with the founding of navies "were depicted in animated terms" as the reporter drily put it. The vote against recommitting had been 48–41; for passage it was 50–39. Abraham Baldwin, Connecticut-born, Yale-bred Representative from inland Georgia, had suspended judgment but now voted nay. It is very likely significant that Frederick Augustus Muhlenberg of Philadelphia and John Watts of New York City, both Republicans, voted aye.[106]

There apparently was never a doubt of passing the Senate, where, after a few amendments readily accepted by the House, approval was voted (19 March) without a division.[107] So confident had the Senate sponsors been that six days earlier they had passed the criminal code with its reference to the presidential use of the "naval forces . . . of the United States." [108]

"An act to provide a naval armament . . . Approved March 27, 1794," had nine brief sections which (1) authorized the six ships, (2, 3, 4) set the numbers, grades, and ratings of officers and men, (5) gave the President his choice of buying or building the ships, (6, 7, 8) laid out the details of pay and rations, and (9) provided the suspension of the Act upon negotiation of peace with Algiers. The preamble said the Act was for the purpose of protecting commerce from the Barbary powers.[109]

Harold and Margaret Sprout, the pioneer students of the subject, found meaning in the sectional distribution of the House votes on the Committee Report, 11 February, and on the Bill, 10 March. New England almost unanimously favored the founding of a navy, the Middle States were for it two to one, the South Atlantic states opposed it almost three to one, and the frontier states, Kentucky and Vermont, were unanimously against it.[110]

The question was asked then and often since why so little of the Anglophobia of that season was to be heard in the speeches of the sponsors of the Navy Bill. Contemporary opponents explained it with the epithets "Tories" and "monocrats."[111] The answer seems to be that the sponsors, commercial and exporting Federalists for the most part, knew that national credit depended on a high level of imports for national revenue by way of customs duties, which, in turn, depended on a high level of trade with Great Britain. If the Hamiltonian financial design was to endure, Anglophobia was a luxury they could not afford.[112] As for their own businesses, suffering at the hands of British and African despoilers, their thinking can be formulated in what one could call the Theory of the Certain Loss. They were for chastising the Algerines because, as things stood, they were certain to lose money by piratical seizures, but naval expenses were not a certain loss. They opposed any reprisals against the British because hostilities with Britain would mean the certain loss of money while sporadic spoliations were not a certain loss on the final balance of their books. There could be no profit in any relations with the pirates; there could be profit in even very restricted trade relations with Great Britain and her West Indies.

The Naval Act of 1794 was part of a general strengthening of the American state, a strengthening undertaken with reluctance. The additions to the Army, the acquisitions of ordnance, the erection of harbor batteries were each a continuation or expansion of an existing practice or institution. The creation of the Navy was an abrupt change of policy. At the adjournment of the Second Congress one could not have foreseen that the Congress would "provide and maintain" a regular Navy only 371 days later. The Congress had been maritime-minded but had been content to rely on a naval potential as a deterrent to foreign powers. American ships had been seized by pirates before 1793 but there was no excitement[113] until new seizures threatened the otherwise bright prospect of large wartime profits.

It is improper to dismiss the rural Republican opposition as narrow. Their reasoning, no doubt, has an antiquarian, rusty creak today, but for their era they had a respectable case which must be examined if one is to have an approximately correct understanding of the popular thought of the past. It should be noted that they supported every defense measure of the session except the enlargement of the regular Army and the founding of the regular Navy.[114] It is safe to conclude that their opposition came from the ancient dread of regular establishments and love of militia.

The roll calls showed their basic weakness. They were unable to hold their city members. The Naval Act temporarily split the "farmer-labor" alliance which was becoming the Republican Party.[115] The general support of the measure by Bache's otherwise raging Republican paper, the *General Advertiser*, the votes of Republicans Muhlenberg of Philadelphia and Watts of New York City showed this.[116] Whether the seaport Republicans wished for the fleshpots of naval contracts or were influenced by a naturally more cosmopolitan outlook is impossible to say.

NOTES FROM PAGES 48 TO 59

1. Robert Greenhalgh Albion and Jennie Barnes Pope, *Sea Lanes in Wartime; the American Experience, 1775–1942* (New York, 1942), 65–67; Washington to Rochambeau, 29 Jan. 1789, George Washington, *Writings*, ed. John C. Fitzpatrick, 39v. (Washington, 1931–1944), XXX, 188.
2. Circular letter to the Consuls of the United States, 21 March 1793, Jefferson papers, Library of Congress (hereafter abbreviated to: LC); Jefferson to Washington, 1 April 1793, *ibid.*; Hamilton to Washington, 5 April 1793, Washington papers, LC.
3. Papers related to Genêt's annoying behavior make up a large fraction of the Washington papers, April–December 1793. The President and his cabinet officers also had absorbing personal distractions.
4. Jefferson to Madison, 23 June 1793, Jefferson papers, LC.
5. Knox to Washington, 6 Sept. 1793, Washington papers, LC. The paper is marked as approved by Jefferson and Attorney General Edmund Randolph.
6. The memoranda were by Washington, Hamilton, Randolph and Jefferson, all undated, bound in Washington papers, LC, November 1793.
7. Samuel Flagg Bemis, *Jay's Treaty, a Study in Commerce and Diplomacy* (New York, 1923), 185–187; although news had been coming from the Mediterranean and elsewhere (mostly bad) Benjamin Franklin Bache's *General Advertiser* (later *Aurora*) said on 3 Jan. 1794 that the country had been three months "without intelligence from either England or France." He was piecing out his columns with anecdotes of the Burgoyne campaign and a description of the "Hot springs of Iceland."
8. Alexander White to Madison, 28 Dec. 1793, Madison papers, LC. White had been one of the Virginia representatives who switched their votes on Assumption as part of the "national capital deal."
9. 3 Cong. 1 Sess., 5 Dec. 1793, *Annals of the Congress, 1789–1824*, ed. J. Gales and W. W. Seaton, 42v. (Washington, 1834–1856), 15, 136–137. Hereafter cited: *Annals*. All subsequent references are to the first session of the Third Congress unless otherwise noted.
10. Edward Channing, *A History of the United States*, 6v. (New York, 1932–1936), IV, 124.
11. Bemis, *Jay's Treaty*, 187; Thomas Jefferson, "The Anas," 11 March 1792, Thomas Jefferson, *Writings*, ed. A. A. Lipscomb, 20v. (Washington, 1904–1905), I, 299.
12. Channing, *A History of the United States*, IV, 126–127.
13. Nathan Schachner, *The Founding Fathers* (New York, 1954), 292.
14. Lear to Washington, 8 April 1793, Washington papers, LC; King to Ham-

ilton, 24 April 1793, Rufus King, *Life and Correspondence,* ed. C. R. King, 6v. (New York, 1894–1900), I, 440; undated memorandum, *ibid.,* I, 441. This self-denial was practiced even before the news of the neutrality proclamation reached Britain. Subsequent references to the King publication will be cited: King, *Life and Correspondence.*
15. Jefferson to Thomas Pinckney, 4 June 1793, Jefferson papers, LC.
16. *Ibid.;* Monroe to Jefferson, 27 June 1793, James Monroe, *Writings,* ed. S. M. Hamilton, 7v. (New York, 1898–1903), I, 266–267; Madison to Monroe, 15 Sept. 1793, Madison papers, LC.
17. Brackenridge to Washington, *National Gazette,* 15 May 1793, quoted in C. M. Newlin, *The Life and Writings of Hugh Henry Brackenridge* (Princeton, 1932), 132–133.
18. Barlow to Jefferson, 2 Dec. 1793, Jefferson papers, LC.
19. Manning J. Dauer, *The Adams Federalists* (Baltimore, 1953), 12–13. The American whaling fleet, based in part on French ports, prospered despite its unique French connections.—Edouard A. Stackpole, *The Sea Hunters: the New England Whalemen during Two Centuries, 1635–1835* (Philadelphia, 1953), 169–175.
20. Jefferson papers, April–December 1793, LC.
21. Eugene Perry Link, *Democratic-Republican Societies, 1790–1800* (New York, 1942), 133–141; an excellent example was the audacious work of M. A. B. Mangourit, Genêt's agent, who tried to promote the Florida Republic.—R. R. Palmer, "A revolutionary Republican," *William and Mary Quarterly,* third series, IX (Oct. 1952), 483–496.
22. Link, *Democratic-Republican Societies,* 141.
23. See Chapter III.
24. O'Brien to Bulkeley, "March the 26th 1793 & 8th of captivity," Washington papers, LC; Humphreys to Jefferson, 26 Sept. 1793, *American State Papers,* ed. Walter Lowrie and Matthew St. Clair Clarke, 38v. (Washington, 1832–1861) Class I, *Foreign Relations,* I, 295. Hereafter cited: *ASP: For. Rel.*
25. Humphreys to Washington, 21 March, 4 April, 5 May 1793, Washington papers, LC.
26. Church to Jefferson, 12 and 14 Oct. 1793, *ASP: For. Rel.,* I, 296; see also, Jefferson to the Congress, 28 Dec. 1790, *ibid.,* I, 105.
27. Humphreys to Jefferson, 26 Sept. 1793, *ibid.,* I, 295.
28. Same to same, 8 Oct. 1793, *ibid.; General Advertiser,* 12 Dec. 1793. For a collection of the rumors which were immediately afloat, *ibid.,* 27 Dec. 1793.
29. Jefferson to the Congress, 28 Dec. 1790, *State Papers and Publick Documents of the United States,* 3d ed., 10v. (Boston, 1819), X (*Confidential State Papers*), 45–47, hereafter cited, *State Papers and Pub. Docs.;* Montgomery to Jefferson, 26 July 1791, *Naval Documents Related to the United States Wars with the Barbary Powers,* I, 33; O'Brien to the Congress, 28 April 1791, *ASP: For. Rel.,* I, 129–130; O'Brien to Humphreys, 12 Nov. 1792, quoted in R. W. Irwin, *The Diplomatic Relations of the United States with the Barbary Powers* (Chapel Hill), 57–58.
30. Lawrance to King, 15, 18 Dec. 1793, King, *Life and Correspondence,* I, 506; Alsop to King, 23 Dec. 1793, *ibid.,* I, 508; Gore to King, 23 Dec. 1793, *ibid.,* I, 508–509.
31. Gore to King, 24 Dec. 1793, *ibid.,* I, 510–511.
32. *General Advertiser,* 4 Jan. 1794.
33. *Ibid.,* 1 Jan. 1794.
34. Humphreys to Jefferson, 23 Nov. 1793, in Irwin, *The Diplomatic Delations of the United States with the Barbary Powers,* 61; see also, Chapter I.
35. The Tunisian pirates apparently stayed in the Mediterranean during these years. The Moroccans had an Atlantic coast but were fighting a civil war and neglecting their ships.—Jefferson to Washington, 16 Dec. 1793, *ASP: For. Rel.,* I, 295.
36. Humphreys to Washington, 30 Nov. 1793, Washington papers, LC; *American Minerva,* 15, 17 Jan. 1794 (the text of the Queen's order was printed in the issue of the 17th); Church to Jefferson, 22 Oct. 1793, *ASP: For. Rel.,* I, 299.
37. Humphreys to Washington, 23 Nov. 1793, Washington papers, LC.
38. Even a partial list of believers makes a remarkable cross-section of parties and mixture of places. For the sake of brevity only the names, dates of expression, and

sources are given below: David Humphreys, 7 Oct. 1793, Washington papers, LC; Joel Barlow, 2 Dec. 1793, Jefferson papers, LC; Edward Church, 12, 14 Oct. 1793, *ASP: For. Rel.*, I, 296; John Lawrance, 10 Dec. 1793, King, *Life and Correspondence*, I, 503; John Alsop, 12 Dec. 1793, *ibid.*, I, 505; Pierce Butler, 19 Dec. 1793, Griffith J. McRee, *Life and Correspondence of James Iredell*, 2v. in 1 (New York, 1949), II, 403–404; Tobias Lear, 25 Dec. 1793, Washington papers, LC; William Findley, 15 Jan. 1794, *Annals*, 234; James Madison, 20 April 1795, *Political Observations* (Philadelphia, 1795), 5; Thomas P. Carnes, 2 May 1794, Carnes papers, Duke University (Carnes's letter located for me by James Morton Smith).

An almost equally large number of pseudonymous allegations of the same guilt was harvested from just two newspapers, one Federalist and one Republican.

Just to keep the record straight it should be added that the Portuguese-Algerine truce was probably made on the sole initiative of Consul George Logie, and for the reasons given by the British Foreign Office. Logie appears to have received no instructions on the subject. M. S. Anderson, Highgate, England, to the writer, 22 September 1957, citing the relevant documents in the Public Record Office, FO 3/7. On the discretion allowed to Consuls in Africa at the time see Hilda I. Lee, "The supervising of the Barbary Consuls during the years 1756–1836," *Bulletin of the Institute of Historical Research*, XXIII (1950), 193–194.

39. Church to Jefferson, 12 Oct. 1793, *State Papers and Pub. Docs.*, X, 279; Humphreys to Washington, 31 Jan. 1794, Washington papers, LC; Thomas Pinckney to Washington, 25 Nov. 1793, *ASP: For. Rel.*, I, 327; Gardner Weld Allen, *Our Navy and the Barbary Corsairs* (Boston, 1905), 47–48; Irwin, *The Diplomatic Relations of the United States with the Barbary Powers*, 58–60.
40. For example, Leacock to Jefferson [1793], Jefferson papers, LC.
41. For example, Lear to Washington, 25 Dec. 1793, and Gordon of St. Neots, England, to Washington, 7 March 1794, Washington papers, LC; Stanley Lane-Poole, *The Story of the Barbary Corsairs* (New York, 1890), chapter 19, considers the European toleration of the pirates.
42. "Americanus," No. 2, *Gazette of the United States*, 29 April 1789; Representatives Nicholas and Clark, 16 Jan. 1794, *Annals*, 243, 246.
43. Under heading "BOSTON, Dec. 25" in *American Minerva*, 1 Feb. 1794; a hint is in "Abstract of Weekly Intelligence," *ibid.*, 12 Feb. 1794.
44. Federalist Representatives said this in opposing Madison's commercial resolutions.
45. Simultaneously the executive branch launched a diplomatic offensive by sending James Monroe to Paris, John Jay to London, and Thomas Pinckney to Madrid. These missions led to Jay's and Pinckney's treaties and Monroe's recall in temporary disgrace.

   A list of the twenty-one ports to be garrisoned is in *Annals*, 479–480.
46. 2 Jan. 1794, *Annals*, 154–155. Madison wished the debate to be public but lost without a division.
47. 16, 24 December 1793, *ibid.*, 20–22.
48. Harold and Margaret Sprout, *The Rise of American Naval Power, 1776–1918*, rev. ed. (Princeton, 1944), 29, 29n. The Federalists were Thomas Fitzsimons (Pa.), Benjamin Goodhue (Mass.), Francis Malbone (R.I.), Jeremiah Wadsworth (Conn.)—these were the shipowners—Elias Boudinot (N.J.), and Uriah Forrest (Md.). The Republicans were Josiah Parker (Va.), Nathaniel Macon (N.C.), and Richard Winn (S.C.). Parker later became a Federalist.
49. Franklin Delano Roosevelt, "Our first frigates, some unpublished facts about their construction," *Transactions* of the Society of Naval Architects and Marine Engineers, XXII (1914), 139–140.
50. 20 Jan. 1794, *Annals*, 250; *ASP: Naval Affairs*, I, 5. It was proposed to change the *ad valorem* rate of articles paying seven and one-half per cent to eight and one-half per cent. Specific duties were to be added: five per cent on stone, marble, stoneware and earthenware; three cents a bushel on salt; six cents a ton on American ships in foreign trade;

and twenty-five cents a ton on foreign ships.

51. *Annals,* 432. The debate in Committee of the Whole occupied 6, 7, 10, and 11 Feb. 1794.
52. Gates to Madison, 13 March 1794, Madison papers, LC; Monroe to Jefferson, 16 March 1794, Jefferson papers, LC.
53. Robert R. Livingston to Monroe, 4 Jan. 1794, Monroe papers, LC.
54. *General Advertiser,* 12 Feb. 1794.
55. *Ibid.*, 20 Dec. 1793, 6 Jan. 1794.
56. *Ibid.*, 24, 25 Jan., 5, 16 Feb. 1794.
57. *American Minerva,* 21, 25, 26 Feb., 3 March 1794.
58. *Ibid.*, 14, 19 Feb. 1794; *General Advertiser,* 17 Feb. 1794.
59. Oliver Wolcott, Sr., to Oliver Wolcott, Jr., 13 Jan. 1794, George Gibbs, *Memoirs of the Administrations of Washington and John Adams,* 2v. (New York, 1846), I, 126, hereafter cited: Gibbs, *Memoirs;* Church to Jefferson, 12 Oct. 1793, *State Papers and Pub. Docs.*, X, 280.
60. *Biographical Directory of the American Congress, 1774–1949* (Washington, 1950). The Massachusetts man who spoke against the Report was William Lyman of Northampton, a newcomer to the House.
61. Abraham Clark, N.J., 6 Feb. 1794, *Annals,* 433–434; John Nicholas, Va., 7 Feb., *ibid.*, 439; William B. Giles, Va., 10 Feb., *ibid.*, 447, 10 March, *ibid.*, 490–492.
62. James Madison, Va., 11 Feb., *ibid.*, 449–451.
63. Abraham Baldwin, Ga., 6 Feb., *ibid.*, 434.
64. Giles, 10 March, *ibid.*, 490–492.
65. Giles, *ibid.*, 486–490; Nicholas, 6 Feb., *ibid.*, 434.
66. Giles, 10 Feb., *ibid.*, 446–447.
67. Madison to Col. James Madison of Orange County, 21 Feb. 1794, Madison papers, LC.
68. Madison, 6 Feb., *Annals,* 433.
69. John Hunter, S.C., 10 Feb., *ibid.*, 446.
70. William Lyman, Mass., 10 Feb., *ibid.*, 445; Madison, 6 Feb., *ibid.*, 437; the quotation is from John Smilie, Pa., 7 Feb., *ibid.*, 439.
71. Giles, 10 March, *ibid.*, 497. A year later Madison wrote an anonymous pamphlet, *Political Observations* (Philadelphia, 1795), in which he added more arguments, although it was then too late to do much more than to keep the fires of opposition burning. Among the arguments were the following: (1) The expense was greater than had been estimated, (2) the profit of the trade must be greater than the naval expense in order to justify the naval expense, (3) no other branch of trade would be helped, (4) the United States could move into whatever trade was vacated by nations moving into our lost trade, (5) and the ships would not be ready in time for any use. (p. 21–22.)
72. Irving Brant has an excellent account of "Mr. Madison's Resolutions" in *James Madison, Father of the Constitution* (Indianapolis, 1950), chapter 30.
73. William L. Smith, S.C., 10 March, *Annals,* 494–497; Thomas Fitzsimons, Pa., 7 Feb., *ibid.*, 438–439, 441; Samuel Smith, Md., 6, 10 Feb., *ibid.*, 434–435, 447–448.
74. Zephaniah Swift, Conn., 7 Feb., *ibid.*, 439–440.
75. William Vans Murray, Md., *ibid.*, 441.
76. Uriah Tracy, Conn., 11 Feb., *ibid.*, 448–449.
77. Fitzsimons, 7, 11 Feb., *ibid.*, 438–439, 449; Benjamin Goodhue, Mass., 7 Feb., *ibid.*, 441.
78. Samuel Smith, 6, 10 Feb., *ibid.*, 434–435, 447–448.
79. William L. Smith, 10 March, *ibid.*, 494–497.
80. Samuel Smith, 6 Feb., *ibid.*, 434–435; Fitzsimons, 7 Feb., *ibid.*, 438–439.
81. Samuel Smith, 10 Feb., *ibid.*, 447–448.
82. William L. Smith, 10 March, *ibid.*, 494–497.
83. *Ibid.*
84. Murray, 7 Feb., *ibid.*, 440–441. At least one influential Federalist expected to use the frigates against other enemies than the pirates.—Lawrance to King, 12 Jan. 1794, King, *Life and Correspondence,* I, 541–542.
85. Shearjashub Bourne, Mass., 10 Feb., *Annals,* 445.
86. Murray, 7, 10 Feb., *ibid.*, 440–441, 446.
87. James Hillhouse, Conn., 10 Feb., *ibid.*, 445.
88. Goodhue, 7 Feb., *ibid.*, 441.
89. Fitzsimons, 7 Feb., *ibid.*, 438–439; Goodhue, *ibid.*, 441.

90. Hillhouse, 10 Feb., *ibid.*, 445.
91. Murray, 7 Feb., *ibid.*, 440–441.
92. William L. Smith, 10 March, *ibid.*, 492–494.
93. Samuel Dexter, Mass., 10 Feb., *ibid.*, 445–446; Hillhouse, *ibid.*, 445. "Concluded" is here used logically, not chronologically.
94. Tracy and Goodhue, 11 Feb., *ibid.*, 448–449, 451.
95. Ames, 6 Feb., *ibid.*, 436; Samuel Smith, 6, 10 Feb., *ibid.*, 435–436, 447–448.
96. William L. Smith, 10 March, *ibid.*, 494–497.
97. Fitzsimons and Swift, 7 Feb., *ibid.*, 438–440.
98. William L. Smith, 10 March, *ibid.*, 492–494.
99. *ASP: For. Rel.*, I, 413, 418; *State Papers and Pub. Docs.*, X, 311, 325.
100. *Annals*, 481.
101. Bemis, *Jay's Treaty*, 188, 192; Albion and Pope, *Sea Lanes in Wartime*, 71–74; Rufus King's figure was "more than" two hundred.—King, *Life and Correspondence*, I, 517–518.
102. It was this news from the West Indies, the latest in an accumulating series of exasperations, which caused leading Federalists to propose what became Jay's mission. See, Goodrich to Wolcott, Jr., 10 March 1794, Gibbs, *Memoirs*, I, 130, and a Rufus King memorandum in King, *Life and Correspondence*, I, 517–518.
103. Giles "had observed more votes in favor of the bill since the receipt of late intelligence than before . . ."—10 March, *Annals*, 489.
104. "An act to provide a naval armament," Section 9, *Annals*, 1428. Giles mentioned the existence of Section 9 on 10 March, the day the bill passed the House, hence it was not a Senate amendment.—*ibid.*, 490.
105. Madison said that Section 9 meant that no other use could be made of the frigates without the permission of the Congress, which would probably be denied.—Madison, *Political Observations*, 22–23.
106. *Annals*, 485–486, 497–498.
107. *Ibid.*, 65, 71.
108. *Ibid.*, 68.
109. *Ibid.*, 1426–1428.
110. Sprout and Sprout, *The Rise of American Naval Power*, 31.
111. For the opposing conspiracy theories which unhappily imprisoned the thought of both embryonic parties see Marshall Smelser, "The Federalist period reconsidered as an age of passion," in a forthcoming issue of *American Quarterly*, and, "The Jacobin Phrenzy: Republicanism and the Menace of Monarchy, Plutocracy, and Anglophilia," in a forthcoming issue of the *Review of Politics*. The ugly hatreds and suspicions were not quite so apparent in the congressional party struggles where the rules of debate enjoined the proprieties.
112. Dauer, *The Adams Federalists;* Joseph Charles, "Hamilton and Washington: The origins of the American party system," *William and Mary Quarterly*, third series, XII (April, 1955), 227.
113. The previous seizures were in 1785.
114. *Annals, passim,* and Madison, *Political Observations.*
115. As we have been taught by Link's valuable *Democratic-Republican Societies.*
116. Frederick Augustus Muhlenberg, acting as chairman of the Committee of the Whole, in April 1796 broke a tie by casting his vote in favor of the Jay Treaty. He was not re-elected in 1796 and was replaced by Blair McClenachan. His defeat was attributed to his Jay Treaty vote.—Paul A. W. Wallace, *The Muhlenbergs of Pennsylvania* (Philadelphia, 1950), 285, 291. His volatile constituency made no difficulty about his naval vote.

V

Madison's "Commercial Propositions"

From colonial times to the present day the use of commercial discriminations in maritime trade [1] has been favored by the Americans as a tool of foreign policy. It was used before the War for Independence to exert pressure for a change in British policy, and it is used in the 1950s in the hope of affecting the strength of the totalitarian nations.

Commercial discrimination, considered as an international pressure, had no more ardent supporters than James Madison and Thomas Jefferson. They made their most memorable use of it on the eve of the War of 1812, but they had tried to put the policy into effect in the 1790s. As we have seen, after secret debates late in December 1793 the Congress, on 2 January 1794, adopted resolutions to prepare a bill for the creation of a naval force.[2] One day later, Representative James Madison introduced a series of resolutions aimed at enacting commercial discriminations against the trade of nations which discriminated against the trade of the United States. It was not accidental that the nation which most neatly fitted Madison's specifications was Great Britain. Thus launched almost simultaneously, the debates on the Naval Bill and the commercial resolutions went on at the same time [3] and it was probably to be expected that some observers would see them as rivals. Before looking into the argument two facts should be noted. First, although Madison was a leader in the opposition to the Naval Bill he did not take an intransigent, "either-or" position on the two projected policies. Second, some of his supporters came to regard the set of commercial resolutions as a desirable alternative to the Naval Bill.

The commercial resolutions were intended to give practical effect to a report on foreign trade prepared by Secretary of State Thomas Jefferson and sent to the Congress on 16 December 1793. Jefferson had given notice of his conclusions to the other members of the Cabinet late in 1791, and the notion of commercial retaliation against British trade restrictions, he said, had been heatedly opposed by the Secretary of the Treasury, Alexander Hamilton.[4] It was then known that Great Britain was sending a Minister to the United States. Since his coming might lead to the negotiation of a settlement of Anglo-American differences, Jefferson's commercial report was laid aside.[5] Now, two years later, he revived it on the ground that attempts to negotiate had been wholly unsuccessful. The Report summarized the state of the trade of the United States with the nations which were its leading customers or suppliers. It showed that each discriminated against the trade of the United States to some degree and suggested two alternate remedies, reciprocal trade treaties or retaliatory measures. Jefferson said Great Britain had everything her own way in her American trade and therefore had nothing to gain by negotiation. The French had promised to negotiate a trade treaty but their internal tumults had distracted them.[6] The Secretary of State introduced a question of naval policy when he wrote that foreign trade was more than a business matter. By hampering the development of American commerce the discriminations handicapped national defense—keeping down the number of American ships, seamen, and shipbuilders.[7]

Madison's Resolutions of 2 January 1794 applied Jefferson's principles concretely. His preamble said that the United States should enact "further restrictions and higher duties, in certain cases." Then followed seven specific proposals.[8] It is not necessary to carry in mind the details of Jefferson's Report and Madison's Resolutions in order to understand the debate which followed, so far as it concerned the naval policy. What mattered was that the authors intended to constrain British trade in the same way the British treated American trade, and—equally important—everyone concerned thoroughly understood that the measures were anti-British.

British behavior had been exasperating. Early in 1793 the Foreign Office refused to promise to protect American seamen from impressment although simultaneously demanding protection of British ships and seamen from French privateers in American waters.[9] In June the British ruled that breadstuffs were contraband, and neutral ships carrying flour to French ports were seized and purchased for British use.[10] Worse was to come but this was enough to arouse American indignation, which was easily inflamed, as Jefferson recorded, since France and Britain, the old friend and old foe, were at war.[11] James Monroe thought the administration showed a shameful "subservience" to British views, or was "impotent and contemptible," sacrificing national honor in exchange for a good credit rating.[12]

As for Madison, ever since the First Congress he had been dissatisfied with the commercial relations of the United States and Great Britain. He wished for true reciprocity, not equality with other victims of British mercantile policy.[13] The proclamation of American neutrality in the spring of 1793 angered him as an act of "Anglomany." [14] He was not convinced that the alarums and excursions of the Algerine pirates were the greatest dangers to the United States. The building of six frigates was "pointed at one only of our evils." What was needed was "some safe, but powerful remedy, that might be applied to the root of them; and with this view the Commercial Propositions were introduced." [15] His attitude was stated bluntly to Monroe: "G. B. has made war on our commerce." [16]

Although he had long had the idea of using trade regulations for diplomatic ends, it was Jefferson who encouraged him to act when he did. Near the close of the Second Congress, two and a half months before the British defined food as contraband, Jefferson wrote to Madison that he expected Great Britain and the naval powers would prevent "supplies even of provisions" from entering France. This would justify war. He hoped the Congress was to be called into session because it should have the right to deliberate on the question, although he himself did not hope for war. The United States should appeal to interest not to arms. He would like to see the United States "instantly exclude from our ports all the manufactures, produce, vessels, and subjects of the nations committing this aggression, during the continuance of the aggression, & till full satisfaction be made for it." [17]

When the Resolutions came to the floor of the House of Representatives some saw in them a weapon which could be used to attack the Naval Bill. They argued that the best reply to the Algerine depredations was to retaliate against the nation which had unleashed the pirates.[18] John Nicholas of Virginia compared the British use of Indians and pirates, and concluded that British behavior gave the country only a choice of war or commercial reprisal.[19] William Branch Giles of Virginia was sure the Resolutions would bear so heavily on Britain that she would be glad to call off her pirates.[20] Nicholas thought the Naval Bill, alone, put too much reliance on frigates and neglected other useful regulations for the safety of American shipping.[21] Madison said the southern members were eager for "promoting our navigation" because the South was so exposed to attack that it needed the "protection which results from extensive marine resources." Such resources either prevented attack or were easily converted to "the means of repelling it." [22] This speech was a forensic jewel—implying that he and his friends were more solicitous for genuine naval strength than were the supporters of the Naval Bill. Giles said that justice could not be had in England. Therefore the United States should exercise its right to legislate in its own interest or should revert to the status of colonies again. "He would rather hazard a war, than give up that right." [23]

Out-of-doors, friends of Madison and of his colleagues assumed that the "Commercial Propositions" were intended to be substituted for the Naval Bill. Robert R. Livingston, in New York, saw British policy as motivated by "envy & hatred" and by strategic considerations which led them to destroy our commerce because it increased the number of American seamen and lured British seamen into the American merchant service. Britain, he thought, also hoped to frighten the Americans into throwing themselves on her protection. Furthermore, if Britain could cut the revenue of the United States (most of which came from customs duties) the public credit would decline and the American capacity for defense be thereby weakened.[24] A Richmond correspondent said he agreed with Madison "on the subject of the Algerine business, and highly approve the resolutions which you have offered . . ." [25] Spencer Roane advised an invasion of Canada; if that were not feasible he urged support of "Mr. Jefferson's plan of reciprocating commercial prohibitions & restrictions," which would probably lead to a British revolution and the establishment of free trade.[26] General Horatio Gates, writing from New York, put the prevailing assumption most plainly: "In regard to The Algerines, I approve your plans, preferable to that of raising a Naval Armament." [27] This harmony of the Virginia majority and the New York minority had a prophetic significance for the rise of the Republican Party.

The group we now call the Federalists devoted more thought and energy to countering Madison's proposals than they did to promoting their pending Naval Bill. It has been said that war is a continuation of policy by other means. Madison was accused of defining commerce as war carried on by other means. The central argument of the Federalists was that the enactment of Madison's proposals would precipitate war with Great Britain.[28] Fisher Ames of Massachusetts referred to them as "the war regulations" [29] which only made war more likely and diminished the preparation for it— "Our policy should be precisely the reverse." [30] Robert Troup, the New Yorker who has seemed best informed on Hamilton's thinking, wrote to Rufus King, "they will lead us into war." [31] The leading New York Federalist newspaper listed the remarkably inflated prices-current in the Caribbean area and drew the business-like conclusion that peace must be preserved.[32]

If Madison intended war, to what purpose? The answer was easily given: to help France. "It is all French that is spoken in support of the measure," wrote Ames. "I like the Yankee dialect better."[33] Oliver Wolcott, Jr., of Connecticut, said the Virginians "hate the English because they owe them money; they love the French from consanguinity of character." Therefore American trade was to be channeled "to display certain romantic affections and gratify resentments."[34] The "most artful and wicked calumnies" were spread in the middle and New England states to the effect that Madison was the tool of the tactless and imprudent French Minister, Edmond Charles Genêt, and had been a French agent since the days of the War for Independence.[35] French detentions of American ships in French ports were blamed for American naval weakness[36] but the severity of French counter-regulations was not much emphasized, probably because everyone knew that the French could not enforce them in the future, being bottled-up by the British Navy.

William Vans Murray of Maryland voiced another and curious strategic objection to the Madison program: if enacted into law, Great Britain would have no motive "to interpose her good offices"[37] to extricate the United States from its maritime troubles.

Addressing themselves to the Republican arguments for the "Commercial Propositions" as an alternative to the creation of a navy, the Federalists observed that the alleged provocations by the British were not proved.[38] If the British behavior really were as villainous as charged, commercial reprisal was a weak reply—"the insolence of Britain is contrasted with American weakness."[39] If the Madison proposals could accomplish anything their weight would not be felt soon enough.[40]

The Republican rebuttal centered on the alleged danger of war and insisted that the Naval Bill was much more likely to provoke war than was any system of commercial retaliation.[41] The British could not afford to break their business links with the United States.[42] Giles added what he thought was the clincher—if commercial reprisals provoked Great Britain to war on the United States, the fault would be in British obstinacy.[43]

When the Naval Act passed the House, on 10 March 1794, this aspect of the debate on commercial policy came to an end, but the Madisonians did not give up. "The foolish frigate scheme I see is adopted," wrote Robert R. Livingston, "but let it not prevent our doing something better."[44] They did try to do "something better" and they kept the pressure on the Federalists until the Federalists devised Jay's Mission as a sedative for Anglophobes,[45] but that does not concern us here.

Whether or not the Madison program would have provoked a war with Britain, it certainly provoked a huge eruption of words in the House of Representatives. The greater part of the argument was on the economic issue, and strategic considerations took but a small fraction of the time. This was the way the Federalists wished it. They were very reluctant to be drawn out on the subject of British excesses and tried, with partial success, to confine the discussion of the "Commercial Propositions" to commerce only.

However it does not help our understanding if we attempt the same separation. The debate on the commercial resolutions brought out the sectional and partisan split on economic and foreign policy, and was an important episode in the growth of the party system. The Naval Act was a landmark in the progress and development of American naval policy. The commercial resolutions and the Naval Act are usually treated separately, but the contemporary debaters were unable to keep them in separate compartments. The Republicans, especially, insisted on combining strategic and commercial considerations, an insistence which gave a somewhat old-fashioned mercantilist cast to their thought.

To some of the Republicans the choice was not merely whether to vote yea or nay on a Naval Bill, but was a choice of the better way to proceed in their current crisis—whether it was better to build a navy or to try the alternative of bringing mercantile pressure to bear on British trade. It was therefore a choice of villains, to determine which was the greater enemy, Great Britain or Algiers.

NOTES FROM PAGES 64 TO 68

1. The phrase "commercial discrimination" as used here refers to a foreign-trade policy which intentionally favors one or more foreign nations over others, as a way of exerting economic pressure in order to achieve some national purpose in foreign relations.
2. See Chapter IV.
3. The interweaving of the parliamentary business of the two measures is shown by the calendar below. The Naval Bill was before the House of Representatives on the dates which are printed in boldface, and the "Commercial Propositions" on the italicized dates. *Annals of the Congress, 1789–1824,* 42v., ed. J. Gales and W. W. Seaton (Washington, 1834–1856), 3 Cong., 1 Sess. (All references to the *Annals* are to the first session of the Third Congress. All dates are in 1794 except where otherwise given.)

1794

January

S	M	T	W	T	F	S
			1	**2**	*3*	4
5	6	**7**	8	9	10	11
12	*13*	*14*	*15*	*16*	17	18
19	**20**	21	*22*	*23*	*24*	*25*
26	*27*	*28*	*29*	*30*	*31*	

February

S	M	T	W	T	F	S
						1
2	*3*	*4*	*5*	**6**	**7**	8
9	**10**	**11**	12	13	14	15
16	17	18	19	**20**	**21**	22
23	24	25	26	27	28	

March

S	M	T	W	T	F	S
						1
2	3	4	**5**	6	**7**	8
9	**10**	11	12	13	*14*	15

4. Thomas Jefferson, "The Anas," 11 March 1792, Thomas Jefferson, *Writings*, ed. A. A. Lipscomb, 19v. (Washington, 1903–1904), I, 299.
5. Samuel Flagg Bemis, *Jay's Treaty, a Study in Commerce and Diplomacy* (New York, 1923), 187.
6. The possible retaliations were in five groups. (1) Match high duties and prohibitions on American trade, especially where the imports into America competed with American produce and manufactures. (2) Bar the merchants and factors of any nation which barred those of the United States. (3) If the Americans were permitted to carry only their own products into a foreign land the same rule should be applied to the commerce of the restricting nation, on entering the United States. (4) If a foreign government classified as American ships only those built in the United States, the Americans should apply the same rule of identification to the other nation's ships. (5) If a foreign nation barred even American produce carried in American ships, that nation's ships should be barred from American trade.—Jefferson to the Congress, 16 Dec. 1793, *American State Papers*, Class I, *Foreign Relations*, ed. Walter Lowrie and Matthew St. Clair Clarke (Washington, 1832–1861), I, 300–304.
7. *Ibid.*, I, 303.
8. The Madison resolutions may be summarized as follow: (1) Raises *ad valorem* were to be enacted for manufactures using twelve listed materials—leather, metals, textiles. (2) Tonnage taxes were to be raised on the ships of nations not in treaty with the United States. (3) Tonnage taxes on the ships of nations in treaty were to be lowered. (4) If a foreign nation required that ships must be built in America in order to be classed as "American," the same rule applied to the classification of their ships, unless they happened to be using ships built in the United States. (5) If the foreign nation barred American produce unless carried in American ships, the same prohibition was to be applied to their produce—although not immediately. (6) If a foreign nation admitted American produce or manufactures but only in the ships of the foreign nation, the same prohibition should eventually be applied to their exports to the United States; meanwhile the duty on spirits should be raised. (7) If American citizens suffered losses by the regulations of other countries, contrary to international law, the United States government should reimburse them.—2 Jan., *Annals*, 155–156. The preamble was the only part brought to a vote. It was approved.
9. Jefferson to Thomas Pinckney, 4 June 1793, Jefferson papers, Library of Congress (hereafter abbreviated: LC).
10. Robert Greenhalgh Albion and Jennie Barnes Pope, *Sea Lanes in Wartime; the American Experience, 1775–1942* (New York, 1942), 71; Edward Channing, *A History of the United States*, 6v. (New York, 1932–1936), IV, 135.
11. Jefferson to Monroe, 5 May 1793, Thomas Jefferson, *Writings*, ed. Lipscomb, IX, 75–76.
12. Monroe to Jefferson, 27 June 1793, James Monroe, *Writings*, ed. S. M. Hamilton, 7v. (New York, 1898–1903), I, 266–267.
13. Brant, *James Madison, Father of the Constitution*, 252–253.
14. Madison to Jefferson, 10 June 1793, James Madison, *Writings*, ed. Gaillard Hunt, 9v. (New York, 1900–1910), VI, 127n.–128n.
15. James Madison, *Political Observations* (Philadelphia, 1795), 5.
16. Madison to Monroe, 15 Sept. 1793, Madison papers, LC. It is curious to note that the Anglophile Gouverneur Morris had earlier suggested that the only way to affect British policy was to threaten commercial retaliation.—J. S. Bassett, *The Federalist System, 1789–1801* (New York, 1906), 59. In December 1793 Joel Barlow thought (and hoped) such a policy might even produce a British revolution analagous to the French revolution, but his letter probably did not arrive in time to influence his friends' thinking.—Barlow to Jefferson, 2 Dec. 1793, Jefferson papers, LC.
17. Jefferson to Madison, 24 March 1793, Jefferson papers, LC.
18. Thomas Hartley, Pa., 24 Jan., *Annals*, 291, 293. It will be recalled that Senate debates were not reported at that time.
19. John Nicholas, Va., 24 Jan., *Annals*,

310–311; William Findley, Pa., 25 Jan., *Annals,* 325, also saw the choice as between commercial retaliation and war.

20. William Branch Giles, Va., 6 Feb., *Annals,* 436.
21. Nicholas, 16 Jan., *Annals,* 239.
22. Madison, 14 Jan., *Annals,* 222.
23. Giles, 4 Feb., *Annals,* 423–424.
24. Robert R. Livingston to Monroe, 4 Jan., Monroe papers, LC.
25. Dawson to Madison, 20 Jan., Madison papers, LC.
26. Roane to Monroe, 25 Jan., Monroe papers, LC.
27. Gates to Madison, 13 Mar., Madison papers, LC. Although the shipowners almost unanimously opposed Madison's resolutions the men who went down to the sea in their ships did not. Joshua Barney and twenty-one other shipmasters "forcibly detained" in Jamaica applauded Madison.—Barney *et al.* to Madison, 9, 13 March, Madison papers, LC.
28. "It is wrong to make our trade wage war for our politics."—Fisher Ames, Mass., 27 Jan., *Annals,* 347. See also, William L. Smith, S.C., 10 March, *Annals,* 494–497, for a hint of the same.
29. Ames to Gore, 28 Jan., Fisher Ames, *Works,* ed. Seth Ames, 2v. (Boston, 1854), I, 133.
30. Ames to Gore, 25 Feb., *ibid.*, I, 136.
31. Troup to King, 13 Jan., Rufus King, *Life and Correspondence,* ed. C. R. King, 6v. (New York, 1894–1900), I, 542.
32. Noah Webster's *American Minerva,* 3 March. The main attack on the Madison project (mostly economic rather than strategic) was delivered in the House of Representatives by William L. Smith of South Carolina but ghost-written by Alexander Hamilton.—Nathan Schachner, *The Founding Fathers* (New York, 1954), 299. Hamilton's notes will be found in Alexander Hamilton, *Works,* ed. Henry Cabot Lodge, 9v. (New York, 1885–1886), III, 423–441.
33. Ames to Thomas Dwight, 17 Jan., Ames, *Works,* I, 133. The food supply of France was straitened owing to bad harvests and internal disorganization, from which fact it could be deduced that mercantile pressures were intended to cause a relaxation of the British blockade. It seems quite likely that some of the Republicans thought the Madison proposals would be a desirable way of getting around the neutrality proclamation which Madison so detested. The tone of the Republican speakers throughout the long parliamentary struggle supports this view.
34. Oliver Wolcott, Jr., to Wolcott, Sr., 18 Jan., George Gibbs, *Memoirs of the Administrations of Washington and John Adams,* 2v. (New York, 1846), I, 127.
35. Madison to Jefferson, 2 March, Madison papers, LC, confirmed by scanning the *American Minerva* and the *General Advertiser* (New York and Philadelphia, respectively) for these weeks.
36. *American Minerva,* 4 March.
37. William Vans Murray, Md., 7 Feb., *Annals,* 440–441.
38. Elias Boudinot, N.J., 24 Jan., *Annals,* 309; Ezekiel Gilbert, N.Y., 25 Jan., *Annals,* 324; James Hillhouse, Conn., 25 Jan., *Annals,* 318.
39. Jonathan Dayton, N.J., 24 Jan., *Annals,* 312–313; see also, Uriah Tracy, Conn., 24 Jan., *Annals,* 302.
40. William L. Smith, 10 March, *Annals,* 492–494.
41. Madison, 6 Feb., *Annals,* 433; Abraham Clark, N.J., 6 Feb., *Annals,* 433–434; Giles, 10 March, *Annals,* 486–490.
42. Madison to Gates, 24 March, Madison, *Writings,* VI, 209.
43. Nicholas, 24 Jan., *Annals,* 312.
44. Robert R. Livingston to Monroe, 13 March, Monroe papers, LC.
45. Madison thought the Senate contrived Jay's mission as a substitute for his "Commercial Propositions." Madison to Colonel Madison of Orange County, 4 May, Madison papers, LC. Chief Justice John Jay was sent to England in the Spring of 1794 to attempt to negotiate a reconciliation of all outstanding Anglo-American differences. The negotiation produced "Jay's Treaty" and a controversy so heated that it is a principal watershed in the history of American party politics.

VI

The First Construction Program

The Congress having authorized the building of six ships by the Naval Act of 1794, it now became the charge of the executive to see to the building. The man directly responsible under the President was the Secretary of War, Henry Knox of Massachusetts, who held that office from 1789 until 1795. He had been George Washington's chief artillery officer during the War for Independence. His department had been given responsibility for naval affairs when it was created in 1789. Thomas Jefferson had a low opinion of his talents, saying of him, "a fool as he is . . ."[1] A more recent critic has described the rotund Secretary of War as no statesman, but a good soldier and administrator, with "a bit of inflation about him . . . and like some of his own guns, his range was not equal to his caliber."[2]

Knox had been pondering naval matters for several years and had consulted officer-veterans of the Continental and state navies, as early as 1790. Among them were John Foster Williams of Boston, Captain John Barry, and Joshua Humphreys of Philadelphia.[3] Williams, formerly a Captain in the Massachusetts Navy, had estimated the cost of a nine hundred ton frigate for Knox in 1790.[4] Joshua Humpherys is the best remembered, although he was not necessarily the most competent designer of the day, as has been said.[5] He had formulated a design theory early in 1793. It was his notion that the best way for the Americans to achieve a naval weight in the world would be to build a new class of ships, fast enough to run from all bigger ships, strong enough to take on all ships of the same theoretical rating,[6]—a "pocket-battleship" theory.

After the passage of the Naval Act, Knox was ready with proposals for the approval of the President. The Act, it should be noted, gave the President the option of buying and converting merchant vessels, but no interest was shown in that method of acquiring a force, although it would have been much quicker and probably cheaper.[7]

The Secretary proposed to construct super-frigates superior or equal to any such European classes. After suggesting the number of guns—three forty-fours and three thirty-sixes—and stating the dimensions, he recommended special framing of the ships in order to carry such a weight without hogging.[8] Having ventured into a new field of naval design he had consulted Captain Barry and several designers but found them in some disagreement. Therefore he proposed to secure the services of a consultant, John Hacket, builder of the wartime frigate *Alliance,* which Barry valued as the best ship of the Continental Navy.

He did not think the building should be let out to private contract. Such a procedure would "excite the ill will and envy of those who had no part in it," who would raise the cost of labor. This would "occasion great embarrassments if not ruin to the undertakers." Furthermore, if the Philadelphia builders declined to bid, the government would be unable to let a contract elsewhere. The best way to go about it would be to get "Agents respectable for their intelligence, activity and integrity" and let them build the ships as a government operation.

Political considerations weighed heavily when it came to selecting the possible sites for the construction. Said Knox, ". . . it is just and wise to proportion . . . benefits as nearly as may be to those places or states which pay the greatest amount to its support." Saving "a few thousand dollars in expences [*sic*] will be no object compared with the satisfaction a just distribution would afford." He named six ports which seemed to meet both political and technical requirements.

The cost-estimates which Knox sent to the President turned out to be of little value, being preposterously optimistic. However he included a saving clause: if the European war continues "it is very questionable whether the actual cost will not considerably exceed the estimate."[9] (This was a significant prophecy.) He had previously settled on the salary for the constructors or master-builders, two thousand dollars a year.[10]

Washington replied on the day he received Knox's memorandum. Knox was to go ahead as soon as the design problems were settled and the money was available. But the President had a political amendment. It would be better to build a "forty-four" at Norfolk and a "thirty-six" at Baltimore (Knox had it the other way around), unless Baltimore had some special advantage which was lacking in Norfolk, because Virginia was a richer and more populous state.[11]

With a design-theory established and the designers at work the construction program could be expected to move ahead with "all sail set and everything drawing." But the War Department immediately had specifications trouble. It had been decided to use live oak (*Quercus virens* or *Quercus Virginiana*) for knees and short timbers, because its life was estimated at five times that of white oak.[12] This tree grew on a coastal strip twenty miles wide, from Virginia to Louisiana, the best specimens being found on the Georgia coastal islands.[13] The appropriation was not available till June 1794 at a time when the sickly season was beginning in Georgia. The cutters (from Connecticut) could not get to work there until October.[14]

The lack of progress brought complaint in the Congress. All that Knox could do was to explain the troubles. (He resigned shortly thereafter, but not for this reason.) In the summer of 1795 the live oak supply was still short. Knox's successor, Timothy Pickering of Massachusetts, on his own initiative cut the program back to two ships because he could not get timber for more.[15] Actually this exertion to assure the use of a durable material was probably not wholly necessary. The wood is not as durable as they thought it was and the supply was more limited than they knew. In the end much white oak and other hard wood went into the ships and what dry rot occurred probably was the fault of improper seasoning.[16]

After the passage of the naval legislation in 1794 foreign affairs had continued in a swirl. The events which produced the successful Naval Act and the unsuccessful Madisonian resolutions, were still with the people, still provoking anger. Through March and early April 1794, the Federalist leadership had a real fear that popular indignation at the abuse of neutrals by the British Navy would sweep the country into war.[17] Much was hoped from the mission of John Jay to London, but the President intended to go ahead with military preparations. The Jay Mission, he wrote, was not a signal to end them. "My objects are . . . to provide *eventually*, such measures [military], as seem to be now pending in Congress, for execution, if negotiation in a reasonable time proves unsuccessful." [18] Jay himself, on arriving in Britain, cautioned his friends "not to relax in military preparation." [19]

Representative Jonathan Dayton of New Jersey had moved to sequester British debts, that is, to have American debtors pay the money into the United States Treasury as a pledge to indemnify American citizens for property seized by the British.[20] This appealed to the representatives of a fleetless nation.[21] The arch-Federalist Theodore Sedgwick of Massachusetts even introduced a resolution for a provisional army and tacked on a "rider" giving the President power to embargo the exports of the United States so as to threaten to cut off supplies to the British forces in the West Indies.[22] In a moment of enthusiasm a House Committee was instructed to bring in a bill to authorize privateering against Algiers, Tunis, and Tripoli [23]—a bit of foolishness since the Barbary corsairs had almost no merchant shipping to tempt privateers. Most of this heat was cooled by the expectations of the success of Jay's Mission.

However a thirty-day embargo was enacted. When it expired it was not renewed. James Madison thought it was a sop to the bellicose. The thirty days was a cooling-off period; after it expired, the public confidence in the President (and the use made of him) could not be successfully undermined by the Republicans.[24]

A leading New York Republican also thought his group had been outmaneuvered by the Federalists. Robert R. Livingston wrote to James Monroe that the passivity of the United States actually strengthened Great Britain. By not granting letters of marque and reprisal the United States afforded Britain a strength equal to that of five thousand seamen, enough to man ten ships of the line. Not one American ship went into British waters without losing men by impressment. This was a good argument for stopping all intercourse with Britain, but an embargo or non-intercourse act would also deprive this country of seamen. Adoption of the Madison resolutions would have been better because they would have had a permanent effect. For the United States to keep its seamen, work must be found for them. Work would be had if the United States sent out its own privateers and if it would "connive at the fitting out of privateers under french [*sic*] colours, by giving a more liberal construction to the words of the [French] treaty." This latter tactic would be a very good one because much time would be wasted in remonstrances and protests before any open rupture could occur. The government might also consider holding British ships and men in American ports as hostages for our own shipping in British ports. But these things, he concluded sadly, were only dreams.[25]

A few reprisals and defense matters which were more directly related to the use of naval force came before the Third Congress before the first session adjourned on 9 June.

On 18 March the two chambers jointly authorized the President to use the revenue cutters of the Treasury Department as "despatch boats." [26]

The Senate passed a bill for the construction of galleys (small shallow-draft rowing vessels with single guns mounted in their bows), cost and number not specified, which arrived in the House on 3 June. Representative Josiah Parker of Virginia opposed the idea whole-heartedly.

He complained of galleys on the basis of experience in the War for Independence; galleys drew pursuers who invariably landed and ravaged neighboring coasts. He continued:

> It was true, that galleys were not to be attacked; for they commonly got into such situations as to be out of the reach of any enemy except the mosquitoes. Brave men would fight as well in a galley as any where else; but no man of spirit would place himself in them.[27]

William Lyman, a rare bird, since he was a Republican Representative from Massachusetts, said he had just heard from a friend in Britain who believed the war was going badly and therefore, Lyman concluded, Great Britain was more likely to need galleys for defense than the United States was. James Hillhouse of Connecticut thought galleys unnecessary. Abraham Baldwin of Georgia said they were needed in Georgia and South Carolina, where they did good service during the late war; Representative Parker need not fret, he went on, the President would not send them where they were not wanted. Thomas Fitzsimons of Pennsylvania praised the war record of galleys against the British in the Delaware River. Jeremiah Wadsworth of Connecticut said twenty years of experience at sea had convinced him of their utility. After another day of this penetrating analysis the number of galleys was fixed at ten, and the sum of eighty thousand dollars was appropriated for them. The amended Act was signed by the President on 5 June.[28]

As a hindrance to impressment William Vans Murray of Maryland proposed, on 19 May, the registration of all American seamen. He could get no support and his proposal died; apparently a majority thought such a program could not be administered. In arguing for his motion, Murray said it would give the United States a list of the "seafaring citizens, on whom she may rely in time of war." [29]

Out in the shipyards and forests the construction of the frigates moved along very slowly through 1794 and 1795. Alexander Hamilton's successor at the Treasury, Oliver Wolcott, Jr., whose department did the purchasing for the government, blamed the war in Europe for the frequent delays. Supplies were very hard to get. The shortages were a national danger. What supplies there were in America were liable to be suddenly withdrawn by belligerents' purchases. The competition of the warring nations drove prices up. It was impossible to import the necessary materials. Indeed the supply problem at the moment was "such as forbids the idea of war, even if on other accounts it might reasonably be adjudged to be necessary." The United States must have some system of purchasing everything which could not be manufactured in the country, especially durable items which could be stored against emergencies. Furthermore the country ought to have its own foundries and arsenals, since the art of casting guns, well advanced in the 1770s, "has deplorably declined." [30]

The snail's progress of the construction program provoked some restiveness in the Congress, but not enough to embarrass the administration.[31] Secretary of War Pickering (soon to be translated to the office of Secretary of State) in December 1795 proudly reported the acquisition of much of the necessary canvas and cordage, and the laying of all six keels. No ship was yet framed. This was a report to the Fourth Congress, delivered seventeen months after the appropriation had been voted.[32]

The President's message at the opening of the first session of the Fourth Congress, 8 December 1795, included a reference to Algiers and hopes for a "speedy peace." [33] No more was heard of this until the following March, when he sent word that Joel Barlow had completed a treaty with the Algerines. This revived all of those questions of naval policy which had been temporarily resolved by the passage of the Naval Act. Section Nine of the Act provided for halting the construction program if peace were made with Algiers. The President did not now assume the construction Act was voided but asked the Congress what it wished him to do.[34]

The navy-minded members had not been idle. Taking the hint in the Message of 8 December, William Loughton Smith of South Carolina had moved, on 11 January, the drafting of a bill to repeal Section Nine of the Naval Act, but his motion was tabled, because there was a select committee, headed by Josiah Parker of Virginia, working on naval policy at the moment.[35] Two weeks later Parker was ready with a report which recommended the completion of one "forty-four" and one "thirty-six." The surplus perishable materials should be sold (prices had gone up, there would be no loss) and the unneeded durable materials should be put in storage.[36] The cut from six frigates to two frigates did not represent a Federalist retreat; it represented the harsh reality of the War Department's difficulty in finishing even two frigates.

Parker's report achieved nothing for the moment. On the day scheduled for its consideration (3 February) the House was deeply locked in a debate on Indian policy from which it roved into District of Columbia affairs and never found its way back to its calendar. There was a bill on the same subject being prepared in the Senate in these weeks. Federalist leaders in the more volatile House probably "sat on" Parker's report.

In the middle of March, a week after the arrival of word of the

Algerine Treaty, William Loughton Smith tried to revive the question and hinted at the possibility of compromise. Albert Gallatin of Pennsylvania scented a rat and leaped forward with a resolution calling on the President to suspend construction under Section Nine. This was tabled on motion of the Republican Representative from Baltimore, Samuel Smith.[37] There the matter hung, with the anti-navy and the navy people eyeing each other suspiciously, and perhaps not very trustful of their own colleagues. But an acute observer might well have concluded the naval construction program was now on the defensive.

Over in the Senate the President's African intelligence had been entrusted to a committee headed by William Bingham of Pennsylvania, with whom served George Read of Delaware and George Cabot of Massachusetts—all very othodox Federalists.[38] They produced a bill (passed on 28 March) which provided the completion of two "forty-fours" and a "thirty-six," and allowed the President to complete the other three frigates which had been authorized in 1794, at his discretion. The unexpended money from the Act of 1794 and the eighty thousand dollars intended for the galleys, was to be used for the job.[39] Percentage-wise no President has ever been delegated more authority—permission to double the naval strength of the country at his own discretion! Whether it was so intended is not clear, but the Senate's discretionary clause would have been an effective contrivance for keeping the Dey of Algiers in suspense regarding the naval strength of the United States.[40]

The Senate Bill was put on the House calendar for 29 March. The House got in around to debating it in Committee of the Whole on 7 April,[41] and spent most of three days on it. The debate did not attract as much attention as it might have received, because of exceptional circumstances. The appropriations for putting the Jay Treaty into effect were also before the House. For six weeks, beginning in mid-March, the big congressional story in the press was the Jay Treaty argument.[42]

Ordinarily the pro-navy leadership would have fallen to Fisher Ames by right of talent and zeal, but Ames, complaining of illness, was often absent.[43] William Loughton Smith, Hamilton's front-man in the battle against Madison's "Commercial Propositions," became the paladin of naval policy. On the other side anti-naval members had a new spokesman, Albert Gallatin, a Swiss-born Pennsylvania Republican.

Gallatin was new to the House of Representatives. As a Genevan Swiss his native tongue was French, which automatically made him suspect as a revolutionary. Treasury Secretary Oliver Wolcott, in a letter to his father, said "it is neither unreasonable nor uncandid to believe that Mr. Gallatin is directed by foreign politics and influence." [44]

Gallatin's passion for economy caused him to be classed as an obstructionist.[45] He saw two divisive issues in this Congress, the European war and the Navy. "The true question," as Gallatin saw it, "was whether the creation of an efficient navy should be postponed to the payment of the public debt . . ."[46]

The economy-minded members had sufficient matter for serious reflection. The Congress had so far appropriated $688,888 of which $459,000 had been spent by 1 January 1796. Of the expenditures about $113,000 had gone abroad for "copper and sundry other materials"—a disquieting commentary on American industrial resources.[47] Earlier appropriations had been made with the expectation of the money going for standard frigates. The pocket ship-of-the-line, or super-frigate, was about a fourth larger than the usual frigate, with costs greater in proportion (hence there was to be a necessity for periodic appropriations above the original estimates).[48] The cost of the Algerine treaty was a shocker, too—nearly a million dollars, including $525,000 for ransom, bribes, and miscellaneous expenses,[49] and several hundred thousand dollars for an American frigate to be the flagship of the pirate fleet. For all of this expenditure the United States could show a hundred ransomed captives, a treaty with a gang of sea-going racketeers, three commissioned Captains, on the "navy list," a sheaf of draughtsmen's drawings, several heaps of miscellaneous naval construction supplies, two hulls barely started, three hulls nearing completion, and a file of correspondence explaining why so little had been accomplished. Of course the hulls were *United States, Constitution,* and *Constellation,* and the Captains were Barry, Dale, and Truxtun, and who will put a price on them today?

The consideration of the Senate Bill began with the reading of Parker's committee report which had recommended the completion of two frigates. The first speaker, William Loughton Smith, moved to strike out the clause of the Senate Bill, which authorized three frigates. If his motion carried, he said, he would then move to build the six frigates previously allowed.[50] Smith's motion was a clever stratagem. It diverted the argument into the whole field of naval policy and tempted the opposition either to argue against the entire naval program or to support the Senate's proposal for only three ships. A good many anti-navy men voted for the Senate Bill in the end. Whatever Smith's motive was, it worked out as the old technique of asking for much, so as to be able to compromise on a lesser number, which was the number really sought. Now the debate became triangular: for Smith's motion, for the Senate Bill, or against any navy at all.

Smith and his principal supporter, John Swanwick of Pennsylvania, argued as follows: six ships were needed to keep Algiers in an agreeable frame of mind, further treaties were not to be desired because they send money abroad which could be better spent on the domestic ship-building-industry, and six ships, although not many, would give the country "a kind of Naval Academy." [51] For the Senate Bill, unamended, its supporters said the other three ships could not be finished before the next session of the Congress; therefore there was no need to act on them now. Three would be enough to affect the African states, since there were only the lesser looters of Tunis and Tripoli yet to deal with.[52] At this stage of the argument the attack on the entire naval program was carried by John Williams of New York who said American agriculture did not need a merchant marine to carry its produce away; foreigners would come to get it "whilst eating is in fashion." He proposed to rely on privateers, harbor forts, and floating batteries to protect the country against foreign foes.[53] General Samuel Smith of Maryland replied to Williams: Citizens have a right to the protection of their government, a claim not satisfied by reliance on privateering. If no money were spent to defend commerce it would be hard to justify spending money to defend westerners against Indians. Neither commerce nor agriculture could do without the other.[54]

At this point, the ground of the argument shifted slightly. James Madison, probably fearing the passage of Smith's somewhat extravagant amendment, gently deprecated the naval program of 1794 but hinted the Senate Bill might be acceptable if the discretionary power of the President were stricken.[55] Theodore Sedgwick of Massachusetts pressed for Smith's motion. To cut the program from six to three would appear vacillating and would arouse the "cupidity" of the African pirates.[56] On the other side John Nicholas of Virginia moved to the position of Madison; however, he preferred the two-ship report of the House's own committee, and hoped this legislation was *not* the beginning of a great naval establishment.[57] Madison and Nicholas, although speaking in strongly anti-navy tones, had made a signal from the Virginia bastion which any Federalist could read. If the Federalists would abandon Smith they could have two or three ships without further bother. The battle was practically over.

Three more extended speeches were made in favor of Smith's resolution, although they were a waste of breath. Swanwick (who often fought at other times under the Republican standard) predicted the United States would be a naval power equal to any nation by the 1950's. Smith himself made what surely must have been an offensive remark,—no one took Section Nine of the Naval Act seriously at the time they passed it —"it was never seriously thought that the building . . . would be discontinued." Fisher Ames, in one of his rare addresses of the session, said a navy would promote the creation of an American nationality. The Romans had been strong because each thought himself equal to a king. A national sense of brotherhood in American citizenship was needed to hold together the Union which "so many repulsive passions were now in full activity to sever." [58] No surprise was recorded at this endorsement of *fraternité* by *Citizen* Ames but one may imagine the exchange of sardonic smiles among those members who had been so often castigated by Ames for alleged Francophilia.

Gallatin's oratorical contribution was first, to accept two frigates, and, next, to give a financial report on the United States which concluded with an aphorism: to pay the national debt was the best way of building American prestige abroad. William Branch Giles of Virginia agreed to the latter notion.[59]

Smith lost his motion without a division. Gallatin then moved to reduce the number of frigates to be finished from three to two and lost by only one vote, 43–44.[60] The President's discretionary power to finish the remaining three frigates was stricken from the Senate Bill, and he was authorized to sell the perishable surplus and to put the durable supplies in storage.[61] This was done without debate or division, an abruptness which probably shows the clause had been dealt out as part of the price of the unobstructed passage of the more important clauses, very likely in an arrangement with Madison and Nicholas.

On the next day (8 April) the House considered the report of the Committee of the Whole. The irrepressible Smith brought up his motion again and had the dubious satisfaction of hearing it beaten on a roll call, 36–55.[62] Since Smith had a roll call, Gallatin would have one, too. He repeated his motion to cut from three to two ships, which had lost 43–44 on the previous day, and he made an unpleasant discovery. Overnight some ferment had been working among the Republicans. Although he could get forty-three to stand anonymously with him on the seventh, he could only get twenty-five to pin their names to their votes on the following day, and so he lost this time 25–57.[63]

Smith was by no means discouraged. Apparently without preconcert he now brought out an amendment to encourage the building of merchant ships which would be easily convertible to privateering. He proposed to pay a bounty for each ship so built, the receiver to post a bond to refund the bounty if the vessel were sold abroad. The Collectors at the ports of departure were to administer the law.[64] Although he was also unsuccessful in this maneuver it is worth examining because the debate illuminated some of the corners of naval thought.

Smith mustered three vocal supporters. They said Great Britain had profited by a similar practice and had achieved good results against pirates. Since the bounty would be payable out of tonnage taxes it would be an inexpensive defense precaution. John Williams, in particular, was pleased at the notion—he observed there would be "no officers, no sailors, no materials to provide," and he added a plea for his system of harbor forts, floating batteries, and privateers. William Vans Murray of Maryland said the project had come up in 1794 at which time it had received Virginian support; by the Senate Bill the country was losing three frigates and this amendment offered a substitute for the lost strength. Smith himself pointed to about 2500 American square-riggers: What a great thing, if only a fifth of them were convertible to privateering! And the amendment could harm no one; it left the matter to the option of the builders.[65]

A bipartisan file of speakers rose, each speaking briefly against the proposition, soaking it in cold water. It was technically impractical, the amendment was brought forward at the wrong time, the proposition could not be made financially attractive to the merchants since—if adhered to—it would cut their cargo capacities in half.[66]

Smith reluctantly withdrew the amendment, with a promise to bring it out again.[67] However he had brought to the surface the incorrigible militia-mindedness of the age, as shown by the eagerness with which John Williams had taken up the proposal.

The Senate Bill as amended was read for the third time on 9 April. Nothing new was brought out in the debate that day. The vote on passage was 62–23.[68] When the Bill was returned to the Senate, with the amendments, the Senate concurred immediately.[69]

The only other naval debate of the session was occasioned by the appropriation bill which was considered some seven weeks later. On 27 May the new Ways and Means Committee (Gallatin's brain child) [70] was told to bring in a section on a naval appropriation in their bill appropriating for "Military and Naval Establishments." [71] It was considered by the House on the thirtieth, the actual sum being left blank in the Ways and Means bill.

William Loughton Smith again took the lead. He moved to fill in the blank with $113,025 for the pay "of the officers, seamen, and Marines." Because the ships would not be finished during this session John Nicholas countered with a motion to strike out Smith's figure and insert "the pay of the captains of the three frigates." Even this was objected to by Jonathan N. Havens of Long Island, New York, who said there was no reason to pay them anything—ship-building was not their business—these posts were "mere sinecures." (This was unfair of Havens; the captains were needed as supervisors.) Smith meekly suggested adding the subsistence of the Captains, making the total five thousand dollars, which was "agreed to." [72] Smith had seen his "budget" cut ninety-six per cent in a few minutes.

The Senate accepted the appropriation bill without much difficulty.[73] On naval affairs in the first session of the Fourth Congress the United States Senate was a very harmonious body. In voting on the naval measures of 1796 not one motion required a division, much less a roll call.

Thus three of the six frigates which had been authorized in 1794 survived the making of peace with the pirates of Algiers. If the War Department had found it easier to build the ships there might have been stronger support of Smith's plea to persevere in the building of the authorized six.

The warmest opponents of the naval policy must be found among those twenty-five who voted with Gallatin, on roll call, to reduce the Senate's three ships to two. The strongest pro-navy element was the group of thirty-six which voted on roll call with Smith in a preliminary move to raise the figure from three to six ships. There were about forty members in the intermediate position, of whom twenty-three actually voted against *both* Smith's and Gallatin's motions. To find Robert Goodloe Harper of South Carolina and Nathaniel Macon of North Carolina allied in this group is, it must be confessed, a surprise, because they were usually at opposite extremes on any naval question. It is less surprising to find Thomas Blount of South Carolina and Robert Rutherford of Virginia voting nay on every proposal—they simply wished to have no navy. There seems no rational explanation of the behavior of Roger Griswold of Connecticut who voted with Smith to raise the number of ships, with Gallatin to cut the number, and then voted aye on passage of the Senate Bill.[74]

The American naval controversy of the eighteenth century has been described as an intersectional struggle of east versus west. As it happened, of the twenty-three members of the anti-navy bloc (anti-navy at least in preferring the smaller to the larger number of ships) seven were elected by tidewater constituencies, or lived within a day's travel of the sea, including one from Connecticut and one from Long Island. Thomas Blount, a most inveterate opponent, lived only thirty miles from salt water.[75]

A sectional tabulation of the vote shows naval sentiment progressively weaker from north to south:

	Yea	Nay
New England:		
New Hampshire	4	0
Vermont	1	1
Massachusetts	9	1
Rhode Island	1	0
Connecticut	4	1
	19	3
Middle States:		
New York	6	3
New Jersey	2	0
Pennsylvania	8	2
Delaware	1	0
Maryland [76]	5	1
	22	6
South:		
Virginia	9	9
North Carolina	5	3
South Carolina	3	2
Georgia	2	0
	20	14

No state gave a majority to the opposition, although Virginia turned up nine members who would not go along with Madison and Nicholas, and who formed the only large bloc of opponents.

NOTES FROM PAGES 72 TO 83

1. Thomas Jefferson, "The Anas," 1793, *Writings,* ed. A. A. Lipscomb, 19v. (Washington, 1903–1904), I, 350–351. An edition by Lipscomb is also dated 1904–1905, and appears to be the same text with the addition of an index-volume.
2. James Schouler, *History of the United States of America under the Constitution,* 5v. (Washington, 1880–1891), I, 109. Senator William Maclay, habitually censorious of persons in his diary, found Knox likable. William Maclay, *Journal,* ed. E. S. Maclay (New York, 1890), 310.
3. Howard Irving Chapelle, *The History of the American Sailing Navy; the Ships and Their Development* (New York, 1949), 117–118. Hereafter cited: Chapelle, *Sailing Navy.*
4. Charles Oscar Paullin, "Early Naval Administration under the Constitution," *United States Naval Institute Proceedings,* XXXII (1906), 1002–1003; Franklin Delano Roosevelt, "Our First Frigates, Some Unpublished Facts about Their Construction," *Transactions of the Society of Naval Architects and Marine Engineers,* XXII (1914), 139. Roosevelt hereafter cited, "Our first frigates."
5. Chapelle, *Sailing Navy,* 119–120.
6. Ira N. Hollis, *The Frigate Constitution* (Boston, 1931), 34–37. Humphreys's views were stated in detail in a letter to Senator Robert Morris of Pennsylvania, 6 Jan. 1793, *ibid.,* 35–36. Apparently no one suggested building ships of the line this early.
7. Harold and Margaret Sprout, *The Rise of American Naval Power, 1776–1918,* rev. ed. (Princeton, 1946), 33–36.
8. They *were* heavy, for frigates. *Constellation*'s draft was more than twenty-two feet, "which renders it impossible for her to go into any Port in the United States southward of the Chesapeake, without taking out her Guns." Truxtun to McHenry, 23 June 1798, Dudley W. Knox, ed., *Naval Documents Related to*

the Quasi-war between the United States and France, 7v. (Washington, 1935–1938), I, 132. Hereafter cited: Knox, *Quasi-war*. The theoretical problems of naval architecture were treated in Chapelle, *Sailing Navy*, 118–134.
9. Knox to Washington, 15 April 1794, Washington papers, Library of Congress (hereafter abbreviated: LC).
10. Knox to the House of Representatives, 27 Dec. 1794, *American State Papers*, ed. variously, 38v. (Washington, 1832–1861), Class VI, *Naval Affairs*, I, 6. Hereafter cited: *ASP* with the name of the class.
11. Washington to Knox, 16 April 1794, George Washington, *Writings*, ed. John C. Fitzpatrick, 39v. (Washington, 1931–1944), XXXIII, 333. Hereafter cited: Washington, *Writings*.
12. Knox to the House of Representatives, 27 Dec. 1794, *ASP: Naval Affairs*, I, 6.
13. Robert Greenhalgh Albion, *Forests and Sea Power, the Timber Problem of the Royal Navy, 1652–1862* (Cambridge, Mass., 1926), 23.
14. Barry, Truxtun and Dale to Knox, 18 Dec. 1794, *ASP: Naval Affairs*, I, 8.
15. Washington to Knox, 23 Dec. 1794, Washington, *Writings*, XXXIV, 70, to Butler, 7 Jan. 1795, *ibid.*, XXXIV, 79; Roosevelt, "Our first frigates," 143–144, quoting Pickering.
16. Chapelle, *Sailing Navy*, 168.
17. Gore to King, 15 March 1794, Rufus King, *The Life and Correspondence of Rufus King*, ed. C. R. King, 6v. (New York, 1894–1900), I, 552–553; Leroy to King, 19 March 1794, *ibid.*, I, 554–555; Lawrance to King, 23 March 1794, *ibid.*, I, 556. Hereafter cited: King, *Life and Correspondence*.
18. Washington to Randolph, 15 April 1794, Washington, *Writings*, XXXIII, 329–330.
19. Jay, indirectly quoted in Hamilton to King, 17 Sept. 1794, King, *Life and Correspondence*, I, 573.
20. 3 Cong., 1 Sess., 27 March 1794, *Annals of the Congress, 1789–1824*, ed. J. Gales and W. W. Seaton, 42v. (Washington, 1834–1856), 535. Hereafter cited: *Annals*.
21. William Loughton Smith, *ibid.*, 539–540. Smith opposed it.
22. *Ibid.*, 500–501, 503–504.
23. 2, 7 April 1794, *ibid.*, 559, 562.
24. Madison to Jefferson, 25 May 1794, James Madison, *Letters and Other Writings*, 4v. (Philadelphia, 1865), II, 17.
25. R. R. Livingston to Monroe, 16 May 1794, Monroe papers, LC. This letter is bound with the letters of May 1793.
26. 3 Cong., 1 Sess., 18 March 1794, *Annals*, 524.
27. 4 June 1794, *ibid.*, 108, 765.
28. 3–4 June 1794, *ibid.*, 122, 760–762, 764–766, 1454–1455.
29. *Ibid.*, 703, 772–774.
30. Wolcott, Jr., to Washington, 8 Dec. 1795, George Gibbs, *Memoirs of the Administrations of Washington and John Adams*, 2v. (New York, 1846), I, 284. Hereafter cited: Gibbs, *Memoirs*.
31. HR 4 Cong., 1 Sess., 31 Dec. 1795, *Annals*, 184–185.
32. Pickering to the Vice President and the Senate, 12 Dec. 1795, *ASP: Naval Affairs*, I, 17–19.
33. Washington to the Congress, 8 Dec. 1795, *Annals*, 11.
34. 8 March 1796, *ibid.*, 50, 52–53.
35. *Ibid.*, 233.
36. *Ibid.*, 272.
37. 15 March 1796, *ibid.*, 790–791.
38. *Ibid.*, 54.
39. *Ibid.*, 60, 61, 62.
40. Representative Benjamin Bourne of Rhode Island suggested this motive during the House debate on the Bill. *Ibid.*, 872.
41. *Ibid.*, 802, 869.
42. This is deduced from a scrutiny of each day's issue of two Boston newspapers, the *Independent Chronicle* and the *Columbian Centinel*, of violently opposing views, from 16 March to 30 April 1796. In the *Annals* these debates occupy over 350 columns.
43. Ames arrived in Philadelphia two months after the session opened, taking sixteen days for the journey from Dedham. Ames to Thomas Dwight, 11, 16 Feb. 1796, Fisher Ames, *Works*, ed. Seth Ames, 2v. (Boston, 1854), I, 185–186. "I am not able to stay in the House all the time." Ames to Gore, 11 March 1796, *ibid.*, I, 189.

He appears to have saved his small energies for the debates on the appropriations to carry out the Jay Treaty, a battle which he won for the Federalists (by three votes) with a famous speech on the horrors of an Anglo-American war. J. S. Bassett, *The Federalist System* (New York, 1906), 134–135.

44. Wolcott, Jr., to Wolcott, Sr., 18 April 1796, Gibbs, *Memoirs*, I, 327.
45. Henry Adams, *The Life of Albert Gallatin* (Philadelphia, 1879), 180.
46. *Ibid.*, 157.
47. 3 March 1795, 3 Cong., 2 Sess., *Annals*, 1527; Francis to Pickering, 13 Jan. 1796, *ASP: Naval Affairs*, I, 21, and Nourse, memorandum, 9 Jan. 1796, *ibid.*, I, 22. Truxtun later complained of the quality of American-made anchors. Truxtun to McHenry, 23 June 1798, Knox, *Quasi-war*, I, 132–133.
48. Parker's select committee report, 29 Jan. 1796, *ibid.*, I, 19.
49. Gardner Weld Allen, *Our Navy and the Barbary Corsairs* (Boston, 1905), 56.
50. 7 April 1796, 4 Cong., 1 Sess., *Annals*, 869.
51. Swanwick, *ibid.*, 869–871; W. Smith, *ibid.*, 876–877.
52. Bourne, *ibid.*, 871–872; Parker, *ibid.*, 875–876.
53. Williams, *ibid.*, 872–874.
54. S. Smith, *ibid.*, 874–875.
55. Madison, *ibid.*, 877–878.
56. Sedgwick, *ibid.*, 878–879.
57. Nicholas, *ibid.*, 879.
58. Swanwick, *ibid.*, 881; W. Smith, *ibid.*, 885; Ames, *ibid.*, 882–883.
59. Gallatin, *ibid.*, 883–884; Giles, *ibid.*, 885.
60. *Ibid.*, 886.
61. *Ibid.*, 885–886.
62. 8 April 1796, *ibid.*, 886–887.
63. *Ibid.*, 891.
64. *Ibid.*, 887.
65. Swanwick, *ibid.*, 887–888; Williams, *ibid.*, 889; Murray, *ibid.*; W. Smith, *ibid.*, 890–891.
66. Parker, Goodhue, Madison, Kittera, Harper, Hillhouse, *ibid.*, 887–889.
67. W. Smith, *ibid.*, 890–891.
68. 9 April 1796, *ibid.*, 893.
69. 12 April 1796, *ibid.*, 70.
70. R. V. Harlow, *The History of Legislative Methods in the Period before 1825* (New Haven, 1917), 154–164, examined the rise of the standing committee system.
71. 27 May 1796, *Annals*, 1464.
72. 30 May 1796, *ibid.*, 1485.
73. 31 May, *ibid.*, 119.
74. In fairness, it would seem that any doubts of his mental stability arising out of his later physical brawls on the floor of the House with Matthew Lyon, the "Beast of Vermont," might well be resolved in favor of Lyon.
75. *Biographical Directory of the American Congress, 1774–1949* (Washington, 1950).

    It is impossible to recreate past events for study but it is possible to tally a House roll call in the same order as the Clerk first recorded it. On the passage of the Senate Bill, 9 April 1796, after eighteen names had been called the vote was even; after thirty-six had been called it was two to one in favor of passage; when the roll call had been completed it was three to one for passage. This may have been accidental but it appears as if the band-wagon climbers, after initial letter "C" had been passed, were true to their nature.
76. Although historians have usually regarded colonial Maryland as practically identical in culture and interest with Virginia, the voting behavior of the Free State delegations in the Congresses of the 1790s seems to require that Maryland be then classified as a "Middle State."

VII

The Struggle to Finish the Frigates

The Naval Act of 1796 had provided for finishing three frigates. To pay for this construction the War Department was to use the unexpended funds from previous appropriations and the eighty thousand dollars originally set aside in the spring of 1794 for building ten galleys. If earlier estimates had been reasonably correct the ships might have been quietly built without further argument, but the cost figures had been estimated far below what was actually needed, or, at least, what was actually spent. The naval history of the United States from mid-1796 to the spring of 1797 is the story of a struggle to get more money to finish the authorized program.

The year 1796 was chosen as the time for the administration to present to the public an over-all view of American naval policy. One of the vehicles for the presentation was President George Washington's "Farewell Address," on which he and Alexander Hamilton had been working since spring. The remarks on naval policy appear to have been written by Hamilton (as was most of the Address).[1] The Address, which was made public on 19 September, reminded the country the north found southern produce a help to its "Maratime [*sic*] and commercial enterprise." This enterprise caused southern agriculture and exports to expand. The whole process strengthened the merchant fleet, which also carried the produce of the west and helped thereby to link the west to the other parts of the country. When the country was so united it had greater security from foreign powers, and would need none "of those overgrown Military establishments" which so endangered liberty.[2]

Having planted the thought of the great unifying value of a trade on the high seas, the President, some hundreds of words later, brought home the idea of adequate armed forces contributing to national independence and to the preservation of the country's desirable isolation: "Taking care always to keep ourselves, by suitable establishments, on a respectably defensive posture, we may safely trust to temporary alliances for extraordinary emergencies." [3]

If trade were as necessary as Washington said, one of those "suitable establishments" would have to be a navy. This conclusion was brought out in the next presentation of the administration's views, which was the President's message at the opening of the second session of the Fourth Congress, delivered on 7 December 1796. Hamilton provided much of what went into this message, too.[4]

On naval matters the message said, in summary: Foreign commerce needed naval protection, whether a nation was at war or was a neutral in wartime. Possession of a naval force might enable a neutral to stay at peace. American Mediterranean trade would never be secure without naval protection. The United States should therefore begin to establish a navy. Its trade would provide the seamen, and its advantageous geographical location would allow considerable influence to be exerted by a relatively small force.[5]

It was customary at the time for each chamber to make a ceremonious reply to presidential messages at the beginning of a session.

In the House of Representatives the second session of the Fourth Congress opened with a harshness of tone not heard before. Long before fatigue could account for it, in the first fortnight of the session, venomous discourtesy was almost the rule of debate. There was a three-day argument on the wording of the House's reply to the President, a very bitter argument, best remembered for the speech of William B. Giles of Virginia in which he expressed pleasure at the prospect of the President's retirement, mostly because the President had handled foreign relations so poorly. John Swanwick of Pennsylvania agreed, and pointed to Washington's recommendation of a navy as showing that the country was not at peace.[6] From this the discussion went on to review the conduct of foreign policy, raging all one day, full of oblique personalities which were just barely, if at all, within the limits of parliamentary law. The Republicans proposed many amendments to a draft reply, intended, they said, to expunge the idolatries in it. Most of these amendments were lost. In the end they approved a reply which made no reference to naval power, by a vote of 67–12.[7]

The Senate-reply explicitly agreed with the President by saying American "commerce demands a naval force for its protection . . ." [8]

The acrimony so quickly revealed was the product of the presidential election campaign which was just then being completed. The performance of the French Minister, Pierre Auguste Adet, had angered the Federalists, and with some reason. In October he had informed the United States the French government would treat American ships as the United States allowed them to be treated by Great Britain. This was a slash at the Jay Treaty which permitted British seizure and purchase of enemy cargoes in American ships. This "note" was handed simultaneously to the leading Republican newspaper, Benjamin Franklin Bache's Philadelphia *Aurora.* The Federalists said it was an electioneering trick, arranged by the American enemies of the Jay Treaty, to help the candidacy of Thomas Jefferson against John Adams.[9]

On their side, the Republicans had a fiscal grievance. As Thomas Jefferson put it, the Bank of the United States had "completely saddled and bridled" the American people. Albert Gallatin had discovered what other Republicans had not been sure of, that the national debt had been increasing at the rate of about a million dollars a year.[10] (Actually, in the years 1791–1796, the increase amounted to more than eight million dollars.) [11] So much paper money had been put in circulation as to drive up the prices of imported commodities by fifty per cent [12]—always a sensitive point among southern planters. In the same year, 1796, Treasury Secretary Oliver Wolcott, Jr., had offered six per cent bonds at a fifteen per cent discount and had been unable to raise two per cent of the sum of money he had intended to get. For current expenses he had to dispose of some of the government's stock in the Bank of the United States.[13]

Through January 1797 the private correspondence of some Federalist leaders showed a spirit of foreboding. John Adams, now narrowly elected to succeed Washington, wrote of "a country Impotent at Sea tho Powerful at Land," injured contemptuously and insolently. To another correspondent, he doubted the loyalty of a great many Americans if there were a French invasion of the country.[14] Fisher Ames wrote complainingly to Hamilton,—the Americans were unwilling either to protect or to abandon their foreign trade. "An European would be ready to believe we are in jest in our politics . . ." [15]

This sort of irritation was plain in the press and on the floor of the House. Hamilton was writing regular installments of a pseudonymous tract, "The Warning," in which he said the United States had sufficient maritime strength to make it unnecessary to put up with French depredations.[16] The Boston *Independent Chronicle* said the cut from six to three frigates, and the construction of a frigate as a gift to the Dey of Algiers, showed the passage of the Naval Act of 1794 to have been for the purpose of building Federalist patronage, not for defense against Algiers.[17] The New York *Diary* plumped for an embargo instead of a fleet—"To fit out a navy of considerable force, is an undertaking too expensive for the resources of an infant country." [18] When it was proposed to raise the salary of the Secretary of War by five hundred dollars because, among other reasons, naval business had increased his burdens, Representative James Holland of North Carolina hoped the Secretary would not have much naval business in the future and promised to do what he could to avoid troubling him in that way. The measure failed to pass by five votes.[19]

Despite the widespread veneration of the chief spokesman for Federalist naval policy (Giles's views on Washington were not generally held) it was obvious the intentions of the Federalists were suspect among Republicans. And the Republicans, who, by three electoral votes only, had just missed electing Thomas Jefferson to the presidency, were by no means powerless. When the House Reply to Washington's message could make no statement at all on naval policy it was an ill omen for the navy. Representative Uriah Tracy of Connecticut believed the Republicans hoped to destroy the country by encouraging the French to destroy foreign trade. Then they would prevent the raising of a domestic revenue, thus "introducing their beloved confusion." [20]

For good or ill the country had a naval construction program going and the House could not ignore *that.* A naval committee was appointed to inquire into the state of the equipment ordered by former acts of the Congress, and to look into the question whether any navy was necessary. It was headed by Josiah Parker, Virginia Federalist. The other members were Edward Livingston of New York, Robert Goodloe Harper of South Carolina, and J. S. Sherburne of New Hampshire.[21] The latter made little impress on his times, but Livingston was an ardent Republican and Harper an even fiercer Federalist. The Committee's first step was to ask Secretary of War James McHenry for a report.

The Secretary gave them a description of the state of each of the three frigates, with estimates of the money needed to complete them and to man them. He gave a table of the materials on hand and a table of the materials sold with the prices received. He named the Captains: for *United States,* John Barry, for *Constitution,* Samuel Nicholson, for *Constellation,* Thomas Truxtun, each of the three supervising the civilian constructor of his own ship. (Richard Dale had taken leave to make a China voyage.) In McHenry's opinion each of the ships could be made ready for sea about two months after launching, although none was launched yet. He thought the government ought to acquire a preserve of live oak against a probable price rise, and should also have its own navy yard.[22] To the House of Representatives the most interesting part of the report was McHenry's request for much more money, two hundred thousand dollars above the six hundred-odd thousand dollars which had been spent already, to finish the three frigates, and the sum did not include the cost of manning and provisioning. The Committee recommended "blank" dollars, for the ships, for a navy yard, and for purchase of a stock of live oak and red cedar.[23]

It would take weeks before the House could work its way through a bill of that kind. Meanwhile what was needed was what is now called a "deficiency appropriation." As the Secretary of the Treasury wrote in a memorandum, the funds for construction were down to twenty-four thousand dollars as of the first of the year. Therefore the self-appointed naval leader in the House, William Loughton Smith of South Carolina, moved a temporary appropriation in blank for both army and navy.[24] It was objected to by Joseph B. Varnum of Massachusetts who said there would be time enough when the regular appropriation came up. Smith listed the parliamentary hurdles the regular appropriation would have to clear, all of which would take so much time that the public service would suffer. The House then went into Committee of the Whole on the temporary appropriation. The wording of Smith's motion included the phrase "Military and Naval Establishments." [25]

Albert Gallatin of Pennsylvania next moved to strike out the word "Naval," because the House might not choose to continue building the ships. If it were decided to finish them he would vote to restore the word.[26] This certainly primed the oratorical pump; eleven speakers made seventeen speeches on Gallatin's motion.

The supporters of Gallatin's motion made out an effective case.[27] The Army and the Navy ought to be separated in this matter because the Army is a settled thing and the Navy is not. Before making any appropriation it should be decided whether the frigates should be finished. A temporary appropriation was not the proper, orderly way to go about it. In fact, it was not legal to appropriate before the passage of a naval act; therefore a vote for Gallatin's motion was not a vote against finishing the frigates but against finishing them by this means. Any appropriation should be an itemized appropriation, not a lump sum.

According to the opponents if the workmen were discharged it would damage the public interest. If the frigates were now abandoned the members would be the "monuments of their own folly." The "truest economy" would be to go ahead. Trade was needed to bring in tariff duties. The frigates were needed to protect the trade. Therefore the frigates were needed to bring in the public revenue. To stop because the estimates were too low would be like leaving a house unfinished for the same reason. To strike the word "naval" would be to encourage "piccaroons" to ravage the coast. Even if it were to be decided not to have a navy it would still be best to finish the frigates, rather than to let them rot. The question was not, shall the country have a navy? but, should the Congress finish the frigates?

The opponents attacked the arguments of the Gallatin group specifically. It was certainly legal to appropriate in this fashion because the Naval Act of 1796 incurred this expense; meanwhile the country was defenseless and it was time to start "supporting our dignity." If appropriations must be itemized, how was it the other side only attacked the lack of itemization in a naval matter and not in the case of the Army? As for needing the money, they had the word of the Secretary of the Treasury.

The rebuttal of the supporters of the motion to strike the word "naval" made two points: they were not trying to prevent the building of a navy but to get it done by the proper parliamentary means, and, second, if the previous naval acts left them no choice but to go ahead, why bother to appropriate at all?

Although Gallatin mustered only two speakers from north of the Mason-Dixon line and found his other five all in the Virginia delegation, his motion seemed to have a wide appeal, for it was carried, 42–34.[28] There was to be no "deficiency" appropriation for Secretary McHenry's naval constructors. They would have to await the grinding of the congressional mills.

What was left before the House was the naval committee's report which had transmitted Secretary McHenry's request for two hundred thousand dollars to finish the frigates, plus unspecified sums for the manning and provisioning, for a navy yard, and for a live oak forest-preserve. On 10 February 1797 the House went into Committee of the Whole to consider these matters.[29]

Parker opened for his committee, proposing to fill in "blank dollars" with the figure $172,000. This would not be enough to man the frigates and send them to sea but would be enough to finish the construction. Probably another Congress would meet before manning and provision posed their problems.[30]

Joshua Coit of Connecticut promptly diverted the discussion from one on the amount of money to a discussion of the purposes of the spending, by a motion which would have had the effect of ordering the little squadron to be finished and then put in moth-balls. Specifically he moved to repeal all parts of the Naval Act of 1794 which concerned officers and crew. This would no doubt be an action very distasteful to the Senate because it would appear to require them to repeal an Act, willy-nilly, or do without any naval force.[31] After some parliamentary wrangling the Chair ruled Coit's motion out of order and suggested that its mover's end could only be accomplished by first amending the Parker committee's recommendation so as to omit a reference to the frigates being equipped for sea. John Nicholas of Virginia so moved.

Opponents protested the unfairness of making a single package of the three separate ideas of finishing, equipping, and manning, but Nicholas's motion carried. Now the Committee of the Whole was on record as favoring the completion of the ships but was silent about equipping them for sea.

The ground being cleared Coit next renewed his motion, rephrasing it in such a way as to prohibit manning but not abolish the appointments of the three captains already commissioned. William Loughton Smith professed to be outraged at this use or abuse of the purse power indirectly to change national policy, but Nicholas reminded him this was the theoretical purpose behind the practice of frequent appropriations. Nicholas favored completion of the ships but no more. The ships could be sold for a good price, and, anyway, they could not be manned because the country was not prepared to compete with the high wages now being paid for merchant seamen. Samuel Smith of Maryland said seamen's wages would be lower except for the hazard of impressment into the Royal Navy. If the United States had a navy the hazard would not exist. If the ships could be launched in 1797 he would vote to do it. If they could not, the discussion was unnecessary.

Chairman Parker of the naval committee now rose and patiently explained his committee's stand. He had no doubt the ships could be at sea by October, if the Congress wished. The United States could do without these ships only if it wished to adopt the Chinese policy and have no foreign commerce. Actually the country was better able to found a navy now than Great Britain or Spain had been when they founded theirs. Meanwhile "we are the sport of all nations . . ." He concluded by urging the Members not to be "fickle boys." More argument on the broad bases of naval policy followed, but merely repeated premises which were already well known to both sides.

Then General Henry Dearborn of Massachusetts reached what seemed to be the heart of the subject. He thought the Congress had been very generous. It had been estimated that the ships would cost a hundred thousand dollars each, but they had spent three hundred thousand dollars and still heard a call for more. He thought only the hulls should be finished. The ships could have been built in four months but it was now near four years since they had been authorized.[32] For some reason they seemed to cost twice as much as British men-of-war. He could only conclude that there had been much waste—waste, not error, because men skilled in ship building could hardly have been that much in error. The only recourse of the Congress was to appropriate from point to point as the construction proceeded.[33]

Following this attack on the delays in the construction program Coit's motion to repeal the personnel sections of the Act of 1794 carried, receiving fifty-eight ayes.

Dearborn rose again and moved to finish "the hulls" only. Opponents reminded the Committee of contracts which had been let for rigging. Another thought the treaty with Algiers would soon be obsolete if the Dey learned the United States was to have no naval force. Parker made the most moving speech against Dearborn's motion. Most of the materials needed to finish the ships were on hand and the Naval Committee only asked $172,000 for the rest of the work. He admitted the frigates cost more than any ships he had ever heard of, and Britain paid only one thousand pounds per gun for its warships, but there were two good reasons for the high cost of the American frigates: labor was paid much more in this country, and these were the largest frigates in the world. If the two "forty-fours" were given another deck each, they would be two "seventy-fours." He knew they would be "an ornament to the country . . . he had never seen vessels equal to these." [34]

This appeal was effective, and Dearborn's motion was lost.

The Committee of the Whole reported to the House on the next day (11 February). It approved of striking out the reference to equipping for sea, and also voted to repeal the manning provisions of the Act of 1794, except for the captains already commissioned. The Federalist said it would be improper to combine in one bill the project of finishing the ships and the repeal of the manning provisions because it would be unfair to those who wished to vote in favor of one and to vote against the other. It would also be unfair to the Senate and the executive for the same reason. The Republicans said they were willing to vote to finish the ships but would rather see them burned than manned.[35] The problem was temporarily thrust aside by instructing the Naval Committee to bring in "a bill or bills" incorporating the sense of the House.[36] Chairman Parker no doubt sighed with relief when his $172,000 remained untouched. He could not say the same for his navy yard and live oak supply.

On the previous day the prospect of owning a navy yard was greeted coolly in the Committee of the Whole, the chill being induced by the review of naval costs which had just been completed. However there were always Members who were ready to canvass the whole field of naval policy and two of them, Harper and Gallatin, spoke at length, presenting an excellent contrast of Republican and Federalist views.[37]

Harper opened with the rhetorical question, should the United States aim to achieve naval strength? Commerce appeared to need protection. Some men said commerce should go on and take its risks. If so, the men engaged in commerce would give it up. If the government offered no protection the people would lose respect for the government. Should commerce be abandoned entirely? Many men were trained for it and would refuse to abandon it. Should privateers be relied on for protection? This would add to the cost of trading, which would raise the price of commodities. If the United States copied China and carried no cargoes but left its trade open to all, the strongest nation would compel the Americans to trade with its merchants only. On the other hand, a navy yard—in addition to providing a place in which to season ship timbers, and generally making building less expensive—would have a good effect on the thinking of foreign powers. Action should be taken now or the people who needed protection would begin to think the Congress would never provide it.[38]

Gallatin, on the other side, had doubts whether commerce needed the protection of a navy. After four years of depredations without naval protection the United States was the third-ranking commercial power (behind Great Britain and the Netherlands). Hamburg was a leader in world commerce and had no navy. Navies were "the instruments of power, more calculated to annoy the trade of other nations, than to protect that of the nation to which they belong." The gentleman from South Carolina contradicted himself when he said commerce needed protection, but without protection the men engaged in it would refuse to abandon it. As for the Chinese, they had much maritime trade but made no long voyages. The United States could not support a navy, a judgment which had been confirmed by the great cost of the three frigates then being built. The United States could not man a navy without impressment, a method impossible in the United States. Considering the claim for a navy as needed to protect the public revenue nearly all of which came from tariff duties, two-thirds of the revenue went to the charges of the national debt. If that debt were paid the United States would have great respect abroad and would have plenty of money for a navy.[39]

On the following day the first action was to kill the resolution to buy a navy yard. It received only twenty-three ayes.[40]

The idea of a live oak preserve seems to have originated with the builder-designer, Joshua Humphreys, in 1794, when he wrote to Secretary of War Henry Knox that much of this prized timber was being cut merely to clear the land. If it were not all destroyed he feared that agents of some foreign naval power would come to America and buy it all. If the United States bought several islands covered with live oak, the land could be sold after the trees were cut, for enough money to recover the first cost.[41]

In the Committee of the Whole the opposers of the live oak preserve said the project was presented very vaguely; its sponsors did not agree on the price of the land, nor on the quantities of timber needed or available. This charge of vagueness was probably the most effective argument. However the attack went farther. As for the danger of European purchases General William Heath of Massachusetts said he would be "glad if they would purchase all our forests," and he dismissed the forest proposal as bureaucratic and monarchical.[42] Other opponents said ownership of the timber would be used as an argument to support an even larger construction program, to embark on a large land-purchase would encourage speculators, and live oak could be kept out of European hands by forbidding its export.[43]

The defenders reverted again to the general question of naval policy. The *Notes on Virginia* of Vice President Thomas Jefferson was quoted as favoring a navy for the United States, as large as eighteen ships, but Jefferson's friends disposed of this by saying the book was written during the war with Great Britain and the naval part was not applicable to the needs of the 1790's. From here the argument ranged over and synopsized the whole of the naval debate since the Constitutional convention. Tempers were frayed, as revealed when John Nicholas said the Act of 1794 had been passed by alleging its necessity as a protection against Algiers, a danger no longer cited—"protection from the Algerines was a mere pretence to set the building of a fleet on foot."[44]

At length the live oak preserve was brought to a vote and decisively rejected, 31–55.[45] The report of the Committee of the Whole was then considered by the House of Representatives, which accepted it by rejecting the navy yard proposal, 69–21, and the live oak preserve, 62–29.[46] William Loughton Smith tried to salvage something from the debacle by a resolution offered on 14 February to prevent the export of live oak "for a limited time," but the resolution was tabled and never brought up again.[47]

Thus far the House of Representatives in the second session of the Fourth Congress had stripped the executive of authority to commission or enlist any more men than the three captains, Barry, Truxtun, and Nicholson. It had discarded the projects for a live oak preserve and a navy yard. All the administration had won was a tentative promise of $172,000 to finish the ships, with the understanding they would not go to sea. At this moment, comically late, Secretary McHenry asked the help of Hamilton in formulating propositions to submit to the Congress, concerning a navy yard and ship timber. (Of course the House had yet to receive "a bill or bills" from its Naval Committee, but it was very unlikely the yard or the trees would receive any more consideration.) The harassed and perplexed Secretary had found the discussion very embarrassing. As he said,

> It is however no easy matter to account for the great expenditures that have taken place beyond what had been expected, and not involve predecessors in some censure, and at the same time insinuate a belief or expectation that similar expences may in future be avoided . . .[48]

The Naval Committee had two "bills" ready on 13 February but they were not considered until the eighteenth.[49] One bill had a "blank dollars" provision, and the other would repeal the manning provisions of the Act of 1794, saving the three captains. Once more the House went into Committee of the Whole. The bill to repeal the manning provisions was considered first.[50]

Now the Federalist side of the House was put through a course of humiliation. First the manning bill was amended so as to apply its repeal to all manning provisions of all naval legislation. Then the Republicans refused to substitute the word "suspend" for the word "repeal," by a vote of 30–51. By this time John Swanwick of Pennsylvania was so angry he challenged the anti-navy forces to put a stop to construction of the frigates if that was what they wished. The Republican reply was a motion by A. B. Venable of Virginia to connect the two bills, making them one. From this motion flowed an argument which had little to do with naval policy or constitutionality. It was simply a tactical operation by which the Republicans overwhelmed their opponents in order to make the Federalists in the House and Senate vote for the repealer if they were to get their ship-money. They carried the union of the two bills, 41–36. This was the lowest vote-total of the day.

The Committee of the Whole then reported to the House of Representatives what it had done. The House proceeded to vote on the Committee's report. The Federalists struggled in agony against the necessity of voting for the repealer in order to get the $172,000 but in the end, of course, they had to do it.[51] An analysis of the vote would yield little fruit. Basically the issue was one of national "housekeeping," and some voted aye only because the country had sunk so much money in these ships they could not bear to leave them unfinished.

A fortnight later the admirable Truxtun, writing to McHenry about the professional training of officers, let off a growl when he incidentally mentioned "the pusillanimity of Congress . . ."[52] The whole circumstance must have been mortifying to the three captains. As late as the end of August *United States* (launched on 10 May) was guarded by a detachment of soldiers from Fort Mifflin.[53]

The bill had yet to be considered by the Senate, which received on the twentieth, "An act repealing so much of an act supplemental to an act, entitled 'An act to provide a Naval Armament,' as relates to the officering and manning the frigates building in the United States; and appropriating money for the purpose of finishing the frigates United States, Constitution, and Constellation." It is not easy to learn what happened in the Senate because its debates were not published, although they had been open to the public for several years. From an examination of the long-hand changes made in the Senate on the face of the engrossed House Bill, and from a reading of the cryptic Senate reports in the *Annals* by the light of those long-hand changes, the sequence of events can be determined but not the reasons for it.

The title of the bill was changed by striking out the word "Repealing" and inserting "Suspending." Next, and mysteriously, the appropriation was stricken out. Then the repealing-text was changed so the manning provisions were not "repealed" but "suspended until the end of the next session of Congress." The exception of the three captains was retained, but to it was added: "& the Employment of such persons as may be necessary for preserving the said Frigates." [54]

In this surprising form the bill returned to the House, for concurrence in "several amendments." [55] The Republicans took one look and would have none of it. Gallatin moved to postpone action on the bill until the first Monday in December, because as the Senate had phrased it, the President could man the ships under cover of the provision to engage as many men as were needed to preserve them. The motion carried, 43–29.[56]

Harold and Margeret Sprout, the most recent students of this subject, said matters had now come to an "impasse." [57] The word is perhaps too strong. Gallatin had taken the tide of Republican anger at the flood, and it appeared, had killed the navy by his motion to postpone the consideration of the Senate's amendments to the House Bill. But the Senate's move seems to have been well considered from the Federalist point of view. The earlier naval statutes were still intact. In the following fortnight the Republicans must have had some uneasy reflections at the thought of the three beautiful frigates, so nearly finished, being left to rot in the sun and the rain, representing, as they did, so many hundreds of thousands of dollars of public money. Perhaps they had been hasty.

On 2 March the routine bill appropriating for the armed forces was brought up. It included the usual five thousand dollars for the pay and subsistence of the three lonely captains. William Loughton Smith slyly moved to insert $172,000 to finish the frigates. His motion was easily carried in both Committee of the Whole and in the House of Representatives although the debate was of the sort the reader would expect, and included a repeat performance of the Jay Treaty wrangle, and a good many nasty personal attacks very thinly disguised as quasi-polite discussion. At one point a motion to finish only "the hulls" was lost by the casting vote of the Speaker.[58]

The Senate was pleased to accept the money [59] and the "lame duck" session of the Fourth Congress adjourned *sine die* in the evening of the next day, an hour before its and George Washington's terms expired.

Although the repeal of the manning-provisions had been beaten off, the session was hardly a glorious one for the navy-minded members. The appropriation of $172,000 would not be enough to do more than finish the ships, and would leave them naked of seamen. The naval force had three unfinished ships, three captains, no crews, no live oak forest, no navy yard.

Anti-navy thought had found a spokesman of rare ability in Gallatin. Gallatin, by his significant equation of the city-state of Hamburg with the United States, had exploited the continuing appeal of the "little America" type of isolationism, earlier revealed in the ratification controversy. Statistically considered, Gallatin may have been correct in his low estimate of the value of a navy to American commerce in his generation. But the United States Navy was not solely a problem of accountancy. As Henry Adams said, when Gallatin's Party had controlled the executive branch for twelve years the three frigates were the only national glory. The Americans would have sacrificed the public financial credit and much else before parting with the fame of the ships. Gallatin himself later "found that his country had no national dignity abroad except what these frigates had conquered." [60]

The executive had come off badly in its contest with the Republicans. It had been publicly derided and castigated as incompetent or wasteful, because of the unexpected great expense of the construction program. Captain Truxtun, a year later, explained the costs pretty well. All the building operations south of Philadelphia were excessively expensive. He had protested in the beginning to Secretary Knox, who himself had said to build in the south would increase the cost by a quarter, but President Washington wished to spend the money throughout the country. South of Philadelphia labor was "scarce and indolent," materials cost more, and supervision was more difficult because the few skilled workmen were not skilled at ship building. In Truxtun's considered professional judgment good small vessels could be built on the Chesapeake but the region was not suited to the building of large ships.[61]

The Republicans in this session showed themselves more fiercely antinaval than ever before. The reason for this intensification of their opposition is not to be found solely in the arguments on naval policy. They feared the Federalists. Specifically they feared the centralization of power by increasing debts and increasing taxes. They also suspected the administration of intending to use its armed force on the side of monarchical Britain against republican France. As Irving Brant succinctly phrased it, they voted against sending the frigates to sea because they thought they would "start a war they couldn't finish." [62]

More than these specific fears, they were jealous of civil liberty. An exaggerated concern for internal security had led each side to doubt the patriotism of the other, which in turn brought a political perversion of honest patriotic sentiment, expressed in contumely, slander, and abuse of the honor of those of differing political beliefs. In this electric atmosphere, with the sides approximately even in strength, defense preparations were almost paralyzed by political hatreds. But passions were to rage much more furiously before they spent themselves.

NOTES FROM PAGES 87 TO 100

1. Victor Hugo Paltsits, *Washington's Farewell Address*, 176, 184.
2. George Washington, *Writings*, ed. John C. Fitzpatrick, 39v. (Washington, 1931–1944), XXXV, 220–221.
3. *Ibid.*, XXXV, 235.
4. The President asked Hamilton's assistance, and expressed a doubt whether there should be any naval reference beyond the need for protecting the Mediterranean trade. Washington to Hamilton, 15 November 1796, *ibid.*, XXXV, 272–273. Hamilton went a good deal beyond it in a long undated reply, to be found in the Hamilton papers, Library of Congress (hereafter abbreviated: LC). The complete naval comments of each will be found hereafter in Appendix B.
5. 4 Cong., 2 Sess., 7 Dec. 1796, *Annals of the Congress, 1789–1824*, ed. J. Gales and W. W. Seaton, 42v. (Washington, 1834–1856), 1593–1594. Hereafter cited: *Annals*. Dates will be given where necessary for clarity.
6. *Ibid.*, 1615, 1630.
7. 13–15 Dec. 1796, *ibid.*, 1607–1668.
8. 10 Dec., *ibid.*, 1520.
9. James Madison, quoted in Irving Brant, *James Madison, Father of the Constitution* (Indianapolis, 1950), 445.
10. Jefferson to Monroe, 12 June 1796, Thomas Jefferson, *Writings*, ed. A. A. Lipscomb, 19v. (Washington, 1903–1904), IX, 337–338. The edition by Lipscomb, 1904–1905, appears to be the same text with an index-volume added.
11. United States. Bureau of the Census. *Historical Statistics of the United States, 1789–1945* (Washington, 1949).
12. Jefferson to Monroe, 12 June 1796, Jefferson, *Writings*, IX, 337–338.
13. George Gibbs, *Memoirs of the Administrations of Washington and John Adams*, 2v. (New York, 1846), I, 371. Hereafter cited: Gibbs, *Memoirs*.
14. John Adams to Smith, 18 Jan. 1797, to Welsh, 19 Jan. 1797, Adams papers, reel 117, LC. Quoted by permission of the Adams Manuscript Trust, Boston, Mass.
15. Ames to Hamilton, 26 Jan. 1797, Hamilton papers, LC.
16. Hamilton, "The Warning," 27 Jan. to 27 March 1797, Alexander Hamilton, *Works*, ed. Henry Cabot Lodge, 9v. (New York, 1885–1886), V, 363–392.
17. Boston *Independent Chronicle*, 26 Jan. 1797.
18. New York *Diary*, 28 Jan. 1797, quoted in Boston *Columbian Centinel*, 11 Feb. 1797.
19. 26 Jan. 1797, *Annals*, 1987–1990, 2010–2011.

20. Tracy to Wolcott, Sr., 24 Jan. 1797, Gibbs, *Memoirs*, I, 439.
21. 16 Dec. 1796, *Annals*, 1671.
22. *Ibid.*, 1913; *American State Papers*, ed. Walter Lowrie and Matthew St. Clair Clarke, 38v. (Washington, 1832–1861), Class VI, *Naval Affairs*, I, 25–28. (Hereafter cited: *ASP:* followed by the name of the class.) For the convenience of the reader it may be noted that the keels were laid in 1795. The launchings of 1797 were as follows: *United States*, Philadelphia, 10 May; *Constellation*, Baltimore, 7 September; *Constitution*, Boston, 21 October. Gardner Weld Allen, *Our Naval War with France* (Boston, 1909), 48.
23. 25 Jan. 1797, *Annals*, 1983–1984.
24. 31 Jan., *ibid.*, 2049.
25. *Ibid.*, 2049–2050.
26. *Ibid.*
27. The temporary appropriation debate, 31 Jan., *ibid.*, 2050–2056.
28. *Ibid.*, 2056.
29. 10 Feb., *ibid.*, 2111–2113.
30. *Ibid.*, 2113.
31. The debate in Committee of the Whole, which followed Coit's motion, 10 Feb., *ibid.*, 2113–2122. The probable reaction of the Senate was argued by William Loughton Smith, and Samuel Sewall of Massachusetts.
32. The ships had been authorized two years and eleven months earlier. The expenditure thus far on the ships alone was a little less than two-thirds of a million dollars. *ASP: Naval Affairs*, I, 26.
33. *Annals*, 2119–2120.
34. *Ibid.*, 2121.
35. 11 Feb., *ibid.*, 2148.
36. *Ibid.*, 2148–2149, 2151.
37. The navy yard debate, 10 Feb., *ibid.*, 2122–2130. Bernard C. Steiner, *The Life and Correspondence of James McHenry* (Cleveland, 1907), credited McHenry with proposing the purchase of a navy yard. *Ibid.*, 180n.
38. *Annals*, 2126–2128. If it were discovered that Harper spoke from a brief prepared by Hamilton this writer would not be at all surprised.
39. *Ibid.*, 2128–2130.
40. 11 Feb., *ibid.*, 2131.
41. Humphrey to Knox, 23 Dec. 1794, *ASP: Naval Affairs*, I, 9.
42. 11 February 1797, *Annals*, 2134.
43. The live oak debate, *ibid.*, 2131–2148.
44. *Ibid.*, 2146. Jefferson's endorsement of a navy while Secretary of State could more effectively have been quoted.
45. *Ibid.*, 2148.
46. *Ibid.*, 2149–2150.
47. 14 Feb., *ibid.*, 2154.
48. McHenry to Hamilton, 12 Feb., Hamilton papers, LC. A year later McHenry told the House Naval committee it would have been much cheaper to have built the ships at one place, successively. The desire for quick results, he said, had dictated the decision to build them simultaneously at different places. McHenry to Livingston, 22 March 1798, *ASP: Naval Affairs*, I, 37–38.
49. 13 Feb. 1797, *Annals*, 2151; 18 Feb., *ibid.*, 2200.
50. The debate on the Naval Bill of 1797, *ibid.*, 2200–2209.
51. *Ibid.*, 2208; 20 Feb., *ibid.*, 2209.
52. Truxtun to McHenry, 3 March 1797, in Bernard C. Steiner, *The Life and Correspondence of James McHenry* 251–254.
53. McHenry to Barry, 30 August 1797, United States Navy, Miscellaneous manuscripts, LC.
54. Senate records, 22, 27 Feb. 1797, Legislative records, National archives; *Annals*, 1553–1554, 1556–1557, 1561–1562.
55. *Ibid.*, 2326.
56. 28 Feb., *ibid.*, 2329.
57. Harold and Margaret Sprout, *The Rise of American Naval Power, 1776–1918*, rev. ed. (Princeton, 1944), 38.
58. 2 March, *Annals*, 2339–2352.
59. *Ibid.*, 2358.
60. Henry Adams, *The Life of Albert Gallatin* (Philadelphia, 1879), 171–172. Adams, writing in the 1870s, believed most of the money spent on the Navy in the previous eighty years had been "uselessly expended."
61. Truxtun to McHenry, 20 May 1798, McHenry papers, LC. See page 73 for Knox's own encouragement of the President in this matter of spreading the expenditure over the country for political advantage. Perhaps this was the first McHenry had heard of the political motivation of the decentralized building program. See note 48, *supra*.
62. Irving Brant, *James Madison, Father of the Constitution* (Indianapolis, 1950), 448.

VIII

The French Imbroglio and the Navy

1797

Relations with France had steadily worsened since the making of the Jay Treaty. In July 1796 the French had resolved to treat neutral shipping in the way neutral shipping allowed itself to be treated by Great Britain. This policy was written in large plain letters by a decree of 2 March 1797 which authorized the seizure of neutral vessels laden in whole or in part with enemy property. To the Americans the French government justified this policy by saying the Jay Treaty was contrary to the spirit of the Franco-American commercial treaty of 1778.[1] The protests of Pierre Auguste Adet, the French Minister in Philadelphia, were coolly received, as "feeble in themselves, and more feebly urged."[2] He privately blamed President George Washington for "blind submission" to King George III and said Hamilton was the President's Pitt, who would lead the United States "back under the yoke of England."[3] Adet's formal note of protest, at the time of the presidential election of 1796, has been mentioned[4] as an irritant to Federalists. It was almost an ultimatum and was intended more for the public than for the Department of State.[5]

The conception of American policy in the minds of the responsible French officers went about like this: The United States, in return for a small concession in the British West Indian trade and a share of the Far Eastern trade, contracted to admit British vessels into American ports on an equality with France. Thus the Americans abandoned the cause of freedom from British monopoly and threw away the best weapon, the discrimination against British shipping, in exchange for small immediate advantages. The surrender was accomplished in secrecy, concealed even from the United States Minister to France. Therefore it was a deliberate insult to France, an insult apparently delivered with pleasure by such leading Americans as Alexander Hamilton and John Jay.[6]

For once the French were able to damage American shipping seriously. The British found their commitments in other parts of the world so insistent that in 1797 and for several years thereafter they quit harassing French West Indian shipping in its home waters and contented themselves only with defending their Caribbean commerce.

The effect of French spoliations on American commerce was grave. Insurance on a Jamaican voyage rose to forty per cent of the value of the ship and cargo.[7] The records of the seizures showed looting by French captors, improper prize-court procedures, and occasional personal atrocities.[8] The French government was supposed to pay for the ships condemned but it paid in depreciated paper currency, if at all.[9] Even provision-ships sent to French islands by the French consuls in the United States were condemned.

The key to French indignation was the clause of the Jay Treaty which allowed the British to seize (and buy) provisions. Food had been explicitly protected from seizure in the Franco-American Treaty. Therefore the French could say they were being treated unequally, and American Republicans agreed.[10] In evaluating the French state of mind it is well to remember the condition of the French population, which was close to starvation because of the blockade by the Royal Navy of Britain. Naturally the French leaders were not wholly dispassionate.[11]

James Monroe, Senator from Virginia (and later President of the United States) had been sent as Minister to France, apparently to keep the French friendly while Jay settled matters in London. He did not know Jay's instructions[12] and the Treaty was a surprise to him. As French anger intensified, the Cabinet in Philadelphia blamed Monroe for not explaining the Treaty correctly. When he was discovered to be writing Republican propaganda to friends for publication in the United States he was recalled invidiously and replaced with Charles Cotesworth Pinckney of South Carolina, a very competent man but one known to favor Britain over France in any contest. Pinckney arrived in Paris in December 1796 but the French, while giving Monroe an ostentatiously affectionate farewell, ignored Pinckney and then dismissed him.[13] The news of Pinckney's rejection reached the United States a few days after the adjournment of the Fourth Congress and the inauguration of John Adams as President, in March 1797.[14]

Both parties in America were inflamed—the Republicans because of the odium attached to Monroe's recall, and the Federalists because of the repulse of Pinckney. The Federalists controlled the executive but felt frustrated since their seaborne commerce was open to French attack, while France had "nothing upon the sea thro' which a blow could be returned."[15] They believed French complaints against the Jay Treaty were only convenient excuses for harassments of the United States as part of a French scheme for world revolution which would probably lead to a Franco-American war.[16] Because of the truculence of Federalist public remarks Alexander Hamilton cautioned his successor in the Treasury Department, Oliver Wolcott, Jr., against giving public grounds for believing the Cabinet wished war.[17]

The State Department's "specialist" on the French Revolution, John Quincy Adams, Minister at the Hague, had long before warned of the existence of a French faction in America, with a strong delegation in the House of Representatives.[18] This was easily believed and its acceptance became an act of faith among Federalists of every degree. For example, ex-President Washington wrote three letters in June 1797 questioning the patriotism of the congressional Republicans.[19]

The French had spies in the United States, among whom was General Georges Victor Collot. Today he would be dismissed from any nation's intelligence system as a "blabber-mouth" type of security risk. He was assigned to make a political and military reconnaissance of the West by Adet, in 1796, but was far too talkative. The United States government knew many of the details of his job even before he left for the Ohio Valley. However, Secretary Wolcott believed Collot was to electioneer for Thomas Jefferson for President, and was to use an itinerary drafted for the purpose by Albert Gallatin.[20] Even the French government believed it might rely on the American Republicans to help France "liberate" the western part of the United States. We know this from the surviving instructions to another French agent, M. A. B. Mangourit, who was told to think of James Madison and Robert R. Livingston as most useful acquaintances.[21]

Thus both the French and the Federalists thought the Republican leadership was at least potentially subversive. Although it is now certain they were not in the least unpatriotic, the publicly expressed doubts of Republican loyalty were understandable. In the colloquial—it figured. It may be doubted whether Vice President Jefferson, Madison, Monroe, or Gallatin (Republican floor-leader in the House of Representatives in the Fifth Congress) would have been "cleared" by a "security check," if there had been such a thing in the years 1797–1798. It is necessary to understand this sorry circumstance in order to understand the tone of the debates in the Fifth Congress.

In these depressing circumstances the Federalists tried to solve the national naval problem. President Adams, on 25 March 1797, issued a call for a special session of the Congress to convene on 15 May.[22] This he followed with instructions to the customs collectors not to clear any outbound armed American merchant vessels unless for the East Indies[23] (where the existence of endemic piracy sanctioned the custom).

The British merchants who traded to America precipitated a partial solution of their problem by appealing to the British government for convoys to protect their ships. Rufus King, the new American Minister to Britain, asked advice of Secretary of State Timothy Pickering, who authorized the acceptance of convoys if offered by the British.[24] So far as the ship owners were concerned the United States might as well have been at war. Underwriters would not insure ships bound for French ports, and required the usual "war premiums" for those sailing to the British West Indies.[25]

Federalist leaders corresponded among themselves on what should be done when the Congress met. Despite their failures of the previous session, they anticipated giving the President enough force to protect American commerce, although they disagreed on details.[26] The most influential memoranda of these weeks were those of Secretary of War James McHenry to President Adams, and Hamilton to Representative William Loughton Smith of South Carolina.

McHenry recorded two sets of observations for the President, as helps to the composition of the message to the special session. He made his calculations on two possibilities, war with France alone, or war with France and Spain. What was necessary was the defense of commerce, the fortification of seaports, and the prevention of a slave insurrection in the south (always a favorite figment of the minds of the anti-French). In addition to the ships then building he advised the construction or purchase of three thirty-two gun frigates and six sloops-of-war of sixteen guns each. The condition of the French fleet precluded the invasion of the United States, but, if the Spanish came into such a war, there would be plenty of Indian trouble, hence the Army should also be enlarged.[27] A second memorandum was in general terms, except for a remonstrance against the prohibition of arming merchant vessels.[28]

Hamilton's memorandum to Smith was a remarkable document. It included the entire defense program which was to be urged in the coming session of the Congress (and more) and thereby showed the continuing strength of Hamilton's influence in the government from which he had resigned more than two years earlier. The paper was sixteen pages long. Three-fourths of it was devoted to reasons for avoiding war, and the best diplomatic tactics to be used in the present crisis. Then he arrived at "preparations for War," given under nine heads. Of these nine suggestions, two were financial and three concerned the army and the proposed fortificatons. On matters specifically naval he wrote urging

> the completion of the three frigates, with all possible speed & the purchase of *Twenty* ships the most fit to be armed and equipped as Cutters & Sloops of War. These will serve to guard our Trade against the Pickeroons of France in the West Indies which are chiefly dangerous. They are to be used in the first instance merely as convoys with instructions purely defensive—prohibited from cruising for prizes or from attacking, or from *capturing except when attacked.*

If negotiations failed the government should try "to purchase from Great Britain or obtain on a loan Two ships of the line and three frigates—" Such a deal would be to Britain's interest, because the Royal Navy had more ships than it could man. "This may be the most expeditious mode to augment our navy." (This notion was not submitted to the Congress.) He also advised "To grant Commissions to such of our Merchantmen as choose to take them authorizing them to arm—and defend themselves, but not to cruise and not to capture unless attacked." He thought an embargo should be enacted in such terms as to give the President authority "to grant licenses to sail, if the vessels go themselves armed, or with Convoys"; whether they were American or foreign convoys made no difference.[29]

As the day for the convening of the session drew near, anticipations varied with the politics of the anticipators. Edward Rutledge of South Carolina thought the merchants should be armed, the frigates completed, the seaports fortified ("which are the primary Depot of your Revenue"), and negotiations renewed with France.[30] George Cabot correctly predicted the indictment of the Jay Treaty by the Republicans as the cause of the French impasse.[31] Washington, in retirement at Mount Vernon, said some men expected an embargo and nothing else.[32] Noah Webster recommended keeping on good terms with the world's foremost naval power because if there were a war it would be a naval war. New England, he said, wished peace but thought war probable.[33]

Republican mass-meetings (no doubt carefully organized) in Green County, Pennsylvania, Norfolk, Virginia, and Essex County, Virginia, spoke of "the hasty call to congress by the President," adopted resolutions favoring peace, the use of an embargo before resort to war, and continued negotiations with France.[34]

President Adams recorded some clues to his naval thinking in these weeks. Writing to General William Heath on the anniversary of Lexington-Concord, he remarked, "The times appear not to me so critical and difficult, as they did on the 19. of April 1775, but they are not without their dangers." Peace was very desirable but war could be "just and necessary." If war came it would not be of our making, "but I know not that we need tremble before any Nation at a thousand leagues distance in a just cause." [35] And in a gentle epistolary debate with Elbridge

Gerry he expressed surprise on learning Gerry's high estimate of French strength. He doubted France's ability to accumulate enough ships to bring thirty thousand men to the United States. As for American strength, "we are double the numbers we were in 1775, we have four times the military skill, and we have eight times the munitions of war." Thirty thousand men would not be enough for French purposes. "As to going to war with France lightly I know of nobody who is willing for it—but she has already gone to war with us lightly. She is at war with us, but we are not at war with her." [36]

The frigate *United States* was launched at Philadelphia on 10 May—a nice coincidence for the supporters of the embryo navy. She made an "appearance in the water truly elegant" to the applause of the assembled militia and a large crowd of citizens. "The pleasantness of the day," wrote one reporter, "seemed to give a zest to the flattering prospect of an American navy." The ship-carpenters and artists dined together afterward, and spent the rest of the day "in the utmost festivity." [37] At last Secretary McHenry had something afloat to show to the convening Congressmen when—as they were sure to do—they questioned his cost accounts.

Six days later President Adams addressed both houses of the Congress. He reviewed the sending of Pinckney, and the French rejection. This, he said was an unfriendly act and a denial of the right of embassy. He went on to charge the French with trying to separate the American people from their government. At the present there were no diplomatic relations with France although the United States was trying to negotiate. The French appeared to hope the United States could not defend itself by naval means, but "A Naval power, next to the militia, is the natural defence of the United States." Its coasts could be more easily attacked and defended by naval force than in any other way. The United States had the necessary skills and materials for such defense. The Congress could allow American ships to defend themselves, should finish the frigates, and provide lesser vessels to convoy what ships remained unarmed. It should also consider the prevention of the building of privateers in the United States, which were intended to receive French commissions in order to prey on American shipping. Some of the men and masters of the privateers were American citizens, as well. The President concluded his remarks on defense by recommending additional land forces.[38]

This program was the farthest limit to which John Adams was prepared to go. It was intended, in his mind, as a psychological support for further negotiations. He thought any expenditure beyond what he asked for would be needless expense.[39]

The Republican reception of the President's message can be satisfactorily traced in the writings of Jefferson. Madison had left the Congress and withdrawn to private life, simultaneously with Jefferson's emergence from Monticello to assume the Vice Presidency. Jefferson not only assumed the Vice Presidency but also the active headship of the Republicans. In the first five months of 1797 his attitude toward Adams made a turn of 180°. In January he wrote, "I do not believe Mr. Adams wishes war with France; nor do I believe he will truckle to England as servilely as has been done." A week later he was writing of "a jealous mind like his." By May he was convinced Adams wished to go to war.[40] On the day after the President delivered the message, the Vice President spent considerable time writing to friends, telling them the executive intended war, and he was probably sincere, since he wrote it to Madison.[41] Two days later he wrote to his son-in-law, saying the Congress was peaceable until the President spoke; now it was shifting, and was in favor of aggrandizing the executive branch.[42]

There was also a hot reaction among the Republicans of the House of Representatives. The debate on the strongly anti-French ceremonial reply to the presidential message took almost all of the time of the House from 22 May to 3 June, time which was once more spent in reviewing the relations of the United States with France and with Britain, in a bitter debate which heard constant and venomous references to the Jay Treaty by the Republicans.[43]

The Senate had little trouble getting a majority to favor its reply, which promised to consider the national defenses—convoys, internal defense, arming of merchant ships, and fortifications—although the Senate did not use the words "navy" or "naval." [44]

Downstairs, in the House, the committee-draft of a reply did not mention seapower,[45] but the members were unable to restrain themselves from a few references to the subject. Harrison Gray Otis of Massachusetts first brought it up explicitly by reminding the Republicans of a day when Britain was making trouble and Federalists had come forward with proposals for "the equipment of a navy, fortifying the ports, and organizing the militia." [46] Otis's remarks were intended to take some of the anti-Frenchness out of the proceedings. John Swanwick of Pennsylvania attacked the idea of arming the merchants because it would lead them to prey on each other, as privateers.[47] William B. Giles of Virginia revived the Algerine theme for a moment by saying "England . . . made a truce for Portugal with Algiers, and this truce has cost us fifteen hundred thousand dollars, besides what it may cost hereafter." [48]

The whole quarrelsome episode portended ill for the accomplishment of the President's purposes. Although the House reply, somewhat modified so as to express hope from negotiation, was adopted by a final vote of 62–36, there had been numerous earlier votes on motions to make the tone of the reply less hostile to the French, at least five of which were beaten by margins of six votes or less.[49] It had not been a naval debate but it was now necessary to try to arrive at naval policy in this thickening atmosphere. Gallatin, who would conduct the Republican scrutiny of the matter in the House, now firmly believed Secretary Wolcott, Secretary Pickering, Smith, Fisher Ames, "and perhaps a few more" were definitely in favor of war, and proposed to get it by smearing the opposition as a disloyal, pro-French conspiracy. He had decided on his tactics: to try to work things around into a situation which would require the President to negotiate. He was optimistic— "I believe that we will not adopt a single hostile measure." [50]

The Vice President was appalled by the tone of the Federalists. He too believed there was an unpatriotic attachment of a political party to a foreign country, but the party and the country were the Federalists and Great Britain. He expected "the burning of our sea ports, havoc of our frontiers, household insurgency, with a long train of et ceteras." [51]

Even Hamilton (and other Federalists) thought the House Federalists had gone too far in forcing across their far-from-unanimous anti-French reply. *"Real firmness* is good for everything," he wrote to Wolcott on 6 June; *"Strut* is good for nothing." [52] If the eighteenth century had been truly an Age of Reason when patricians settled things among themselves by pure logic, as has often been alleged, these Federalists should have been able to defeat their opponents in such a magnanimous way as to conciliate them in the moment of victory. But that routine technique of the modern efficient ward-heeler was never mastered by Federalism. A polite, non-committal reply would have gone through the House in half an hour, and they could have gotten down to the business of defense legislation in good humor. Instead they had wasted half a month and now went to work in an atmosphere charged with hate and acrimony.

Having satisfied their emotional need to denounce the Republic of France in company with the President, the House Federalists next produced their program. It was offered by Smith as a set of nine resolutions, which were substantially those recommended to him by Hamilton. The second, third, fourth, and fifth were on the subject of naval force. The others were on harbor fortifications, the regular army, a provisional army, a public loan, taxes, and a prohibition of the export of munitions. The naval sections were as follow:

> 2. *Resolved,* That further provision be made by law, for completing and manning the frigates United States, Constitution, and Constellation.
> 3. *Resolved,* That provision be made by law, for procuring by pur-

> chase a further naval force, to consist of ____ frigates of ____ guns, and ____ sloops of war of ____ guns.
> 4. *Resolved,* That provision be made by law, for empowering the President to employ the naval force of the United States, as convoys to protect the trade thereof.
> 5. *Resolved,* That provision be made by law, for regulating the arming of the merchant vessels of the United States.[53]

The House went into Committee of the Whole on 5 June and approved the resolution on fortifications. When they arrived at the second resolution the Republicans questioned the ability of the country to meet the competition of merchant seamen's wages, argued in favor of a committee to inquire into the matter (the classic parliamentary tactic of delay), doubted whether the frigates would be ready for manning before the next session, and, finally moved to give the resolution to a select committee, a motion which lost, 34–50. The original resolution was then approved.[54]

For resolution three, to recommend the purchase of frigates and sloops of war, the numbers recommended for the blanks were three "thirty-twos" and six "sixteens." Republicans said these would be enough to get us into war but not enough to convoy a twentieth of the trade. Smith and his colleagues (who gave the impression of being on the defensive already) defended the notion of convoying, and patrolling the coastal waters. They urged purchase rather than construction as being much quicker.[55]

The following day was devoted to bills which were sent down by the Senate.[56] Apparently Smith or Hamilton talked of Hamilton's recommendations to make a kind of "lend-lease" deal with the British, for a garbled rumor appeared in the press, reporting the offer of His Britannic Majesty to lend forty frigates to the United States if the country would go to war against France as an ally of Great Britain.[57] By this time Hamilton was becoming pessimistic of the outcome in the Congress. As he wrote to King,

> I fear . . . we shall remain at the mercy of events without those efficient preparations which are demanded by so precarious a situation, and which not provoking war, would put us in condition to meet it.

He could only hope for a continued improvement of public opinion, which might bring the Congress to act properly.[58]

On 7 June Smith withdrew his resolutions to approve the purchase of ships and to authorize the President to convoy the trade, because the Senate had passed bills on those subjects. The House then proceeded to the fifth resolution, which actually raised the question of allowing merchant ships to be armed. Edward Livingston of New York put the basic objection succinctly when he said it would allow individuals "to determine the law of nations, and of course the peace of the country would be placed at their disposal." The merchants were not all Americans, he warned, and some of them might have an interest in bringing the United States into the war. He said he thought the second and third resolutions had been withdrawn because the sponsors were sure of defeat.[59] Other Republicans hammered on the point of the resolution's warlike tendencies and Gallatin expressed doubt whether the proposal was in accord with international law. Joshua Coit of Connecticut thought the resolution should be rephrased to allow the arming of ships bound only to the East Indies and the Mediterranean. Of course this would have nullified the Federalist purpose, and Smith and Robert Goodloe Harper of South Carolina had to argue for arming the ships in the West Indian trade which was the center of the plunderers of American shipping. As the day drew to a close the Federalists showed their real exasperation at being identified as warmongers.[60]

On the next day the Republicans repeated their doubts of the legality of arming the merchants, argued the probable loss of the ships and their arms, and the use of the ships as privateers against the United States. Swanwick hinted at the use of armed merchantmen against Great Britain which was a worse offender than France. (This of course reopened the old wound received by the body politic during the Jay Treaty quarrels, and feelings hardened.) Otis tried to clarify the international law of the subject: The Congress would not be granting a right but would be modifying it. International law implied the right, and the Congress could regulate its exercise so as to prevent it being a pretext for war. It was also expedient. The alternative was to depend on British convoys, which would be "mortifying." [61]

At long last the question of arming merchant ships as part of the national defense program was brought to the vote in the Committee of the Whole. First, it was moved specifically to permit the arming of ships bound to the West Indies, which lost 35–46. Second, it was moved to limit arming to those merchant ships bound for the East Indies and the Mediterranean, which carried 41–40. "The Committee then rose, and the House adjourned." On the next day, 9 June, after some minor amendments, "The question was then taken on the resolution as amended, and negatived; there being 37 for it, and 45 against it." [62] The Republicans had triumphed by amending the resolution to death. To authorize owners to arm ships sailing for the Far East or the Mediterranean was no advantage; the President's prohibition had already excepted them.

Smith had probably foreseen this outcome, since he had already drafted another resolution to be offered in place of the two he had withdrawn, and he now moved its adoption. It read

> *Resolved,* That it is the opinion of this committee, that the President of the United States ought to be authorized by law to provide a further naval force, whenever, in his opinion, the circumstances of the country shall require the same; and that ——— dollars be appropriated for that purpose.[63]

The debate on this resolution took most of the time of 9 and 10 June.

The opening round of the Republicans was an assertion of the constitutional power of the legislative branch, not the executive, to provide and maintain a navy. The Federalist defense was to compare this delegation of power with others, as, for example, the delegation of the power to borrow money. The sponsors went on to describe the resolution as a warning to privateers of the serious intent of the United States, and to threaten the Republicans with yet another special call of the Congress if the present session failed to provide the required defense. John Nicholas of Virginia doubted the necessity of this sort of resolution but hinted at compromise by suggesting the ships be limited to coastal patrol duties. The Federalists agreed and the resolution was amended by adding the words "if necessary for the defence of our seacoast during the recess of Congress." [64]

In this form the resolution was defended by the Federalists who said it was prudent, it would cost money but the expenditure would save money, and it would save more than public revenue because it would save valuable property. It should not be any more narrowly restricted because definite limits might prevent a close pursuit of an offender who was being chased out of territorial waters. On this point the Congress should recognize the President as Commander in Chief, and should do no more than tell him to defend the coasts, and not to convoy. The rest should be up to him.

On the other side there were two dissimilar attacks. One charged the President with supporting this measure in order to increase his power. Another said the President should not be given the power because it would lay an unpleasant duty on him, rightly belonging to the Congress. Others suggested delay until the sense of the Senate (then at work on the subject) could be known. So far as the costs were concerned, it could not be known for sure whether this program would cost more or less than the amount of revenue being lost by the discouragement of commerce, hence the House was being asked to incur a certain loss to avoid an uncertain one. Swanwick thought it impossible to secure adequate ships by purchase to defend American shipping against the true enemy, Great Britain.

Gallatin revealed the central objection of the Republicans, when he said the word "seacoast" was not clear, and moved another amendment: "to be stationed within the United States." Otherwise, he said, the vague wording would allow the President to use the ships to convoy as a way of protecting the seacoast of the United States. His proposal lost 39–48, and the resolution was approved by the Committee of the Whole with 51 ayes.

On the following day the argument continued in the House, with tempers further inflamed. Samuel Sewall of Massachusetts proposed to meet Republican objections with still another amendment: "to defend the seacoast of the United States, and to repel any hostility to their vessels and commerce within their jurisdiction." Whether the new phraseology or the manifest boredom with the subject was most influential is hard to say, but this amendment was approved without a division. As amended the resolution was approved 68–21, drawing the support of such Republican leaders as Gallatin, Nicholas, Livingston, and Swanwick. The twenty-one die-hards came from ten of the sixteen states, but Virginia and North Carolina accounted for eleven of them. New England and New York produced six nays, among them that of the unfathomable Roger Griswold.[65]

It is now time to turn to the deliberations of the Senate which had been working upstairs in relative obscurity, its debates open to visitors but not published regularly in the press, and therefore lost to posterity. On 29 May the Senate voted to establish four committees on defense matters, including one on the navy and the arming of merchantmen. There was a brief battle on a motion to eliminate the arming of merchantmen from the cognizance of the Naval Committee, a motion which lost 11–17. The Naval Committee was composed of men not one of whom had voted to exclude the arming of merchantment from consideration.[66] It is safe to say there was not a "minority member" on the Committee.

Not being clogged by the cumbersome Committee of the Whole system then used so much in the House of Representatives, the Senate got its business done with relative dispatch. A naval bill was brought in a week later. Its first section provided for the acquisition of up to nine twenty-gun ships; the Republicans lost a motion to strike out this section, 11–18. The majority then changed the bill so as to authorize the President to use the three frigates and any other public ships to protect the ships and cargoes of American citizens, and to guard the harbors and seacoasts in any way not contrary to the law of nations or treaties of the United States. There was a motion to limit this protection to "within the harbors and on the seacoasts" as making it more precise; the motion lost, 13–15. For reasons not clear the bill was then recommitted for four days, after which another Republican assault was made on the nine-ships proviso; again they were beaten back, this time by a vote of 12–15. Two days later "An act providing for the protection of the trade of the United States" passed, 16–13. The opposing roll calls, throughout, had varied only by the number in attendance. There were no conversions, or switches, nor can any compromises be identified. It was a straightforward battle between thirteen who wished no navy, and sixteen who did, and the sixteen won every test.[67]

The exact phrasing of the Bill need not concern us because it was to be much recast in the House but it contained provisions for enlarging the naval force by purchase, up to as many as nine ships, arming the merchants, and using public ships to convoy. Thomas Jefferson, who presided over this process and early predicted the result (but was not enabled to cast a tie-breaking or tie-creating vote) privately hoped the House would not concur. However the outcome was uncertain because the House had been dividing so narrowly.[68]

Secretary Pickering had logged over three hundred seizures of American vessels by French privateers in the past eleven months.[69] In a letter to Minister King in London he expressed hope the House might still do well. The Senate had followed the President's suggestions—not so the House, except "partially." But the increasing number of French "aggressions," while the session continued might stimulate the adoption of the "preparatory measures." [70] Indeed, the date of adjournment might well be a critical point. It was to the interest of Federalists to postpone it as long as possible in order to accumulate evidence of Gallic perfidy, if for no other reason. Gallatin wrote to his Hannah about his suspicion of Federalist motives: Smith wished the session to continue as long as possible so some Republicans would go home and leave the Federalists with a working majority.[71] The first setting of an adjournment date probably was a good test of the political balance. On 22 June the date was set, in the House, for adjournment on the twenty-eighth, by a vote of 51–47,[72] a victory, although a narrow one, for the Republicans.

Nothing more was done with Smith's resolutions because the principal Senate Naval Bill had come down stairs on the sixteenth. After an unsuccessful motion by Joseph B. Varnum of Massachusetts to postpone action "till the first Monday in November" the Committee of the Whole went to work on it on the twenty-second.[73]

The Federalists soon found themselves battling to save some discretionary power for the President, as the Republicans fired off amendments which would have tied him up with restrictions. When Federalists said such restrictions would seem to show the world a lack of confidence in him, Giles was frank to admit he had "not much confidence in the President." [74] The Republicans particularly opposed empowering the President to convoy, as both illegal and warlike. In this and the question of arming the merchant fleet there was a point of international law at issue. The search of neutrals by a belligerent was allowed if done in a legal manner by staying out of gunshot and sending searchers in a boat. If the master of the ship being searched resisted the legal method of search he was acting illegally, and the searcher would not be blamed for using force. Hence to convoy could provoke violence and war, for convoys had no other purpose than to keep strangers away. The Federalists answered by pointing to the right of convoy embodied in American treaties with Sweden and the Netherlands, which, they said, made it the national policy. Since the convoys proposed in 1797 were to protect against French privateers, the citation of Dutch and Swedish arrangements made no impression.[75] In a state of obvious exasperation and frustration, Otis declared the Republican object seemed to be "to prevent anything effectual from being done." [76] This was probably an accurate observation.

Before the Committee of the Whole was ready to report to the House it had knocked out the provision for purchasing up to nine ships of twenty guns and authorized the use of the revenue cutters in their place. This was good tactical thinking because the cutters were built for chasing, not carrying, and were well adapted to hunting down privateers. The decision showed the pervasive but not entirely successful influence of Hamilton, who had written to Smith on the tenth, and suggested the desirability of increasing the number of revenue cutters and using them as anti-privateers.[77] He got the use but not the increase. The cutters' crews were enlarged, and their operations restricted to American territorial waters. The employment of any public ships to convoy was prohibited.

If it seems the Federalists achieved little in this wrangle it will be well to see what they managed to avoid. They defeated a motion which would limit the President to protecting the coast and commerce within the jurisdiction of the United States. They defeated a motion to fix naval pay in detail, and left it to the President to meet the pay-roll within an authorized round sum. They defeated a motion to limit the naval program to one year. This last matter was an ominously close shave; the vote was 46–46 in Committee, made 46–47 by the casting vote of Chairman George Dent of Maryland.[78]

Now these decisions had to seek ratification in the House of Representatives. The going here was equally rough, for the Republicans had tasted blood. The work of the Committee of the Whole was approved by the House with one significant exception. The opposition was determined to put a time limit on the naval program. Smith saw it coming and stood up to it manfully. He successively moved a time limit of five years, four years, three years, and two years, and each motion was "lost by a considerable majority." Finally, on a motion by Coit the time limit was set at one year plus the duration of the next session. Over half of the House membership voted aye.[79] The Bill was ordered to third reading.

For a week Josiah Parker of Virginia had been holding a financial report from Secretary McHenry. It was the same old song. The War Department needed $197,636 more, to get the frigates ready for sea. Pay and subsistence for the crews would be $220,938 annually.[80] Why, asked the outraged Nicholas, did not the $170,000 of last session suffice? Parker said the previous estimate had not included the guns. Gallatin gave up. He would vote no. There could be no excuse for arming these ships at this expense except in time of actual war. Swanwick referred to waste and extravagance which had occurred because there was no agency to supervise the work, but ships would be cheaper in the future, this was a start, someday the country would be "a great maritime Power." John Williams of New York gave all the arguments against the construction program, but said he would vote for it since the times were so parlous. Giles said he wished Williams would make a speech in favor of the program and vote against it. Giles went on to allege the founding of the navy by an alarm, and the steady increase of it by successive alarms. He next foresaw press-gangs roaming the water fronts. It had been the "constant aim of some gentlemen in that House to increase the expenses of our government."

Harper accused Gallatin of trying to measure the national "rights, dignity, and honor . . . by counting-house calculations." John Allen of Connecticut said the men who opposed every good idea since 1789 now opposed the idea of a navy. Nicholas said he had decided to vote for it because only by having a navy could the error be known—"by one year's experience of the plaything" they would learn "that money was of greater value than the frigates"; then "all parties would concur in relinquishing it."

Sewall now precipitated a greater flurry of emotion. The opposition, he said, had proved commerce to be useless. The American people need not pay to protect it, for commerce could protect itself if let alone. Therefore, "Let those States which live by commerce be separated from the Confederacy." Varnum called out, "Point of order!" Sewall concluded by saying the commercial states were rich enough to get along by themselves. Nathaniel Macon of North Carolina insisted Sewall put secession resolutions on the table,—"This is such language as [I] have never heard before in [this] House!"—but the Speaker ruled Sewall wholly out of order and also denied Gallatin recognition to reply to Sewall. Gallatin then mildly said, "these frigates would not afford that protection which was expected of them," and sat down.

They proceeded to vote on the Bill as amended. It passed 78–25. Its title was changed from the one given by the Senate, to "An act providing a naval armament." [81] On the day before passage, the Senate had confirmed the appointments of a three-man Commission appointed by President John Adams, to try to reopen relations with the French,[82] that same trio which was later to report the explosive "X. Y. Z. Affair."

After the Senate had re-read its much-changed Bill it sent word down to the House of its unwillingness to accept a prohibition of convoying or to concur in eliminating the purchase of the nine ships.[83] Smith moved to recede from the objectionable amendments; on the question of convoying he lost 46–48—on the other by a wider margin. There was nothing to do now but for each chamber to appoint a conference committee.[84] The conference committees were unable to agree, so a compromise was worked out on the floors of the chambers. The House gave up its prohibition of convoying, and the Senate accepted all of the other House changes. Parker's argument on the convoying convinced the House. He said "no vessels could be got ready as convoys for several months, when it might probably be too late to use them." Since the Congress was scheduled to meet again in November, and July was almost upon them, this was enough to switch a handful of votes and the convoy-prohibition was given up, 51–47.[85]

"An Act providing a Naval Armament," approved 1 July 1797, had fourteen sections. Section one authorized the President to man and employ the three frigates. Sections two to eleven, inclusive, gave the details of personnel, pay, and rations. Section twelve authorized the strengthening of the crews of the revenue cutters, and their use "to defend the seacoast, and repel any hostility to their vessels and commerce within their jurisdiction, having due regard to the duty of the said cutters in the protection of the revenue." Section thirteen reenacted some related legislation on the use of cutters. Section fourteen set the time limit as determined in the House.[86] The House of Representatives had its way in every matter except the prohibition of the use of the frigates to convoy.[87]

The appropriation went through without a hitch: two hundred thousand dollars to complete and equip the frigates, a hundred thousand for the pay and subsistence of their officers and men, and ten thousand for the extra expenses of the cutters. There was no argument.[88] This Congress also passed laws regulating the import and export of arms, prohibiting the re-registration of American ships taken by privateers, providing artillery, regulating the militia, and authorizing the construction of harbor fortifications.[89] There were abortive attempts to revive the old projects of a navy yard, a live oak preserve, and the construction of galleys.[90]

The first session of the Fifth Congress, called specially by the newly inaugurated President to consider defense problems, had produced some improvement in land defenses. It had gone ahead with the three frigates, making housekeeping rules and appropriating the money needed to send them to sea, fully manned and equipped, to be used at the discretion of the President. It had authorized the use of the Treasury Department's revenue cutters for naval purposes. It had provided some tardily effective means of financing these efforts.

This was not much for a session which lasted practically two months. On balance it must be described as a Federalist fiasco, when it is considered they intended to add as many as nine sloops-of-war to the little fleet.

The two parties established two opposing lines of thought in the Congress. The Republicans claimed the Federalist program was a war-program, and inferior to the Republican policy of exhausting all possibilities of diplomacy before talking so belligerently. The Federalist case could be summarized as favoring the appearance of toughness; otherwise the French would stall any negotiations in order to gather the profits of their privateers.

Manning J. Dauer has said the President's recommendations "were in advance of moderate opinion."[91] The conclusion is supported by a reading of the newspapers for these months. There was much news of French commerce-raiders but very little on the course of the naval legislation through the Congress, and the general tone of the press was peaceable. Even John Fenno's arch-Federalist *Gazette of the United States,* while supporting the Federalist naval program, admitted the French navy was too weak to mount an invasion of the United States. And if it could send an expedition westbound across the Atlantic the British would have to assume it was intended for their West Indies and try to intercept it.[92]

The Federalists in the House were also guilty of absurdly bad management. Even Hamilton referred to their acts of "resentment rather than defense."[93] Professor Dauer's analysis of the composition of this

House is very helpful here. The House had fifty-eight nominal Federalists, but one was the Speaker, Jonathan Dayton (an "irregular"), one was continuously absent, and fourteen others were irregular in their voting. Thus the hard core of House Federalism totaled only forty-two. Of forty-eight Republicans, nine were waverers, and one was regularly absent. Thus instead of the paper figure of 56–48, on the floor the actual working figures were a good deal closer: 42–38. Eliminating Mr. Speaker, and the two absentees, there were but eighty regulars. Twenty-three irregulars, who thought of Dayton as their leader, held the balance of power.[94] To win support from this group the Federalists tried to force a hotly anti-French manifesto through the House as the chamber's reply to the President's message, probably in the belief it would commit the House in advance. They supported it with attacks on the honor and the patriotism of the minority. The only ponderable result was to pitch the whole session on an emotional key and to prove that rage and hatred made poor launching ways for a navy.

The irregulars were probably more affected by a changing tide in European affairs than they were by arch-Federalist vituperation. Austria withdrew from the war against France. The Bank of England teetered on the edge of bankruptcy. The Royal Navy was having trouble enforcing discipline. All in all, a reasonable man could think the world would soon be at peace.[95]

The hyper-Federalists were fuming and frustrated. Senator Theodore Sedgwick of Massachusetts blamed the rout on Republican cowardice, "*a dread of the power & vengeance of the terrible Republic.*"[96] Senator Uriah Tracy of Connecticut proposed secession by New England and the middle states, leaving the south to affiliate with France.[97] Ex-Senator Cabot grumbled to his friend King, "how much we are disgraced by the Congressional discussions of the last session."[98]

Disgust and alarm were mixed in Republican hearts. Jefferson evaluated the session over which he was then presiding: it was inconvenient, it cost sixty thousand dollars for the expenses of the meeting, war was the object but no war ensued—a waste all around. He excoriated the influence of the irregulars:

> A few individuals of no fixed system at all, governed by the panic or the prowess of the moment, flap, as the breeze blows, against the Republican or the aristocratic bodies, and give to the one or the other a preponderance entirely accidental.[99]

Ex-Senator John Taylor of Caroline (who had resigned his seat in disgust at what he alleged was the corruption of Federalism) sat down and wrote a letter to his then Senator, Henry Tazewell, saying, if the New Englanders embroiled the country in a war with France it might be better to "break the Union for the sake of destroying our monarchy." Perhaps it could then be renovated on better principles.[100]

Actually the country was in better hands than the Republicans knew. Over on Philadelphia's Market Street, near Sixth, lived a sturdily honest and able patriot—if not a particularly tactful one—John Adams, second President of the United States. He understood the international situation as well as any American and could probably pronounce the new name Bonaparte better than most. Whatever the alarmed Republican leaders might think, he was not desirous of matching the United States alone against the might of France. Writing to an old friend as the session neared its close he said if Europe had peace while the United States was still on bad terms with France "this country has before it one of the most alarming prospects it ever beheld." [101] John Adams was still hoping and working to keep the peace. Soon his Commissioners, John Marshall and Elbridge Gerry, would join Charles Cotesworth Pinckney for another try at making friends in Paris.

NOTES FROM PAGES 102 TO 120

1. Samuel Flagg Bemis, *A Diplomatic History of the United States,* rev. ed. (New York, 1942), 111–114. Hereafter cited: Bemis, *Diplomatic History.*
2. Edmund Randolph to King, 6 July 1795, Rufus King, *The Life and Correspondence of Rufus King,* ed. C. R. King, 6v. (New York, 1894–1900), II, 15. Hereafter cited: King, *Life and Correspondence.*
3. Adet to Committee of public safety, 2 September 1795, in Gilbert Chinard, ed., *George Washington as the French Knew Him* (Princeton, 1940), 106–109.
4. See p. 23. The index of *American State Papers,* ed. Walter Lowrie and Matthew St. Clair Clarke, 38v. (Washington, 1832–1861), Class I, *Foreign Relations,* I, well summarized the letter: "menaces; reproaches; complaints; allegations against the United States of duplicity, weakness, partiality, insensibility to the claims of justice and honor; with disregarding their neutral obligations; affording an asylum to British ships of war; declining liberal commercial overtures; violating treaty stipulations, and forming in opposition to them a connection with Great Britain; declares that the vessels of the United States shall be exposed to plunder from French vessels of war and privateers; that his ministerial functions are suspended, though this suspension is not to be viewed as an immediate rupture."

   American State Papers is hereafter cited *ASP:* with the name of the class added.
5. H. J. Ford, "Timothy Pickering," in Samuel Flagg Bemis, ed., *The American Secretaries of State and Their Diplomacy,* 10v. (New York, 1927–1929), II, 201–204. Hereafter cited: Ford, in Bemis, *Secretaries.*
6. Arthur B. Darling, *Our Rising Empire, 1763–1803* (New Haven, 1940), 193–194. Hereafter cited: Darling, *Rising Empire.*
7. Edward Channing, *A History of the United States,* 6v. (New York, 1932–1936), IV, 184. Hereafter cited: Channing, *United States.* On British strategical considerations see E. B. Potter, *et al., The United States and World Sea Power* (Englewood Cliffs, N.J., 1955), 158; Herbert W. Richmond, *Statesmen and Sea Power* (Oxford, 1946), 199.
8. Robert Greenhalgh Albion and Jennie Barnes Pope, *Sea Lanes in Wartime: the American Experience, 1775–1942* (New York, 1942), 78–80. Hereafter cited: Albion and Pope, *Sea lanes.*

9. Ford, in Bemis, *Secretaries,* 212–213.
10. J. S. Bassett, *The Federalist System, 1789–1801* (New York, 1906), 221.
11. Darling, *Rising Empire,* 229.
12. Bemis, *Diplomatic History,* 112.
13. Channing, *United States,* IV, 177–179.
14. Jefferson to T. M. Randolph, 11 March 1797, Jefferson papers, Library of Congress (hereafter abbreviated: LC).
15. Cabot to King, 19 March 1797, King, *Life and Correspondence,* II, 160–161.
16. King to Hamilton, 8 March 1797, *ibid.,* II, 154; John Quincy Adams to Hall, 9 Feb. 1797, John Quincy Adams, *Writings,* ed. W. C. Ford, 7v. (New York, 1913–1917), II, 114; Wadsworth to Wolcott, Jr., 26 March 1797, George Gibbs, *Memoirs of the Administrations of Washington and John Adams,* 2v. (New York, 1846), I, 479, hereafter cited: Gibbs, *Memoirs.* John Quincy Adams, at the Hague, had been warning of world revolution for some time. See, for example, his letter to his father, 13 August 1796, John Quincy Adams, *Writings,* II, 25.
17. Hamilton to Wolcott, Jr., 30 March 1797, Gibbs, *Memoirs,* I, 485.
18. John Quincy Adams to John Adams, 21 July 1796, John Quincy Adams, *Writings,* II, 4, to Pickering, 1 Feb. 1797, *ibid.,* II, 99.
19. Washington to Pickering, 12 June 1797, to King, 25 June 1797, to D. Humphreys, 26 June 1797, George Washington, *Writings,* ed. John C. Fitzpatrick, 39v. (Washington, 1931–1944), XXXV, 464, 475, 481.
20. George Victor Collot, "General Collot's plan for a reconnaissance of the Ohio and Mississippi valleys, 1796," tr. with an introduction by Durand Echeverria, *William and Mary Quarterly,* third series, IX (Oct. 1952), 512–520: Wolcott, Jr., memoranda, 19, 21 May 1796, Gibbs, *Memoirs,* II, 350–352.
21. R. R. Palmer, "A revolutionary Republican: M. A. B. Mangourit," *William and Mary Quarterly,* third series, IX (Oct. 1952), 483–496.
22. James D. Richardson, *A Compilation of the Messages and Papers of the Presidents, 1789–1897,* 11v. (Washington, 1900–1902), I, 232–233.
23. Wolcott, Jr., to Collectors, *Federal Gazette and Baltimore Daily Advertiser,* 11 May 1797; Hamilton disapproved of the order—Hamilton to Wolcott, Jr., 13 April 1797, Gibbs, *Memoirs,* I, 491.
24. King to Pickering, 12 March 1797, Pickering to King, 9 May 1797, King, *Life and Correspondence,* II, 153, 178.
25. Pickering to King, 12 April 1797, King, *Life and Correspondence,* II, 164.

Insurance rates, expressed in percentages of the combined value of ships and cargoes:

Year	*To Britain*	*To Mediterranean*
1795	3–10	25
1796	6–8	25
1797	7–10	25

Year	*To West Indies*	*To Asia*
1795	2	3
1796	6–15	5–6
1797	15–25	10

—Albion and Pope, *Sea lanes,* 70.

26. See Sedgwick to King, 12 March 1797, King, *Life and Correspondence,* II, 157–158; Hamilton to King, 8 April 1797, *ibid.,* II, 167–168; Cabot to King, 10 April 1797, *ibid.,* II, 169; Wolcott, Jr., to Wolcott, Sr., 29 March 1797, Gibbs, *Memoirs,* I, 482; Cabot to J. Smith, 17 April 1797, *ibid.,* I, 494–495.
27. McHenry to John Adams, 8 April 1797, McHenry papers, LC.
28. McHenry to John Adams, 29 April 1797, *ibid.*
29. Hamilton to W. Smith, 10 April 1797, William Loughton Smith papers, LC.
30. E. Rutledge to Jefferson, 4 May 1797, Jefferson papers, LC.
31. Cabot to King, 9 May 1797, King, *Life and Correspondence,* II, 180–181.
32. Washington to Wolcott, Jr., 15 May 1797, Washington, *Writings,* XXXV, 446.
33. Webster to King, 30 May 1797, King, *Life and Correspondence,* II, 181–182.
34. *Federal Gazette and Baltimore Daily Advertiser,* 15, 18 May, 2 June 1797. The Norfolk meeting was presided over by the Reverend James Madison, Episcopal Bishop of Virginia.
35. John Adams to Heath, 19 April 1797, Adams papers, reel 117, LC. Quoted by permission of the Adams Manuscript Trust, Boston, Mass.
36. John Adams to Gerry, 3 May 1797, *ibid.* Also quoted by permission.
37. *Federal Gazette and Baltimore Daily Advertiser,* 13 May 1797.

38. 5 Cong., 1 Sess., 16 May 1797, *Annals of the Congress,* ed. J. Gales and W. W. Seaton, 42v. (Washington, 1834–1856), 54–59. Hereafter cited: *Annals.* All references hereafter are to 5 Cong., 1 Sess. Dates will be given where they may facilitate search.
39. Manning J. Dauer, *The Adams Federalists* (Baltimore, 1953), 129.
40. The about-face can be traced in the following series: Jefferson to Madison, 22, 30 Jan. 1797, to Strother, 8 June 1797, to Madison, 15 June 1797, Thomas Jefferson, *Writings,* ed. H. A. Washington, 9v. (Washington, 1853–1854), IV, 162, 167, 181, 183.
41. 17 May 1797, Jefferson papers, LC.
42. Jefferson to T. M. Randolph, 19 May 1797, *ibid.* Curiously enough, Captain Richard O'Brien, the seafaring slave of Algiers, had lately arrived in Philadelphia from his Algerine captivity and a diplomatic errand for the United States. His response to President Adams's message was the composition of a memorandum to Jefferson on what naval force would be adequate for the United States—a total of thirty-two men-of-war. He envisaged six frigates on the original plan, six "twenty-fours," twelve "eighteens," six schooners, and two sloops. For coastal work he also recommended four galleys and fifty to eighty gun boats. He added the personnel requirements, a tactical doctrine, and discussed strategic advantages and problems of the Mediterranean, the West Indies, Florida, the Great Lakes, the St. Lawrence, and the "Bay of fundi." O'Brien to Jefferson, 18 May 1797, Jefferson papers, LC.

    O'Brien was certainly out of touch with the currents of politics. Six years earlier or six years later Jefferson would have been keenly interested. At the moment O'Brien "had the wrong number."
43. The debate occupies 171 columns of the *Annals.*
44. Senate, 23 May 1797, *ibid.,* 13.
45. 22 May, *ibid.,* 67–69.
46. 23 May, *ibid.,* 106.
47. 24 May, *ibid.,* 113–114.
48. 25 May, *ibid.,* 139.
49. 29, 31 May, 1, 2 June, *ibid.,* 193–230.
50. Gallatin to Nicholson, 26 May 1797, Henry Adams, *The Life of Albert Gallatin* (Philadelphia, 1879), 184. Hereafter cited: Adams, *Gallatin.*
51. Jefferson to Thomas Pinckney, 29 May 1797, Thomas Jefferson, *Writings,* ed. A. A. Lipscomb, 19v. (Washington, 1903–1904), IX, 389.
52. Hamilton to Wolcott, Jr., 6 June 1797, Gibbs, *Memoirs,* I, 544; James Schouler, *History of the United States of America under the Constitution,* 5v. (New York, 1880–1891), I, 353.
53. 5 June, *Annals,* 239.
54. *Ibid.,* 241–243.
55. *Ibid.,* 243–246.
56. *Ibid.,* 247–252.
57. *Federal Gazette and Baltimore Daily Advertiser,* 6 June 1797; Norfolk *Herald and Public Advertiser,* 12 June 1797.
58. Hamilton to King, 8 June 1797, King, *Life and Correspondence,* II, 183. His news of the session was probably not later than 6 June.
59. 7 June, *Annals,* 253–255.
60. *Ibid.,* 255–266.
61. 8 June, *ibid.,* 268–270.
62. 9 June, *ibid.,* 280–282.
63. *Ibid.,* 283.
64. *Ibid.,* 285–286.
65. 9–10 June, *ibid.,* 285–297.
66. 29 May, *ibid.,* 15–16.
67. 6, 7, 9, 12, 13, 15 June, *ibid.,* 18–20, 22.
68. Jefferson to Strother, 8 June 1797, Jefferson papers, LC.
69. Thomas A. Bailey, *A Diplomatic History of the American People,* 3d ed. (New York, 1946), 82.
70. Pickering to King, 20 June 1797, King, *Life and Correspondence,* II, 190.
71. Gallatin to Hannah Gallatin, 19 June 1797, Adams, *Gallatin,* 184.
72. 22 June, *Annals,* 358.
73. 16, 22 June, *ibid.,* 324–325, 359.
74. *Ibid.,* 364. The Committee of the Whole debate, *ibid.,* 359–377.
75. See Harper's speech for the presentation of the Federalist side, *ibid.,* 1445–1453 (5 Cong., 2 Sess.).
76. *Ibid.,* 365.
77. Hamilton to Smith, 10 June 1797, W. L. Smith papers, LC.
78. 23 June, *Annals,* 370.
79. *Ibid.,* 370–376.
80. McHenry to Parker, 16 June 1797, *ASP: Naval Affairs,* I, 28–30. The paper was given to the House on the twenty-fourth, although Parker received it on the seventeenth.
81. *Annals,* 378–386.

82. Gallatin to Hannah Gallatin, 21, 23 June 1797, Adams, *Gallatin*, 185.
83. 26 June, *Annals*, 28, 390.
84. 27 June, *ibid.*, 391–393.
85. 27–29 June, *ibid.*, 29–31, 407–410.
86. *Ibid.*, 3689–3692. Section eight of the Act re-established "the rules for the regulation of the Navy" as of 1775, *ibid.*, 3691. These had been principally the work of John Adams, who drew on the British regulations. Gardner Weld Allen, *Our Naval War with France* (Boston, 1909), 59–60.
87. The engrossed bills, with long-hand changes, are in, Engrossed bills of the Senate, 4 March 1795 – 4 March 1805, Legislative records, National archives.
88. 3 July, *Annals*, 434, 440. They refused to raise taxes immediately. A loan of eight hundred thousand dollars was authorized. A salt duty was put on, effective 1 October. A stamp tax was passed, effective 1 January 1798. *Ibid.*, 3693–3702.
89. *Ibid.*, 3685–3704.
90. 17, 19 June, 8 July, *ibid.*, 333, 339–340, 464–465.
91. Dauer, *The Adams Federalists*, 129.
92. Philadelphia *Gazette of the United States*, quoted in *Federal Gazette and Baltimore Daily Advertiser*, 17 June 1797.
93. Hamilton to Smith, 10 June 1797, W. L. Smith papers, LC.
94. Dauer, *The Adams Federalists*, 133, 303. The Speaker did not preside over the Committee of the Whole but was then free to lead and deal.
95. Nathan Schachner, *The Founding Fathers* (New York, 1954), 425; Irving Brant, *James Madison, Father of the Constitution* (Indianapolis, 1950), 452–453; the noticeable friendliness of the House Republicans toward any wavering Federalist was, of course, effective in building Republican strength. Hindman to King, 21 Aug. 1797, King, *Life and Correspondence*, II, 212–213.
96. Sedgwick to King, 24 June 1797, King, *Life and Correspondence*, II, 192.
97. Given in Dauer, *The Adams Federalists*, 207. He and Pickering headed an abortive secessionist movement in 1804.
98. Cabot to King, 17 August 1797, King, *Life and Correspondence*, II, 212.
99. Jefferson to Burr, 17 June 1797, Jefferson papers, LC.
100. H. H. Simms, *Life of John Taylor* (Richmond, 1932), 69.
101. John Adams to Dalton, 1 July 1797, Adams papers, reel 117, LC. Quoted by permission of the Adams Manuscript Trust, Boston, Mass.

IX

"X. Y. Z." and the Navy

With the adjournment of the Congress and the departure of John Marshall and Elbridge Gerry to join Charles Cotesworth Pinckney as Commissioners to France, an atmosphere of suspense and of wary waiting, settled on the country. President John Adams did not expect a formal war with France; Charles Maurice Talleyrand-Perigord, the foxy executive of French foreign policy, could hardly wish war since French advantage would be best served by the appearance of anger and the continued despoiling of undefended American shipping.[1] For that matter, it was not only American shipping which loaded the money-chests of French sea-rovers. The American Consul at Marseilles later reported the condemnation there of over a hundred prizes taken from "the Danes, Sweeds, Russians, Genoese, &c. &c." [2]

The only American naval activity was the seemingly interminable work on the three frigates. *United States* had been launched at Philadelphia in May, *Constellation* was put into the water at Baltimore and at long last *Constitution* was to be launched at Boston, but the first trial was a failure when she stuck fast before wetting her bottom. The Republican poet-editor and ex-merchant skipper, Philip Freneau, was delighted at the fiasco, and exhorted her

> Madam!—Stay where you are . . .
> O frigate Constitution! Stay on shore . . .
> Was man design'd
> To be confined
> In those fire-spitting hells a navy nam'd? [3]

But after a rest in her ways she ignored him and soon floated free and undamaged. The three frigates were finally afloat and needed now to be rigged, armed, and manned.

The second session of the Fifth Congress assembled at Philadelphia late in November and on the twenty-third settled back to hear the President's message.

The President devoted an important part of the message to naval concerns. There was no peace in Europe and no security for American citizens and property at sea, but it was gratifying to know the Americans were determined to support their sovereignty against all attacks. Peace could be preserved by the "exertion of . . . natural resources for defence." The earlier precautions had been proved wise, since depredations were increasing. Regardless of the outcome of the negotiations with France (the Commissioners were then in Paris) there was no reason to think an undefended commerce "will not be plundered." Commerce was essential to the United States and the nation was pledged to protect it. He recommmended "every exertion to protect our commerce, and to place our country in a suitable posture of defence . . ." National defense should be provided for as much as possible by taxes in order to place but little reliance on loans.[4]

In its reply the Senate agreed promptly and whole-heartedly.[5] Adams acknowledged the Senate's statement in a way which showed he was unreservedly for building up the naval power: "A mercantile marine and a military marine must grow up together; one cannot long exist without the other." [6] Down in the House of Representatives a lesson had been learned. Of the five members appointed to draft their reply two were warm Republicans. The House answer told the President he could rely on the "energy and unanimity" of the nation "to exert, upon all proper occasions, their ample resources in providing for the national defence." They agreed with him on the importance of commerce and its right to protection. They hoped the United States could remain neutral, but they felt the danger of war and promised to do what they could in cooperation with the President to avoid it. This time—not having written an exclamatory party-manifesto as in the previous session—they got the whole thing adopted with but one amendment. With only one day's discussion it passed through both the Committee of the Whole and the House.[7] Adams told them he was glad to have harmony on the subject of the importance of commerce.[8]

Albert Gallatin of Pennsylvania, floor leader of the House Republicans, found the contrast with the previous session's rages amusing. He wrote to his wife, Hannah,

> On the subject of the address, it seems to have been agreed on all hands that something general and inoffensive was the best answer that could be given to the wise speech of our President. He was highly delighted to find that we were so polite, and in return treated us with cake and wine when we carried him the answer . . .[9]

The House went into Committee of the Whole to consider the President's recommendations. Robert Goodloe Harper of South

Carolina moved six resolutions, each on a part of the message, each providing for a committee "to report by bill or otherwise." This was approved [10] except in the case of the committee on the protection of commerce which was required to report in general.[11] Chairman Samuel Sewall of Massachusetts, highly respected by Gallatin as "the first man of that party," protested. He wished to be free to report by bill if he and his committee wished. Gallatin insisted the report be general because it was to deal with undetermined principles, while the other committees were furthering settled policies. The real issue seemed to be the attitude of the merchants on the President's prohibition of arming merchantmen; the Federalists feared a general report would have to show the mercantile opposition to the President's policy. It would be better politics, no doubt, merely to bring in a bill to authorize the arming of the merchant fleet. Sewall moved to allow his committee (hereafter, the Naval Committee) to report by bill. The vote was 45–45, and the Speaker voted aye, so it carried. New England favored Sewall's request six to one, the middle states were evenly divided, and the South and West opposed it three to one.[12] However, Sewall preferred greater unanimity and when he did report, in January, he reported by a series of resolutions.

There was no sense of urgency in the early weeks of the session. As the days ticked by there was only the feeling of forever waiting. Gallatin wrote to Hannah, "My greatest leisure time is while Congress sits, for we have nothing of any real importance before us . . ." [13] He and his Republican colleagues kept in forensic trim by hard attacks on any Federalist measures brought forward but these were practice scrimmages so as to be ready "to assume that high tone" needed if the news from France were bad.[14] Outside of Congress Hall the Navy and its Republican belittlers were not forgotten. A Federalist dinner in Boston celebrated George Washington's birthday with a torrent of toasts, including, "The Rising Navy of America May it like *Hercules* strangle serpents who would stifle it in its cradle." [15]

William Loughton Smith of South Carolina, the self-appointed naval leader of the Fourth Congress, had gone to Lisbon as American Minister. A new leader, Robert Goodloe Harper, now offered himself. He was a vain and arrogant man, otherwise competent but not very popular with his Federalist colleagues and doubly detested by the Republicans because he was a renegade from their phalanx. He headed the new Ways and Means Committee. Although the Naval Committee was at work, he anticipated them by moving a resolution for an interim appropriation of "blank" dollars to finish the frigates, on 10 January. The figure he wished was twenty thousand dollars. All he achieved was to afford the Republicans an occasion for charges of waste and mismanagement, and the Committee of the Whole rose without acting on the motion,[16] certainly an inauspicious beginning.

This business of needing a deficiency-appropriation on the eve of a new regular naval appropriation evidently worked like yeast in Republican minds. On the fifteenth they proposed the appointment of a committee to investigate past naval expenditures. After ineffectual opposition from Harper and Sewall the motion carried, with an additional proviso for inquiring into the slowness of construction as well. An investigating committee, headed by Edward Livingston of New York, was named for the work.[17]

The Naval Committee brought in its resolutions on the sixteenth, based on an estimate secured earlier from Secretary of War James McHenry who needed $396,212 to get the frigates to sea. *Constellation* was nearest to being ready: "she may," said McHenry, "be sent to sea at a very short notice." [18] Sewall's bill asked for money for the frigates, their crews, and ammunition, for coast-defense vessels, and for a foundry to cast guns. The figure requested was McHenry's.[19] The matter of the foundry originated in the Senate, where Benjamin Goodhue of Massachusetts headed a Naval Committee which was drafting a bill to authorize the government to cast its own naval guns.

Here the Navy languished. The House had now two things to wait for—news from France and news from Livingston's investigating committee.

Soon other action was overdue. At the end of December the House Naval Committee had brought in a bill to regulate the arming of private ships—the euphemistic way of saying, a bill to authorize the arming of merchant ships. John Nicholas of Virginia moved to make it the order of the day for the first Monday of February and his motion passed (not without ten columns of debate in the *Annals*) by a vote of 40–37.[20] The first Monday of February came and passed, and no notice was taken of the armed-private-ships bill. Gallatin was bored and said he and Nicholas only stayed in this unpleasant Congress because they were needed by the Republican Party—"our side of the House is so extremely weak in speakers and in men of business." [21] Secretary of the Treasury Oliver Wolcott, Jr., found the suspense not so much boring as very depressing.

> I am really pained for the worthy and honourable men who now have any thing to do with public business, especially in Congress. Their situation is humiliating; they can do but little good, and doing nothing, in the present state of our country, is attended with almost as bad effects as would result from bad measures. My hopes respecting the present government are almost extinguished.

He went on to make a colossally mistaken prediction. The French Directory was "too wise and politic to do anything which would rouse and unite the country." [22]

Things had moved slowly. By the first week of March 1798 the Congress had been in session three months. In that time the House had set up a Naval Committee, had approved resolutions to draw bills for the several appropriations—excepting the Navy, had initiated an investigation of the naval construction program, had received a resolution to buy a foundry and a bill to permit the arming of merchant ships. None of these resolutions or bills approached passage. The Senate had a Naval Committee too, which was collecting data on French maritime pillaging and fathering a bill to buy a foundry. The Congress was almost passive in defense matters. The Republicans were weak in the Senate but strong in the House where they had been able to delay at every point.

The long silence from France was a matter for serious reflection by President Adams. At length, sometime between 24 January and 15 February he asked his cabinet secretaries a question, what should be done if the Commissioners were unsuccessful in France? Secretary McHenry fired off the question to his patron and mentor, Alexander Hamilton. Hamilton's reply was passed on to the President as McHenry's. It was a remarkable state paper, foreshadowing most of what was to happen in the next two years.

If it became manifestly impossible to come to terms with the French the following conditions should be noted: (1) The public was averse to war, especially war with France. (2) A formal break would stimulate France to the worst possible evils. (3) A "mitigated hostility" would leave the door open. (4) There would be no profit in "a formal war with France" because it had no trade to capture, no territory to conquer which the United States would wish to keep. (This point was not transmitted by McHenry.) (5) The country should adopt a "truly vigorous defensive plan," at the same time keeping up a readiness to negotiate.

The "truly vigorous defensive plan" envisaged these preparations: (1) Allow the merchants to arm. (2) Acquire up to twenty sloops-of-war. (3) Finish the three frigates. (4) Give the President the authority to acquire up to ten ships-of-the-line "in case of open rupture." These might be had from Great Britain, to be manned and officered with Americans. Provisional talks leading to this end might well be opened with Britain immediately. The authority given by the Congress should be phrased broadly enough so that the President might even take part of a foreign navy into American pay.

The privately armed ships should be permitted to capture all who attacked them, and all French privateers fround "hovering" within a set distance from the coast.

After a further disquisition on the army and on taxes, he concluded by saying he thought the defeat of Britain by France, and the invasion of the United States were "very possible." The government must make calculations on those possibilities.[23]

And so matters rested until, on 5 March, the President lit a fuse which was connected with some very unstable elements. On that day he sent a letter to the Congress, signed by Pinckney, Marshall, and Gerry, dated 8 January 1798, which said in part: "We can only repeat that there exists no hope of our being officially received by this Government, or that the objects of our mission will be in any way accomplished." [24] The letter was printed on the same day in the Philadelphia Federalist organ, the *Gazette of the United States,* which coupled it with a private letter from Gerry, dated 3 January, to the same effect. Another letter, from Bordeaux, 8 November 1797, was printed also, which mentioned the "most shameful neglect" of the American Commissioners.[25] It helps to gauge the effect of this publication to notice a letter in the same paper, 8 March, signed "Ximenes," urging a declaration of war on France and denouncing Gallatin, among others, for his "truc jesuite stile." [26] Although ex-Senator George Cabot of Massachusetts, one of the brainiest and laziest of Federalists, gloomily calculated there would be no results from the news (he based his calculation on the poor showing of the previous session) [27] Federalism was electrified and the Congress began to overcome its inertia.

The Republicans leaped to the intellectual barricades. A correspondent signing himself "Juba," wrote for the Republican New York *Argus,* "A short Question—*Is it worth while to go to war with France?*" The answer, of course, was an echoing "No." He attacked the arming of the merchants (mostly commanded by British subjects and tories) and as for privateering, "The French have no commerce by which our privateers could be rewarded; we must cruise against the wind, and like Ixion we may sieze [*sic*] a cloud." The whole thing was a plot to go to war to help Britain.[28]

Gallatin was acutely alarmed: "May God save us from a war!" he wrote. He saw a rise in naval interest in the Congress, and predicted the authorization of more ships, which would be costly and of little use, except to get the country in "still deeper." It would be much better to bear the losses at sea until it was plain whether there was to be an Anglo-French peace in the spring, or, failing that, to await the results of the probable French invasion of the British Isles.[29] (This expectation of a French invasion of Britain was much in the minds of Americans, none of whom attempted to explain how the French would first dispose of the British home fleet.)

In the House the Federalists wheeled into action to get the naval program moving once more. The Republicans resisted, claiming the facts were not all available. The tone of argument reached a new low in the discussion of 13 March when Sewall moved to go into Committee of the Whole to discuss the Naval Committee's program, which he had attempted to revive several days earlier. As the Republicans urged delay until more could be learned, Harrison Gray Otis of Massachusetts accused them of "inventing apologies for prolonging the state of degradation." When William B. Giles of Virginia said he needed more facts before he made his decision Harper thought it was not unusual for the gentleman from Virginia "to display his ignorance of facts." Giles said he knew the gentleman from South Carolina supposed "he had a monopoly of knowledge."

Since the members insisted on arguing naval policy and each other's motives the Speaker, Jonathan Dayton of New Jersey, twice in a few minutes had to rule offenders out of order but they went at it just as fiercely. Otis announced he considered it an "honor" for Giles to disagree with him. If it were decided, he continued, to abandon the protection of commerce "the country would not long be worth the pains of defence; it would become disunited, and there would be an end of its prosperity." The Republicans, not the Federalists, were the war party, and the war they wished was "civil war." Giles then dared Otis to come outside and say that.

After Giles and then Samuel W. Dana of Connecticut ("the most eloquent man in Congress," Gallatin called him) [30] were successively ruled out of order by Dayton, the House went into Committee and, without further fireworks, agreed to resolutions which authorized the writing of a bill for the completion, equipping, and manning of the frigates, with an appropriation for the pay-roll.[31] At some cost in lacerated feelings the Republicans had effected a compromise; the House would take up the matter of the frigates but would not canvass all of naval policy.

Another illustration of the acidity of the moment appeared in the press at this time. A bill for the salaries of the members of the foreign service being before the House on 5 March, Nicholas tried to put a ceiling of nine thousand dollars on the salaries of Ministers Plenipotentiary. He lost by a vote of 48–52. The New York *Argus* reported it under the heading,

DIALOGUE

A. So, the Foreign Intercourse Bill has passed, hay?
B. 52 to 48.

A. We go on bravely.
B. 52 to 48.
A. Think ye, that we shall arm, and call the *British* to protect our trade?
B. 52 to 48.
A. Patience, patience—Surely you cannot suppose they mean to plunge this country into such irretrievable ruin? [32]

Sewall's committee had its bill ready in twenty-four hours. It proposed to appropriate $115,833 for the three frigates, "to complete, and equip for sea, with all convenient speed . . ." The sum of $268,879 was asked for pay and subsistence of the officers and crews for a year, and for maintenance, ammunition, contingent expenses, the caretakers of the navy yards at Norfolk, New York City, and Portsmouth, New Hampshire. (This latter figure was a maximum, not an appropriation in detail.) The Republicans questioned the meaning of "for sea, with all convenient speed." Was this an order to the President to send them to sea? It was moved to strike out "with all convenient speed," but the motion lost 38–47. After some trifling changes the House approved the bill. Several dates for Third Reading were argued. The Republicans moved the most remote date of those mentioned, but lost that motion too, 42–43. The majority ordered the bill to its Third Reading then and there, and it passed with fifty-seven ayes.[33]

The naval appropriation bill went through three readings in the Senate on successive days, without division or roll call.[34]

The last riposte of the Republican press was an alarum about war and taxes. "The first gun that is fired in earnest about the importation of British ribbons &c. will bring this country in a worse situation than it ever has been. The produce of a farm at market will not pay the taxes on it [the farm]." [35] This specimen of the wayward press ignored the total absence of a federal land tax.

Meanwhile two other naval projects of the Congress were in motion. One was a plan to establish a separate Department of the Navy, the first formal resolution for which was introduced by Sewall on 8 March. The founding of the new Department will be treated in detail later.

The other matter was the business of the House committee to investigate Secretary McHenry's administration of naval affairs, which had been authorized on 19 January and was headed by Livingston, a Republican. McHenry provided Livingston with all the information required, on 22 March, but a curious silence followed. The report of the committee consisted of a very long letter from McHenry (three pages in the large format of the *American State Papers*) plus sixteen pages of tables and reports. The accompanying documents numbered seventeen.

In general, McHenry attributed the delays of the construction program to changes in design, difficulties of getting out the live oak trees in Georgia, accidents, fires, bad weather, yellow fever, and lack of preparation for the program. The increase in costs had the same causes and were made worse by the decision to build the ships simultaneously at separate yards. The wartime rises in the costs of labor and materials were also noted.

This report was not given to the House until five weeks after Chairman Livingston had received it.[36] Speculation on this interesting hiatus is complicated by the fact that Livingston was a Republican. At first glance the report would appear to have been valuable ammunition for Republican salvos against Federalist competence. On the other hand, it would have been useful evidence to support the Federalist allegations of a need for a separate Department of the Navy. Livingston, who heatedly opposed the bill to establish the Department of the Navy, probably decided it was better tactics to hold back the report until after the Act to establish the Department had been disposed of. When he finally submitted it to the House (27 April) it was of no use to anyone except, perhaps, the first Secretary of the Navy, and there is no evidence to show it influenced events in this session.

Outside Congress Hall, heat and pressure were building up. President Adams had at last received dispatches in full from his Commissioners in Paris which proved there would be no accommodation with the government of France within the foreseeable future. On 19 March the President sent a message to the Congress categorically announcing the failure of the mission. He suggested the Congress give its attention to measures he had spoken of earlier, among them those "for the protection of our seafaring and commercial citizens." He also asked the members to notice the difference of the present situation from what it had been when he had prohibited the arming of merchant vessels. He said he now intended to lift the prohibition except in such cases where it seemed the armed ship was "intended to be employed contrary to law." [37] The President's chief purpose in sending this message was to encourage the Congress to get on with the project of strengthening the country's sea power.[38]

The Republicans—although they lived to regret their scepticism—were not disposed to take the President's word as evidence of the hopelessness of further negotiation. In a fierce scene of wrangling and vituperation, on 2 April, the House voted to request a sight of the papers sent by the Commissioners.[39] In this action the Republicans entrapped themselves. When Secretary of State Timothy Pickering had deciphered the papers he hinted of their explosive character to Hamilton, and suggested publication would weaken the Republicans. The effect of this hint is still visible in the roll call in the *Annals,* where the names of John Allen of Connecticut and Harper are listed with the ayes, along with such unlikely political bedfellows as Gallatin, Giles, and Nicholas. A combination of Hamiltonian Federalists and Republicans had overridden the moderate Federalists in passing the call for papers.[40] When the papers arrived on the next day,[41] the Republicans had reason to mourn their deed. For these were the famous "X. Y. Z. Papers," which told in detail how the French agents refused even to begin to negotiate until the Americans had bribed them into compliance. (This was approved diplomatic tactical doctrine in the French Foreign Ministry at the time, but no more palatable to Americans for that reason.)

A fraction of the extreme Federalists now became a war party. They had a newspaper of great influence on their side, John Fenno's Philadelphia *Gazette of the United States,* which editorialized, "To say '*we will not resort to war*' is almost as wise as to say when one's house is in flames, that *we will not resort to water* . . ." [42] There were no restrictions on attacks against the Republicans who were described in the paper's columns: ". . . a large junto of servile jacobins furiously oppose every measure of the executive, are striving to subvert the constitution and destroy the confidence which the people have reposed in the constituted authorities . . ." [43] An anonymous poet scored the dilatory Congress, and hymned:

> Let the red flag of vengeance be display'd,
> And ghosts of ruffians gleam on ev'ry blade;
> While the rude throats of our loud cannon roar,
> And deadly thunder on the miscreants pour;—
> A horde of monsters, whom no faith can bind,
> Pests of the earth, and curse of all mankind:
> When deep tho late shall vengeance' bolts be hurl'd,
> And hosts of murderers crowd the infernal world.[44]

This must be what people mean when they say it is not necessary to use profanity if one has a good vocabulary. And it was strong talk from a third rate power against the nation which had just knocked out the Austrian Empire and promoted a new General named Napoleon Bonaparte.

But there was not to be a declaration of war. Senator Theodore Sedgwick blamed the House Republicans; "the determined and rancorous Jacobins . . . under the *controul* [*sic*] of the Genevese [Gallatin], are a well organized & disciplined Corps, never going astray, or doing right even by mistake." [45] Actually, President Adams and

Hamilton had each independently decided against a declaration of war. Hence the war-minded had no nationally known leadership.

Before the publication of the "X. Y. Z. Papers" the Republicans were putting up a pretty hard fight. For example, Representative John Dawson of Virginia had circularized his constituents with a loaded question, asking what they thought of the President's "important, intemperate, and unconstitutional" message of 19 March.[46] Thomas Jefferson urged the House Republicans to pass a bill to prohibit the arming of merchantmen (which the President now permitted). If it were beaten in the Senate "it would heap coals of fire on their head." He also recommended a recess, as a cooling-off period, "in order to go home & consult their constituents . . ." The whole problem would be accented by the coming invasion of England. Then the public would see who was for war and who for peace.[47] The New York *Argus* announced the message of the nineteenth: "Here is FOOD which will be deemed by many hard to digest—*gun powder* and *red-hot balls.*" The urging of the President to violate neutrality would surely bring the war "to our fire sides." The President was a pro-British warmonger.[48]

But after the publication of the "X. Y. Z. Papers" there was a deepening and depressing sense of crisis in the hearts of the Republicans.[49] An attempt had been made in the House on 27 March by Richard Sprigg of Maryland to counterattack the President's message of the nineteenth. He moved three resolutions: (1) It was not expedient to go to war with France. (2) The Congress ought to restrict the arming of private ships. (3) "That adequate provision shall be made by law for the protection of our seacoast, and for the internal defence of the country." The first resolution was debated off and on for five days. Then the publication of the dispatches occurred, and the Sprigg resolves were dead.[50] All Sprigg had accomplished was to draw Federalist fire. The *Gazette of the United States* discussed his try under the headline: *"THE PLOT DISCOVERED,"* in a short account spiced with such phrases as "disgrace and jacobinism," and "shallow projects," and concluding with a description of the project as the use of *"clamor, virulence* and *falshood* [*sic*], supported by impenetrable impudence." [51]

The Republicans made what they could of an expected *entente* with the old foe Britain. Benjamin Franklin Bache's Philadelphia *Aurora* incorrectly reported the arrival of British agents to arrange for the American rental of some of His Britannic Majesty's warships. The terms would be generous because the British would then drag the United States into the war in order to make peace with the French by sacrificing the Americans. The country had better hurry into the war or it would be too late. Britain was likely to be defeated by invaders "before they have begun their preparations for the *conquest of Mexico.*" [52] The New York *Argus* lamented the fate of American sailors in these lend-lease warships, commanded by British officers, "to be *lashed, shot, or hung* . . . at their discretion or pleasure!" [53] Where these notions came from one can not say, but Hamilton had recently written to Pickering "It would be good policy in [Britain] to send to this Country a dozen frigates to pursue the directions of this Government." [54] And several close friends of Hamilton were interested in a scheme for a joint Anglo-American operation in Latin America.[55] There were no wire-tappers then but some public men of the 1790s suspected their mail was tampered with. In 1800 Aaron Burr, the very efficient Republican leader of Manhattan, proved he had a close-to-perfect system of acquiring information of Hamiltonian Federalist plans—but one can only speculate on these things.

The arming of the merchant fleet was not, of course, a new issue but brought on a continuation of an old debate. Adams had twice written of it as a good idea in the fall of 1797.[56] Having given the Congress advance notice in the message of 19 March, he caused a circular to be issued to the collectors of the revenue, from Secretary Wolcott, to relax the prohibition on the clearance of armed private vessels unless there was reason to think they were to be used "contrary to law." [57] The United States Minister in London, Rufus King, was told to advise shipmasters there to arm before returning home, if they intended to, because there was a shortage of guns in America. They would also be well advised to bring in powder, saltpeter, lead, copper, sail cloth, and hemp, as well.[58]

The Republicans, of course, attacked the policy. Petitions to the Congress to prohibit the practice came in from seven Massachusetts towns during April, most of them presented by Representative Joseph B. Varnum.[59] The Cambridge town meeting said to arm the merchants was "tantamount to war." The general line of argument followed by the towns was the one previously urged. Roxbury feared it would put the peace of the country in the hands of shipmasters "of a great variety of character; that among them are men of violent passions . . ." Peace might depend on the "pride, caprice, or passion of the master of a merchant vessel." [60] Another town, Milton, emphasized the high proportion of British subjects or lately naturalized Americans who commanded in the merchant marine.[61] Perhaps these petitioners had heard of Captain Kidd or of the "War of Jenkins's Ear." Historically considered, the opponents had a point.

A Republican editor warned seamen of their dubious legal position if they shipped in an armed vessel which carried no public commission. What he hinted at, of course, was piracy.[62] Bache questioned the measure's popularity,[63] and "A SAILOR" in the New York *Argus* thought an embargo would be better evidence of true neutrality.[64]

The Federalists replied with counter-petitions, with satire (farmers favored the prohibition so sailors would be out of work and wages would fall),[65] with arguments from international law,[66] with predictions of unparalleled prosperity if the policy remained in effect (headline: "ARM! or STARVE!"),[67] and with proposals for legislative safeguards against the abuses which the Republican petitioners feared.[68]

The most interesting, if rather intemperate, discussion of the pros and cons of arming the merchants occurred under the auspices of the Society for Free Debate, in New York. The Society held periodic public debates, with speakers recognized from the floor, admission one shilling. On 26 April they debated whether it would be better policy to enact an embargo or to arm the merchant ships. About 450 persons attended. The discussion ended in what the New York *Argus* described as a "species of *fracas*." The embargo supporters claimed they listened politely to their opponents, that only two of them hissed and those two were promptly squelched by the Chair. But when their turn to speak came the Society was "kept in a Bedlam for about one hour and a half." The meeting ended with the adoption of a resolution endorsing the arming of merchantmen, to be sent to the President and the Congress. The *Argus* countered by saying it was approved at a time when "almost all orderly citizens had retired." It is pretty hard to say exactly what happened. In the course of the debate the Chairman was impeached and removed from his throne. His replacement handed out a statement for the press entirely unconfirmatory of the account in the *Argus*.[69] However one may safely conclude the issues at stake were not generally regarded apathetically.

It will be noticed most of the reaction recorded above was urban (except the New England town petitions which were probably secured by agents appointed for the purpose). The news of the "X. Y. Z. Affair" was still traveling out through the predominantly rural population like the wave from an exploded island-volcano. It would take a while to learn of its effect. Any day of April 1798 was probably too early to estimate the national impact of the "X. Y. Z. Affair." So far as the Navy was concerned, things had begun to move with the arrival in the Congress of the "no hope" letter, received there on 5 March. Whether more naval strength would be authorized than heretofore would depend to some extent on the national reaction to French insolence.

Some Federalists were pretty cheerful about it. Joshua Humphreys, ship designer to the Department of War, was toastmaster of a Federalist dinner in Philadelphia on 21 April (no Hatch Act then). Among the planned toasts offered were these:

12. The infant navy of the United States—Like the infant Hercules, may it even in its cradle strangle the serpents which would poison American glory.—9 cheers.
13. The American Seamen—May they shew [*sic*] themselves not the mere instruments of commerce, but the able defenders of their country.—9 cheers.
15. May the Atlantic be a Red Sea to all who shall attempt to invade our country—12 cheers.[70]

Matthew Carey, Philadelphia writer, publisher, and editor, took all this grumpily. His report cast a somewhat different light on the affair.

> These *hundred staunch federalists* drank no less than *thirty-two staunch toasts,* to each of which they gave exactly 9 cheers . . . [except one which was given 12] amounting in all, by an exact calculation, *to two hundred and ninety-one* cheers or huzzas, vulgarly called hurraws; each of which was accompanied with the tossing of hats, caps & wigs in the air;—merry-andrew jumps,—and divers other irregularities and violent movements.[71]

On the basis of the evidence, the verdict still stands. The Federalists were feeling good in these weeks, and their buoyancy portended a heyday for the Navy.

NOTES FROM PAGES 124 TO 137

1. John Adams to Pickering, 31 Oct. 1797, Adams papers, reel 117, Library of Congress *et al.* (hereafter abbreviated: LC).
2. Cathalan to Pickering, 24 May 1798, Dudley W. Knox, ed., *Naval Documents Related to the Quasi-war between the United States and France,* 7v. (Washington, 1935–1938), I, 78–80.
3. New York *Time-Piece,* 18 Oct. 1797, quoted in Nathan Schachner, *The Founding Fathers* (New York, 1954), 433.
4. John Adams, 23 Nov. 1797, 5 Cong., 2 Sess., *Annals of the Congress, 1789–1824,* ed. J. Gales and W. W. Seaton, 42v. (Washington, 1834–1856), 630–634. Hereafter cited: *Annals.* Dates will be given where useful. All citations to *Annals* below will be from 5 Cong., 2 Sess.
5. 27 Nov., *ibid.,* 473–474.
6. 28 Nov., *ibid.,* 474–475.
7. 27–28 Nov., *ibid.,* 642–643, 645–648.
8. 29 Nov., *ibid.,* 652.
9. Gallatin to Hannah Gallatin, 1 Dec. 1797, Henry Adams, *The Life of Albert Gallatin* (Philadelphia, 1879), 188. Hereafter cited: Adams, *Gallatin.*
10. *Annals,* 653–654.
11. 11 Dec., *ibid.,* 693.
12. *Ibid.,* 693–701; Manning J. Dauer, *The Adams Federalists* (Baltimore, 1953), 304–309; Gallatin to Hannah Gallatin, 19 Dec. 1797, Adams, *Gallatin,* 188.
13. Gallatin to Hannah Gallatin, 2 Jan. 1798, Adams, *Gallatin,* 189.
14. Gallatin to Hannah Gallatin, 19 Jan. 1798, *ibid.,* 189–190.
15. Philadelphia *Gazette of the United States,* 5 March 1798.
16. 10, 11 Jan. 1798, *Annals,* 818–819, 821–828. A kindly estimate of Harper's personality is Gallatin to Hannah Gallatin, 19 Dec. 1797, Adams, *Gallatin,* 188.
17. 15 Jan., *ibid.,* 831–836.
18. McHenry to Sewall, 26 Dec. 1797, *American State Papers,* ed. Walter Lowrie and Matthew St. Clair Clarke, 38v. (Washington, 1832–1861), Class VI, *Naval Affairs,* I, 32, 33. Hereafter cited: *ASP:* with the name of the class.

19. 16 Jan., *Annals,* 840–841.
20. 26 December 1797, *ibid.,* 764–777.
21. Gallatin to Hannah Gallatin, 13 Feb. 1798, Adams, *Gallatin,* 193.
22. Oliver Wolcott, Jr., to Frederick Wolcott, 27 Feb. 1798, George Gibbs, *Memoirs of the Administrations of Washington and John Adams,* 2v. (New York, 1846), II, 13. Hereafter cited: Gibbs, *Memoirs.*
23. Hamilton to McHenry, n.d., Bernard C. Steiner, *The Life and Correspondence of James McHenry* (Cleveland, 1907), 291–295. For the document as transmitted to Adams by McHenry, with a significant omission, see John Adams, *Works,* ed. Charles Francis Adams, 10v. (Boston, 1850–1856), VIII, 562n.
24. *Annals,* 1201.
25. Philadelphia *Gazette of the United States,* 5 March 1798.
26. *Ibid.,* 8 March 1798.
27. Cabot to King, 21 March 1798, Rufus King, *The Life and Correspondence of Rufus King,* ed. C. R. King, 6v. (New York, 1894–1900), II, 290–292. Hereafter cited: King, *Life and Correspondence.*
28. New York *Argus,* 12 March 1798.
29. Gallatin to Hannah Gallatin, 6, 13 March 1798, Adams, *Gallatin,* 195, 196.
30. Gallatin to Hannah Gallatin, 19 Dec. 1798, *ibid.,* 188.
31. 8, 13 March, *Annals,* 1245–1246, 1252–1265.
32. New York *Argus,* 14 March 1798; 5 March, *Annals,* 1234.
33. 14, 16 March, *ibid.,* 1265, 1267–1270; the text of the act, *ibid.,* 3717.
34. 19–21 March, *ibid.,* 524, 525, 526.
35. New York *Argus,* 22 March 1798.
36. *ASP: Naval Affairs,* I, 37–56; 27 April, *Annals,* 1563. Livingston was very active in the deliberations of April. *Ibid.,* index, 2 Sess.
37. 19 March, *ibid.,* 524, 1272. Wolcott wrote most of the message. Gibbs, *Memoirs,* II, 14–15.
38. John Adams, *Works,* I, 522.
39. *Annals,* 1357–1371.
40. Dauer, *The Adams Federalists,* 141.
41. *Annals,* 1374–1375.
42. Philadelphia *Gazette of the United States,* 28 March 1798.
43. "Eugenius," *ibid.,* 3 April 1798.
44. *Ibid.,* 5 April 1798.
45. Sedgwick to King, 9 April 1798, King, *Life and Correspondence,* II, 310.
46. Edward Channing, *A History of the United States,* 6v. (New York, 1932–1936), IV, 189n.
47. Jefferson to Madison, 21 March 1798, Jefferson papers, LC. Madison cordially endorsed these ideas. Madison to Jefferson, 2 April 1798, Madison papers, LC.
48. New York *Argus,* 22, 23 March 1798.
49. Jefferson to Pendleton, 2 April 1798, to Madison, 6 April 1798, Jefferson papers, LC; Madison to Jefferson, 15 April 1798, Madison papers, LC.
50. The debate covers *Annals,* 1319–1373.
51. Philadelphia *Gazette of the United States,* 28 March 1798.
52. Philadelphia *Aurora,* quoted in New York *Argus,* 23 March 1798.
53. New York *Argus,* 18 April 1798.
54. Hamilton to Pickering, 27 March 1798, Hamilton papers, LC; see also, McHenry to Sewall, 9 April 1798, *ASP: Naval Affairs,* I, 34.
55. Marshall Smelser, "George Washington declines the part of El Libertador," *William and Mary Quarterly,* third series, XI (Jan. 1954), 42–51.
56. John Adams to Pickering, 14 October 1797, John Adams, *Works,* VIII, 554, to Wolcott, Jr., 27 Oct. 1797, Adams papers, reel 119, LC.
57. Philadelphia *Gazette of the United States,* 22 March 1798.
58. Pickering to King, 2 April 1798, King, *Life and Correspondence,* II, 297.
59. 30 March 1798, *Annals,* 1357; 2 April, *ibid.,* 1367–1368; 13 April, *ibid.,* 1413; 23 April, *ibid.,* 1522; New York *Argus,* 12, 13, 16 April 1798.
60. Roxbury petition, 30 March 1798, *Annals,* 1357.
61. 2 April, *ibid.,* 1367–1368.
62. New York *Argus,* 24 March 1798.
63. Philadelphia *Aurora,* 5 May 1798.
64. New York *Argus,* 19 March 1798.
65. Philadelphia *Gazette of the United States,* 5 May 1798.
66. *Ibid.,* 6 April 1798.
67. *Ibid.,* 24 March 1798.
68. *Ibid.*
69. New York *Argus,* 30 April 1798.
70. Philadelphia *Gazette of the United States,* 23 April 1798.
71. Philadelphia *United States Recorder,* copied in Philadelphia *Aurora,* 3 May 1798.

X

A Navy for Defense

March–May 1798

The Federalists were now determined to press vigorously for a more adequate navy. Alexander Hamilton had drafted a naval policy at the request of Secretary of War James McHenry, before the middle of February, which had been transmitted to President John Adams as McHenry's own. There had been little visible result. A month later Hamilton put his quill to the paper again. This time he wrote to Secretary of State Timothy Pickering. Politically this was a good choice of correspondents because Pickering kept up a continuous political collaboration with the congressional Federalists, particularly with those who still looked upon Hamilton, rather than Adams, as their leader. (The Secretaries of State, War, and the Treasury had this same tropism.)

As Hamilton put it, the question was now a question of the independence of the United States. He thought the necessary legislative measures were as follow: (1) Permit the merchants to arm and to capture attackers. (2) Complete the frigates and "a considerable number of sloops-of-war," up to twenty guns each, "to capture all attacking, and privateers found within twenty leagues of our coast." (3) The President to be authorized "to provide and equip ten ships of the line in case of open rupture with any foreign power." There were other points, concerning the army, the militia, harbor fortifications, taxes, and the suspension of the treaties with France.[1] One can be reasonably certain this program was divulged to the Representatives and Senators who would be most receptive to it.

As it happened, the first major legislation to move after the "X. Y. Z. Affair" broke the log-jam was a Senate bill to provide for leasing or buying one or more foundries. This was not a new idea. Secretary of the Treasury Oliver Wolcott, Jr., had recommended it to President George Washington in 1795.[2] In December 1797 Rufus King, in

London, had advised accepting the proffer of the services of the American-born Sir Benjamin Thompson, Count Rumford, who had had "much experience in the establishment of Cannon Founderies" and who had also made improvements in field artillery.[3] Rumford's services were not acquired, but the episode showed that gun-founding was not a forgotten idea.

The Senate's Foundry Bill was introduced by Benjamin Goodhue of Massachusetts, chairman of the Senate's Committee on the Security and Protection of the Commerce of the United States (hereafter, the Naval Committee) on 20 March, and passed its three readings on successive days.[4] When it went down stairs to the House of Representatives it was happily received in the committee headed by Samuel Sewall of Massachusetts—the Committee on the Protection of Commerce and the Defence of the Country, hereafter the "Naval Committee"—which recommended passage without amendments. At this stage the Foundry Bill carried an appropriation of a hundred thousand dollars.[5] Sewall wished quick action but nothing could compete with the lust to talk about the President's message of 19 March which had announced the failure of the mission of Charles Cotesworth Pinckney, John Marshall, and Elbridge Gerry,—the "X. Y. Z. Affair." [6] Within a day or two the Republicans had thought up a good stalling tactic. They successfully moved to call on the President for more facts—specifically they wished to know how many heavy guns the United States had acquired since 1 January 1794, what percentage had been cast in the United States, where they were cast, what sizes, and the prices paid for each size.[7] There the matter rested for twelve days.

Sewall chafed, reflected, and developed a countertactic. It took the form of a resolution, on 9 April, to appropriate "blank" dollars for "cannon, arms, and ammunition." [8] He tried to get action in the Committee of the Whole three days later but failed because the House was still waiting for the gun statistics. That same day the gun report arrived. On the thirteenth Sewall got his hearing in the Committee of the Whole. His proposal now was a House resolution to appropriate money to buy the big guns and much other equipment. Carefully preserved was the power voted by the Senate to be given to the President "to purchase or hire foundries, or armories" if he found it hard to buy the guns.[9]

In Committee of the Whole the Federalists claimed the operation of foundries by the federal government would prevent a conspiracy to raise prices. The best answer of the Republicans was an equally hypothetical argument: the knowledge of the intention of the government to make its own guns would cause a cessation of manufacture in the hope the gun-makers could sell their plants to the government at good prices. But the Naval Committee's resolution passed.[10] Re-written as a bill, it was considered again in Committee of the Whole a few days later. Sewall had a surprise for his colleagues. He proposed to fill in the blank appropriation with the sum of $1,200,000, a matter of a 1200% jump from the earlier Senate figure. Even Harrison Gray Otis of Massachusetts, one of the hyper-Federalist extremists, was astonished. Sewall explained: the money was not to buy guns for the frigates (they had already been provided) but to buy guns for the harbor forts and the new ships he expected the House would authorize and to buy small arms and other military stores. Two hundred thousand dollars would go for copper sheathing. In the end they settled on eight hundred thousand dollars for these purposes, with a hundred thousand dollars extra to buy foundries and armories.[11] The bill passed easily on the next day.[12] The Senate Bill to cast guns had grown into an entire munitions program, with the appropriation multiplied ninefold.

This nine hundred per cent "mark-up" was significant. Before the publication of the "X. Y. Z. Papers" the Senate asked only a hundred thousand dollars. After the publication the House dared to appropriate nine hundred thousand dollars. This was a nice statistical measure of the intensification of feeling caused by the publication of the dispatches from the Commissioners. The Senate made no difficulty when it received the Bill.[13]

"An Act to enable the President of the United States to procure cannon, arms, ammunition; and for other purposes," approved 4 May 1798, had three sections. The first section allowed a maximum expenditure of eight hundred thousand dollars for "cannon," small arms, ammunition and military stores. The second section allowed the President to lease or buy foundries if he found it hard to purchase the equipment. The third section allowed him to spend a hundred thousand dollars for the purposes of section two.[14] Ex-President George Washington immediately began to "lobby" for the erection of a foundry at "the Mouth of the Shenandoah," where the government already owned a proper site[15] (and later established the famous Harper's Ferry arsenal and armory).

A bill to increase the number of ships came out of Senator Goodhue's Naval Committee on 23 March. The prevailing excitement over the failure of the mission to Paris caused consideration of the Bill to be postponed until after the publication of the dispatches from the Commissioners who had been sent to Paris.[16] During these days the lines were being drawn, and policy-positions reconsidered and clarified in the minds of the opponents.

If the Republicans had been in power at the moment their program would have been about like this: to affirm publicly a belief in the possibility of further negotiation with the French, to fortify the principal harbors, and to strengthen the internal defenses by reorganizing the militia and beginning to accumulate arms.[17]

The extreme Federalist position was shown in a letter from Senator Theodore Sedgwick to the American Minister in London, Rufus King. He listed his hopes as follow: the passage of the Foundry Bill (then being much broadened in the House), authority to add sixteen ships to the naval force, fortification of the harbors, establishment of a corps of artillery and of cavalry, authority to capture armed French ships which attacked American ships, authority to capture all armed ships within twenty leagues of the coast, the voiding of the French treaties, passage of an Alien Act, and an increase in the public revenue. The session so far, he thought, had been "a disagreeable one & hitherto almost wholly unproductive . . ." He would not "deem the public safety provided for" unless these measures were enacted.[18]

Senator Humphrey Marshall, Republican of Kentucky, put his party on record in the Senate on 26 March by offering a series of resolutions: (1) to embargo all shipping except fishing vessels; (2) to fortify and garrison the ports; (3) to establish a provisional army (that is, one to be enlisted but not activated until necessary); (4) to supply any deficiencies of arms and military stores. Except for the first, these would have been acceptable to the Federalists and, politically, they would have been well-advised to approve numbers two, three, and four, and to order bills drafted accordingly, in order to bring the Republicans into the family, so to speak. But the Senate debated only the first, beat it by a vote of 5–22, and postponed the others.[19] No Republican was going to be allowed to father Senate military or naval legislation.

The Senate Bill, which was then receiving its series of postponements, provided for the use of naval vessels to convoy.[20] The British were already providing this service to any American merchant captain who asked for it. Secretary of State Timothy Pickering was grateful, but thought "how disgraceful to the United States if we continue to depend on the protection of the British Navy without any reasonable exertion on our part to protect ourselves." [21]

In opposing the Senate Bill to increase the fleet, the Republicans relied on the "economy-in-government" argument. The British Navy pressed men to serve for five dollars a month. The United States abhorred impressment and would not use it. Therefore the Navy would have to compete with merchant ship owners who were even then signing on sailors at Baltimore for twenty-four dollars a month [22]—a financially disastrous differential. Furthermore, if trade with the French West Indies could not be restored the price of flour would drop, damaging the American farmer in order to benefit the British war effort.[23] The Federalists argued the economic question by saying the farmers needed "a free commerce" to keep prices up, and only a navy could keep the export trade free.[24]

At length, on 9 April, the Senate got around to voting on the Bill for increasing the number of ships and rolled over the Republican minority by a vote of 20–7.[25] The Bill provided for the purchase of up to sixteen ships, of not more than twenty-two guns each.[26]

As the Bill moved down to the House, Secretary McHenry tried to strengthen the spirit of the Federalists by a letter to Chairman Sewall which detailed the naval needs.

> France derives several important advantages from the system she is pursuing toward the United States. Besides the sweets of plunder, obtained by her privateers, she keeps in them a nursery of seamen, to be drawn upon, in all conjunctures, by her navy. She unfits, by the same means, the United States for energetic measures, and thereby prepares us for the last degree of humiliation and subjection.
>
> To forbear, under such circumstances, from taking naval and military measures to secure our trade, defend our territory, in case of invasion, and prevent or suppress domestic insurrection, would be to offer up the United States a certain prey to France, and exhibit to the world a sad spectacle of national degradation and imbecility.
>
> The United States possesses an extensive trade; heavy expenses must be submitted to for its protection . . .

He then specifically recommended an increase of naval strength by the addition of two ships of twenty-two guns, eight of twenty guns, and ten of sixteen guns. The President should have authority, if war became open, to acquire six ships-of-the-line or the equivalent in frigates (the equivalent in frigates, it may be noted, would be ten or twelve). The large ships might be acquired in Europe—meaning, of course, in Great Britain. For the twenty smaller vessels he estimated the cost at $1,941,181. He thought it might be well to add six galleys to the list.[27] This was a remarkable letter, asking, as it did, for even more strength than was provided in the rather generous Senate Bill which he must have known would arrive simultaneously.

The comment on the necessity for spending a good deal of money to protect an extensive commerce was a natural anticipation of Republican arguments to the contrary. At about the same time Thomas Jefferson, who was presiding over the Senate, wrote to James Madison, "All . . . which the advocates of peace can now attempt is to prevent war measures *externally*, consenting to every rational measure of *internal* defence & preparation." The program would be very costly, and its sponsors would have to find the money. This letter echoed the decision of a House Republican caucus of the same day.[28]

As the Bill to increase the number of ships entered the appropriating House it was a convenient public display to have *Constellation* sail down from Baltimore to the mouth of the Patapsco River, on her shake-down. She performed well, wrote "an officer" on board; "under double-reefed topsails, coursers, jib, and staysails only, and out of trim . . . [she] run ahead of everything that was in company, going down with all their light sails set." But it was thought necessary to deny a rumor which said *Constitution* had sunk at her mooring in Boston harbor.[29]

In the House the Senate Bill found two principal objections. The Republicans were determined to prevent the use of any ships to convoy because convoying was, they said, a certain prelude to open war. And sixteen ships (to say nothing of McHenry's twenty) were too many.

The House debate on the use of the ships as escorts of the merchant fleet exhibited the Federalists at their most passionate. The opponents of the use of convoys said to convoy was warlike. As John Nicholas of Virginia said, if search were to be allowed, there was no need to convoy; if it were not allowed, there would be war. To convoy was not good economy, either, because it could only protect trade to Great Britain which was worth eight million dollars a year. Yet the cost of protection would be two million dollars a year. Federalists then accused the Republicans of trying to kill the entire Bill. Was it peaceable, they asked, to tell the plunderer in advance they would not defend themselves? Furthermore, if the country were at war with France it would not suffer from French depredations any more than it did at the moment.

Gallatin rose to reply at length. He thought the country must either bear its losses or resist with force leading certainly to war. If war came by act of a foreign power, possession of the ships would mean the country was prepared for war although not to blame for starting it. He reminded Federalists of the condition of trade if there were a war with France. The United States could then trade only with Great Britain and prices would drop accordingly.

This speech of Gallatin's was one of the greatest parliamentary irritants in American history. Speaker Jonathan Dayton of New Jersey (the House had resolved itself into the Committee of the Whole) rose to express his "indignation" at such "tame and submissive language." John Allen of Connecticut said Gallatin's speech showed the same spirit which produced the Whiskey Rebellion. (This was very "personal," because Gallatin had been falsely blamed as ring-leader of the

Rebellion.) After cries of "Order!" had produced a relative calm, Daniel Brooks of New York said American independence would never have been achieved if such advice as Gallatin's had prevailed. Samuel Dana of Connecticut rose to offer a pseudo-apology for Dayton's strong language. It was a natural outburst, said Dana, because, after all, Dayton was a native-born American and a war-veteran.

Gallatin, somehow keeping his temper, now said his only interest was in preserving peace. Little more was done that day.

On the next day, 20 April, Allen renewed the attack on Gallatin with a prepared speech (which ran twelve and a half columns in the *Annals of the Congress*). This was a much quoted speech, describing Gallatin's position as "Jacobinic." As Allen put it,

> Were France herself to speak through an American mouth, I cannot conceive what [she] would say more than what we have heard from certain gentlemen to effect her purpose . . . Is this the language of an American who loves his country? No, sir, it is the language of a foreign agent . . . It is not the language of patriotism . . .

The theme of Allen's violent address was the skill of French diplomacy in creating a French party in the House to oppose the Federalists.

Nicholas mildly advised the Federalists to move a declaration of war, if that was what they wished. Nathaniel Macon of North Carolina thought the Federalist measures were too strong for peace but too weak for war. Gallatin summed up Allen's tirade: the Republicans were told to prove themselves anti-French by voting in favor of every Federalist measure.

In the end the Republicans managed to strike out four sections of the Bill as it had been written in the Senate. One of these explicitly authorized the use of public ships to convoy, and the other three provided regulations for convoying (matters of ships' papers, contraband, destinations). These four were excised without a division of the vote.[30]

Gallatin next moved to write in an explicit prohibition of convoying. This was not acceptable. Apparently the Federalists were willing to throw out the statement authorizing the President to convoy, because some of them thought he had the power without the grant of it. But they were unwilling to accept a prohibition of convoying. When the amendment to prohibit convoys came to a vote in Committee of the Whole it lost 32–49. New England opposed the amendment in a ratio of eight to one, the middle states by almost two to one, while the southern and the two western states favored it better than two to one.[31]

Next they took up the question of the number of ships to be authorized. A motion to cut the number from sixteen to twelve was made by Samuel Smith of Maryland, who urged it because they would be unable to find more than twelve merchant ships suitable for conversion. Josiah Parker of Virginia and Robert Goodloe Harper of South Carolina, both Federalists, agreed with this reasoning. This might have been enough to swing the irregular Federalists to that side but John Williams of New York, a Federalist, added another dimension to the picture. He pointed to the total of defense appropriations thus far, $1,850,000 without having given any consideration to cutters, floating batteries, and other precautions. Eight smaller ships and the three frigates would be enough. Commerce was overextended as it was. If the American farmers had to put up three or four million dollars a year to protect commerce it would be better to have no commerce. The American people had been prosperous and happy in the years 1783–1784 until they began to buy imported goods. Then home manufactures declined and the people went into debt. If the country kept on with this naval program the debt would never be paid. Sobered, the Committee voted to reduce the number from sixteen to twelve, by a vote of 49–27, and reported this action to the House of Representatives on the same day. The irrepressible Edward Livingston said he favored sixteen ships because the entire Federalist program was a war program and sixteen would be none too many. Now he would like to see who the cowards, so much denounced in the House, really were. Livingston was twice in a few minutes ruled out of order, and by vote of 45–37 the House accepted the reduction of the number of ships.[32] A sectional analysis of the vote shows New England to have been the center of defection on this amendment. Instead of the usual ratio of six or eight to one in favor of any naval expansion, the five New England states turned up eleven ayes and only sixteen noes on the amendment. The middle states had an identical total. Therefore when the four southern and two western states voted 28–5 in favor of the reduction, it carried easily.[33] The Senate Bill, as amended to reduce the number of ships and strike out any reference to convoys, passed the House of Representatives on Third Reading, 42–26.[34] After some argument and several divisions (in one of which Vice President Jefferson was privileged to cast a tie-breaking vote in favor of the House change) the Senate accepted the amended Bill as it had been reworked in the House.[35]

"An Act to provide an additional armament for the further protection of the trade of the United States, and for other purposes," approved 27 April 1798, authorized the President to buy, rent, or build up to twelve vessels of not more than twenty-two guns each, allowed him to fix the number and grade of the new officers, provided that navy pay and regulations for them be the same as before, regulated enlistment, provided for recess-commissions for officers, and appropriated $950,000 for these purposes.[36]

The Congress now had a financial problem. The estimated expenditure for 1798 had been a little less than seven million dollars; receipts were estimated at slightly more than eight million dollars. The expenditure-estimate had included $374,000 for the Navy. Now the Congress had added $1,850,000 for the defense of the country (including the $900,000 for foundries and munitions, of which the Navy was to receive a large share). As of 1 May the House Ways and Means Committee recommended using the million dollar surplus which had been anticipated earlier, for these purposes.[37] This left a deficit of almost a million dollars to be met, a matter which was put off until later.

The executive went ahead to acquire the twelve ships. Friends of the project let the press know of Secretary Wolcott's search for suitable vessels which might be purchased by the government.[38]

One other form of naval defense occupied the attention of the Congress in this phase of their work. On 5 February the President had sent over to Congress Hall an account of an outrage in the harbor of Charleston, South Carolina. In the previous October a French privateer had plundered and burned a British ship while the local authorities had stood by helpless to prevent this violation of American sovereignty.[39] The message was given to the House Naval Committe which took advantage of the excitement over the failure of the mission to Paris to report, on 26 March, a resolution authorizing the President to build and equip a number of "galleys or floating batteries . . ." [40] A few days later Senator William Bingham of Pennsylvania moved to add an amendment providing for ten galleys, to the Senate's Bill for sixteen ships, but he withdrew it a few days later.[41]

Near the end of April, the House having taken no action, Senator Goodhue's Naval Committee introduced "An Act to authorize the President of the United States to cause to be purchased or built a number of small vessels, to be equipped as galleys, or otherwise." It passed the Senate without division.[42] This Bill passed the House also without debate or division,[43] probably because it was thought necessary to have some sort of movable defenses which could be used in the shallow waters of the Carolina and Georgia coasts.[44]

The Galley Act authorized the construction or purchase of not more than ten small vessels to be used "as galleys or otherwise," the officers and men to receive the same pay as those of the United States Navy, and it authorized an appropriation of eighty thousand dollars.[45] Later it was decided to leave the ranks and pay scale to be fixed by the

President, and an amending act was passed in mid-June to that effect. As Chairman Sewall of the House Naval Committee said, it was not necessary to equate the galley-men with the Navy—"a much lower rank would be sufficient." [46]

The second session of the Fifth Congress had so far enacted legislation providing for a munitions program. It had continued work on the three great frigates first authorized by the Naval Act of 1794. It had authorized the purchase of twelve ships which we may group as sloops-of-war, and the acquisition of not more than ten galleys for use in shallow southern waters. It had appropriated almost two million dollars for the Navy or in which the Navy was to share.

Considering their narrow majority the Federalists had been fairly effective. On one point the arch-Federalists had gone beyond their rank and file. That was the matter of pushing for sixteen ships. They got but twelve, the cut being partly for practical reasons since it might have been hard to find that many suitable ships already built, partly because the Federalist farmers were becoming restive under the load of these large appropriations, and partly—said Manning J. Dauer—because the Hamiltonians thought it not worth a serious fight. They privately hoped to get ships from Great Britain if needed.[47]

The key to the understanding of the naval program this far in the session was the ease with which the Republicans got rid of the explicit authority to convoy, in the original Senate Bill to acquire ships. Outside of half a dozen or so who were ready to declare war at any time, all hands thought of the Navy as a Navy solely for defense, what one might call the "one-sixteenth Ocean Navy," intended to operate only on the continental shelf, in the westernmost waters of the North Atlantic. On the basis of "scattered returns" of the reaction to the "X. Y. Z. Affair" they felt justified in moving this far. These reactions were so far mostly urban. When the full returns came in, with the country in full cry against France, they were to take another long look at their naval policy and change it to meet the mood of the time.

NOTES FROM PAGES 139 TO 148

1. Hamilton to Pickering, 17 March 1798, Alexander Hamilton, *Works,* ed. Henry Cabot Lodge, 12v. (New York, 1904), X, 275–278. He wrote a similar letter, in more general terms, to Senator Theodore Sedgwick of Massachusetts, *ibid.*, X, 178.
2. Wolcott, Jr., to Washington, 12 Nov. 1795, George Gibbs, *Memoirs of the Administration of Washington and John Adams,* 2v. (New York, 1846), I, 284. Hereafter cited: Gibbs, *Memoirs.*
3. King to Pickering, 8 December 1797, Rufus King, *The Life and Correspondence of Rufus King,* ed. C. R. King, 6v. (New York, 1894–1900), II, 252. Hereafter cited: King, *Life and Correspondence.*
4. 20–22 March 1798, 5 Cong., 2 Sess.,

Annals of the Congress, 1789–1824, ed. J. Gales and W. W. Seaton (Washington, 1834–1856), 525–528. Hereafter cited: *Annals*. Dates, all in 1798, will be given where useful to search.
5. 22 March, *ibid.*, 1296.
6. 26, 27 March, *ibid.*, 1313–1316, 1319.
7. 28 March, *ibid.*, 1333.
8. 9 April, *ibid.*, 1383–1384.
9. 12, 13 April, *ibid.*, 1412, 1414.
10. 13 April, *ibid.*
11. 17 April, *ibid.*, 1427–1439.
12. *Ibid.*, 1440.
13. *Ibid.*, 543, 549, 551.
14. *Ibid.*, 3726–3727.
15. Washington to Pickering, 6 May 1798, George Washington, *Writings*, ed. John C. Fitzpatrick, 39v. (Washington, 1931–1944), XXXVI, 253–254.
16. There were successive postponements on 26, 28, 29 March and 2 April. *Annals*, 530–531, 532, 533, 534.
17. Manning J. Dauer, *The Adams Federalists* (Baltimore, 1953), 146–147.
18. Sedgwick to King, 9 April 1798, King, *Life and Correspondence*, II, 313.
19. 26, 27 March *Annals*, 531–532.
20. Bingham to King, 2 April 1798, King, *Life and Correspondence*, II, 298.
21. Pickering to King, 2 April 1798, *ibid.*, II, 296–297.
22. Philadelphia *Aurora*, quoted in New York *Argus*, 4 April 1798.
23. Irving Brant, *James Madison, Father of the Constitution* (Indianapolis, 1950), 457.
24. Wolcott, Jr., to Frederick Wolcott, 10 April 1798, Gibbs, *Memoirs*, II, 45.
25. 9 April, *Annals*, 537–538.
26. *Ibid.*, 1384.
27. McHenry to Sewall, 9 April 1798, *American State Papers*, ed. Walter Lowrie and Matthew St. Clair Clarke, 38v. (Washington, 1832–1861), Class VI, *Naval Affairs*, I, 34.
28. Jefferson to Madison, 12 April 1798, Jefferson papers, Library of Congress. "I am told the Opposition Party of our House have lately had a Caucus, at which They agreed upon strong internal defensive Measures; when We get upon Vessels of War for the protection of our Commerce I fear They will give Way." Hindman to King, 12 April 1798, King, *Life and Correspondence*, II, 314.
29. New York *Argus*, 13 April 1798.
30. The debate on convoying, 18–20 April, *Annals*, 1440–1519; Allen's remarks quoted from *ibid.*, 1476, 1482, 1483, 1485.

Some of the Federalists thought Gallatin was a paid agent of the French Directory, already implicated in one attempt to start a revolution in America, and always linked with French espionage. When elected to the United States Senate some years earlier he had been refused a seat on technical (and debatable) grounds of insufficient residence in the United States. The shocking tone of the attacks on him quoted above may have been deliberately intended to provoke him to some violent response for which he could have been expelled from the House of Representatives. Later there was to be an attempt to amend the Constitution in order to change the requirements for holding federal office, an attempt generally believed to be aimed at disqualifying Gallatin.
31. Voting table in Dauer, *The Adams Federalists*, 304–309.
32. 19, 20 April, *Annals*, 1462–1466, 1519–1521.
33. Voting table in Dauer, *The Adams Federalists*, 304–309.
34. 23 April, *Annals*, 1522.
35. 23-24 April, *ibid.*, 545–547.
36. *Ibid.*, 3722–3723.
37. Gibbs, *Memoirs*, II, 63–64, 65.
38. New York *Argus*, 1 June 1798. Howard Irving Chapelle, *The History of the American Sailing Navy; the Ships and Their Development* (New York, 1949), 140–178, includes an account of the ships acquired in this way.
39. John Adams to the Congress, 5 Feb. 1798, *State Papers and Publick Documents of the United States*, 2d ed., 10v. (Boston, 1817), III, 439.
40. 26 March, *Annals*, 1312–1313.
41. 3, 9 April, *ibid.*, 535, 537.
42. 25, 26, 27 April, *ibid.*, 548, 549, 550.
43. 1, 2 May, *ibid.*, 1563, 1567.
44. See remarks of Thomas Pinckney, 11 April, *ibid.*, 1398.
45. *Ibid.*, 3727.
46. 7, 13 June, *ibid.*, 1876, 1925; *ibid.*, 3743.
47. Dauer, *The Adams Federalists*, 147–149.

XI

The Department of the Navy

By the spring of 1798 the naval business of the Department of War had become a large part of the department's work. A similar burden fell also on the Department of the Treasury which took care of contracting and disbursing for all military requirements, including the Navy's.[1] Even while Alexander Hamilton was Secretary of the Treasury he found the naval duties onerous, and when he was preparing to retire he wrote to President George Washington to tell him the Treasury's part of the work, if well done, could engage all of the time of one person. He thought an officer should be appointed for that purpose in the Treasury.[2] If a fraction of the work troubled such an able administrator as Hamilton one could be sure lesser men would find it very difficult.

When members of the House of Representatives began to complain of what they regarded as the excessive costs of building the frigates *United States, Constitution,* and *Constellation,* in the summer of 1797, Representative John Swanwick of Philadelphia tried to explain the costs. The country could build merchant vessels economically, he said, therefore the high cost of war vessels must have been caused by waste and extravagance. In his opinion "the extra expense had been owing to the want of some regular establishment to overlook the business."[3] Swanwick's view is of interest here because he was a Philadelphia merchant who usually voted with the House Republicans, but who joined with the Federalists on maritime questions. His viewpoint was changing in 1797. Earlier in the year he had argued against separating the appropriations for the Army and the Navy.[4]

There can be no doubt there were defects in the arrangement up to 1798. Illustrations could be multiplied but a few will suffice. In January 1798 when the House of Representatives was debating the first naval appropriation of that year, a number of Republicans seized the opportunity to denounce the War Department for mismanaging the naval construction program. The accusations were made by the most competent and aggressive men in the Republican group—Albert Gallatin of Pennsylvania, John Nicholas of Virginia, and Edward Livingston of New York. The ablest of the pro-Navy Federalists commented on the charge but did not defend the Department. Among them was Robert Goodloe Harper of South Carolina, who admitted the frigates "had cost by far too much." Samuel Sewall of Massachusetts, chairman of the Committee on the Protection of Commerce (hereafter called the Naval Committee) spoke of "astonishing . . . errors . . . in estimates." Thomas Pinckney of South Carolina (more famous as the able negotiator of "Pinckney's Treaty" with Spain) called the construction program "an expensive business." [5]

On another occasion Albert Gallatin, who was well qualified as an expert in public finance, described the War Department accounts as poorly kept, and was not contradicted.[6] On the very next day Gallatin found an error in War Department arithmetic which required correction and a bill under consideration had to be "reengrossed." [7]

The nephew of Secretary of State Timothy Pickering had a contract to provision *Constitution,* then being rigged, armed and manned at Boston. In a complaint to his uncle he said he found the business almost impossible to manage, owing to the incompetence of the public officials. He had bought "wet provisions" for the frigate four months before and they were still in storage. All the bread would be ready in a few days but "no one has orders to receive or deliver."

> Till there is some system—a Department, and proper agents under & dependent on it I despair of our receiving any benefit, at least, from *this* Frigate. I believe there has been a Scandalous waste of property in building her; owing, I conceive, to the *entire ignorance* in the Agent of all *naval* affairs.
>
> *Economy* of the public money at any time is almost a phenomenon; but where *inattention* was combined with *unskillfulness,* we could not expect a particle of it.[8]

The Navy agent at Boston was Stephen Higginson, a wealthy merchant with much experience in maritime matters, and too powerful a Federalist to be lightly dismissed. In these same weeks *he* was complaining of the incompetence of the commander of *Constitution,* Captain Samuel Nicholson.[9] It is now of no consequence to try to place the "blame"; what is significant is the apparent lack of supervision of the work of the contractors, the Navy agent, and Captain Nicholson. They were receiving no guidance from above. In addition to these illustrations one could describe unaccountable delays, bungled launchings, and faulty guns.[10]

Next to the President, the man responsible for the program was the

Secretary of War, James McHenry. He had been a practicing physician and, as an army officer, had served on Washington's staff during the War for Independence.[11] Not a word against his character or personality has survived, but he was not a huge success in the Department of War.

His predecessors in the office were Henry Knox of Massachusetts (1789–1795) and Timothy Pickering of Massachusetts (1795–1796). When Pickering was appointed to be Secretary of State, McHenry was President Washington's fourth choice for the vacancy, it having been offered to Charles Cotesworth Pinckney of South Carolina, Edward Carrington of Virginia, and Governor John Eager Howard of Maryland. When the offer was made to McHenry he was urged by Hugh Williamson of North Carolina to take it, in a most indiscreet letter:

> Knox, as you know, was considered to be a Man who went on a most expensive Scale. The follies of a gambling wife were passed to the Debit of her Husband, in Addition to his own—no great Stock of Talents . . .
> Since [Pickering] has been advanced, Terror has seized the public mind from the apprehension that we should be reduced to a State of insolvency by Genl. Wayne or Govr. [Henry] Lee [of Virginia] in the Character of Secy. of War.

Both Wayne and Lee had been mentioned for the office and both seemed to want it. Since most of the public money went through the office the people would be relieved to know McHenry had accepted it.[12] McHenry could not help being flattered at being chosen above Light Horse Harry or Mad Anthony, if only as an evangel of economy. He accepted the appointment, was easily confirmed by the Senate, and took the oath on 8 February 1796. It may be added, as the naval spending went ever higher, McHenry was never once referred to in the Congress as an economy-minded official.

His administration did not give general satisfaction. His first superior, President Washington, thrice sent him veiled reprimands, once for slowness of action, once for careless handling of confidential papers, and—when Washington had retired but had then accepted the appointment of Lieutenant General and commander-in-chief—for not answering a letter.[13] Harper, the naval champion of the House of Representatives, urged Hamilton to accept the post of Secretary of War. Although he had no authority to make an offer, he was sure a change would be acceptable to the then President, John Adams. If Hamilton would accept, "Mr. McHenry would give way: and there is no difference in opinion among the federal party on the absolute necessity of his doing so."[14]

McHenry continued in office until dismissed by President Adams in

1800 for maintaining a close political liaison with Hamilton, after Adams and Hamilton had become bitter political opponents. Quite apart from politics his best friends had become McHenry's severest critics, privately and to his face. In 1798 and 1799 some very harsh words were written of his abilities. Secretary of the Treasury Oliver Wolcott, Jr., wrote to Hamilton, "the arrangements of the War Department are all defective," [15] and to President Adams, "The Secretary of War . . . has more affairs on hand than he can attend to." [16] McHenry's beloved leader, Hamilton, wrote a series of critiques to leaders of the Federalists: "McHenry . . . is loaded beyond his strength," [17] he "is wholly insufficient for his place, with the additional misfortune of not having himself the least suspicion of the fact . . . This has been long observed, and has been more than once mentioned to the President [Adams] by members of Congress." [18] Hamilton by this time was a Major General and Inspector General of the Army. He finally wrote to McHenry, gently but firmly, to tell him his "want of a proper organization" coud not "fail to enfeeble and disorder every part of the service." [19]

In 1799 Senator Theodore Sedgwick of Massachusetts, a stout pillar of the Hamiltonian Federalists, thought War Department delays were "shameful and almost unpardonable"; he put the blame equally on McHenry and the President.[20] On the floor of the House, Representative Samuel Smith of Maryland, McHenry's own state, complained strongly of the War Department's "dilatoriness of conduct," [21] in carrying out several Army acts.

By early 1798 Secretary McHenry himself thought there ought to be a change. He did not think himself "insufficient" for his job, but he did think himself overworked. Accordingly in March 1798 he suggested to Sewall the separation of the naval business from his Department. Sewall's Naval Committee then brought in a report and a resolution recommending the establishment of the office of Commissioner of Marine in the Department of War.[22] The Commissioner would have charge of all naval business of the Department.[23] Sewall's report mentioned "the apparently enormous expenses, and the unaccountable delays" of the naval construction program, and remarked, "The Department of War, as at present established, is unsuitable to this purpose, especially considering its stationary situation, and how much it is occupied by numerous cares of a nature very different." [24] The Report was referred to the Committee of the Whole on the State of the Union.[25]

No action was taken in the House on the recommendation to establish a Commissioner of Marine and, after several weeks went by, the matter was brought up in the Senate by William Bingham of Pennsylvania. On 2 April he moved consideration of "the propriety of instituting a separate Executive department for the purpose of superintending and regulating the various objects connected with the Naval Establishment of the United States." A committee was appointed on the next day to bring in a bill to that effect, consisting of Bingham, Benjamin Goodhue of Massachusetts (chairman of the Senate Naval Committee), and Henry Tazewell of Virginia.[26] Bingham and Goodhue were Federalists, Tazewell a Republican. They reported a Bill on the eleventh, which came to a vote on the sixteenth. The handful of Senate Republicans tried to put a time limit on the duration of the Department but lost that motion 10–15. The Bill then passed by a vote of 19–6.[27] Four of the six opponents were the Senators from Virginia and Kentucky. The other two represented North Carolina and New Hampshire.

Downstairs in Congress Hall the House of Representatives did not get around to discussing the Senate Bill until 25 April. As usual, the Bill was first considered in Committee of the Whole, but not an amendment was made in that stage of debate. When the Committee of the Whole reported its agreement to the House the routine motion to order the Bill to Third Reading was made. Third Reading, it will be remembered, was the occasion of voting whether a Bill should finally pass. It was at this point the strategy of the opponents was revealed, when the Republicans then launched a full scale attack against the motion to put the Bill on Third Reading. This was an infrequent but not unknown bit of parliamentary tactics. If the motion was beaten the Bill would be left in suspense, the question of its passing would never be voted on, and it would die with the end of the Congress.

In this debate the case for the Bill was presented by Sewall, Smith of Maryland, Harrison Gray Otis of Massachusetts, and Harper. Their views can be summarized as follow. The Republicans had complained expenses were high because the responsible officials lacked knowledge of the subject. The War Department had so much to do it could not properly attend to the naval business which, indeed, was likely to become greater. The Congress had appropriated so much that the office, therefore, had become necessary because an expert could save much. The new Department's budget would be smaller than the office expenses of the War Department ($18,250) because the two Departments could use the same accountant. Actually the only additional expense would be the salary of the new Secretary, which was intended to be fixed at $3500—one-third of one per cent of the expenses of the Navy, if the Navy cost a million dollars a year. It was necessary to have a Navy Department in order to impress Europe. If it proved to be useless it could always be abolished. It was too much to expect one man to be competent in directing both the Army and the Navy. The question should not be considered as a question of defense policy, it was, rather, a question of economy. The country should get an expert to do the job, just as individuals do in managing their own affairs. It would not create naval business; that business had already been created by the Congress. After all, the establishment of a marine department was the common practice of nations.

The opposition was chiefly voiced by Gallatin, Livingston, and a New York agrarian Federalist, John Williams. They were aided by Nathaniel Macon, Joseph McDowell, and Robert Williams of North Carolina, and by Thomas Claiborne of Virginia. They said, in substance: The Army and Navy were not large enough to need separate Departments. If help was needed, more clerks could be hired. The establishment could not be an economy move because any increase of officials increased expenses, and every institution had a tendency to aggrandize itself. The revenue of the United States was not large enough to support the kind of a Navy which needed this kind of administration. Experts, if necessary, could be added to the Department of War. When the supporters of the proposal argued that it would lead to enlargement of the Navy they gave a good argument against the proposal, since a large Navy would never be wanted. A construction expert was not wanted because the new ships authorized in 1798 were all to be purchased, not built by the government as the three frigates were being built. As to the effect of the establishment on Europe, mere noise and declamation would not alarm an enemy. With regard to Europe, the only interest of the Congress should be the interest of the United States. After all, all large-Navy countries had unpayable national debts. The Bill to establish a Navy Department provided the nucleus of a bureaucracy because, in addition to the Secretary, it proposed the hiring of a principal clerk and others.[28]

Livingston's speech in opposition was a notable *tour-de-force*. He feared a ship builder might be appointed Secretary of the Navy, and he "could not think such a person fit to be one of the great council of the nation; . . . it must be recollected that the person who holds this office will become one of the counsellors of the President on all great concerns." (He obviously thought of a ship builder as a man possessed of manual skills only, practicing a trade by rule-of-thumb.) Livingston continued, if the country must have specialists for these jobs there would be no end to it, the Secretary of War "must be a perfect engineer" and know how to make arms. Next the country would have "commissioners of gun-barrels and of ramrods." Was this the common practice of Europe? If so it was "a bad one, as the navies of those countries had proved the ruin of them." The Republicans in opposing the establishment of the new Department were accused of being opposed to the defense of the country. This argument, he replied, now came up on every issue, and would probably be brought into a debate on the authorization of "a new post office." [29]

Tempers being what they were in that Age of Rage, the 1790s, some of the debaters used personalities freely. Otis said he expected Gallatin to oppose every defense measure. He thought they should argue the question as briefly as possible and let the minority call for the yeas and nays and "find themselves in a minority as usual." [30] McDowell, on the other side, then devoted a good many words to Otis's skill as a calumniator,[31] and Thomas Claiborne invited the majority to expel the minority and go on alone.[32]

Eventually they got to a vote on the question whether the Bill should be ordered to Third Reading, and the motion was carried 47–41. Third Reading was set for the next day, at which time the Bill passed 42–27.[33] "An Act to establish an Executive Department, to be denominated the Department of the Navy," signed by President Adams on 30 April, had five sections, as follow: (1) Established the Department, with the Secretary at its head, and stated the naval duties. (2) Provided for the principal Clerk and other clerks. (3) Authorized the removal of the naval records from the Department of War. (4) Fixed the salary of the Secretary at three thousand dollars a year, and the salaries of the clerks at the same rates as those paid in the Treasury Department. (5) Divested the War Department of its hitherto existing naval powers.[34]

The key vote, the one on whether the Bill should be ordered by the House of Representatives to Third Reading, revealed the sectional alignment on the question of a separate naval establishment (see p. 157).[35]

The centers of frontier expansion and land speculation, New York, Pennsylvania, Virginia, North Carolina, Georgia, Kentucky, Tennessee, and Vermont, accounted for thirty-four of the forty-one votes against the founding of the Department. To men engaged in selling land to the western pioneers, and to the frontiersmen themselves, public benefactions of the maritime trade seemed to be a distraction from the business at hand. It is also worth while to notice the votes of the three states with pressing Indian problems, Kentucky, Tennessee, and Georgia. They gave not one vote aye. They rarely voted aye on a Navy bill, except on a motion to cut or otherwise harass an appropriation bill.

Another matter, one of "housekeeping," was taken care of by the passage of an act to allow the Secretary of the Navy to exercise the franking privilege.[36]

The next step was the appointment of a Secretary of the Navy. The President's first choice was ex-Senator George Cabot of Massachusetts.

Vote on Ordering Navy Department Bill to Third Reading, 25 April, 1798

	Ayes	*Noes*
New England:		
New Hampshire	3	0
Vermont	1	1
Massachusetts	10	2
Connecticut	6	0
Rhode Island	2	0
Total	22	3
Middle States:		
New York	4	4
New Jersey	4	1
Pennsylvania	2	5
Delaware	1	0
Maryland	6	1
Total	17	11
South:		
Virginia	4	11
North Carolina	1	8
South Carolina	3	3
Georgia	0	2
Total	8	24
West:		
Kentucky	0	2
Tennessee	0	1
Total	0	3
Grand Total	47	41

His appointment was confirmed by the Senate and given out to the press but he declined.[37] The next choice was Benjamin Stoddert of Maryland.[38] Fisher Ames, formerly leader of the Federalists in the House of Representatives, but then in retirement in Massachusetts, wrote to Secretary Pickering,

> I cannot be insensible to the difficulty of selecting the best characters for the Navy Secretaryship, as the compensation is inadequate. Some of your countrymen know the weight of the services and toils which the heads of the departments have to sustain . . .
>
> P.S. I have seen Mr. Stoddert, of Georgetown, but I cannot believe he will accept; he appeared to be a man of good sense [39] . . .

Stoddert still appears at this distance of time to have been "a man of good sense"; because of or in spite of this (as Ames seemed to imply) he accepted the call to duty. He was a combat veteran of the War for Independence and had been wounded in the Battle of the Brandywine.

He left the Continental Army with the rank of Major. Charles W. Goldsborough, Chief Clerk of the Department of the Navy for over forty years beginning in 1798, said Stoddert was a man of integrity, discrimination, and industry.[40] In private life he was an importer, and knew ships, which was about as good a preparation for the job as could be had at that time.[41]

The new Secretary took over his office at 139 Walnut Street, Philadelphia, on 24 June[42] (Gardner Weld Allen, *Our Naval War with France,* said he took charge on 18 June.)[43] He knew he was "in business"; for a fortnight he had been hunted down by job-seekers.[44]

Thus was born the Department of the Navy in the midst of a national quarrel with an erstwhile ally. This creation was of the utmost importance to the history of the United States because it "institutionalized" the public fleet and made it as near to a permanent national institution as human beings could devise. This point of the permanence of the Navy explains why the opponents of the Federalist naval policy so vigorously fought the Bill to establish the Department. It has always been much harder to kill an established agency of high rank in the federal government than it has been to starve a subsidiary organ. It was now the country's consensus that the Navy was here to stay. Another important effect of the "Act to establish an Executive Department to be denominated the Department of the Navy" was that it dignified the Navy, making its head a high officer of state, a step above the place which would have been held in the public eye by a "Commissioner of Marine" under the Secretary of War.

Probably a Department of the Navy would have been founded sooner or later. Why it was founded in 1798 rather than later requires an explanation. On the basis of the contemporary evidence one can only agree with Robert Greenhalgh Albion that the "inadequacy" of the Secretary of War made the separation necessary.[45] With the Navy in the opening phase of a maritime war, efficiency was demanded.

NOTES FROM PAGES 150 TO 158

1. Coxe to Hamilton, 22 Dec. 1794, *American State Papers,* ed. Walter Lowrie and Matthew St. Clair Clarke, 38v. (Washington, 1832–1861), Class VI, *Naval Affairs,* I, 9–10. Hereafter cited: *ASP: Naval Affairs.*
2. Hamilton to Washington, 2 Dec. 1794, Alexander Hamilton, *Works,* ed. Henry Cabot Lodge, 12v. (New York, 1904), X, 79–81.
3. 5 Cong., 1 Sess., 24 June 1797, *Annals of the Congress, 1789–1824,* ed. J. Gales and W. W. Seaton, 42v. (Washington, 1834–1856), 381. Hereafter cited: *Annals.* All citations hereafter are to 5 Cong., 2 Sess., unless otherwise noted. Dates are given where they may be helpful to search. All dates of the *Annals* are 1798 unless otherwise noted.
4. 4 Cong., 2 Sess., 31 Jan. 1797, *ibid.,* 2051.
5. 5 Cong., 2 Sess., 11 Jan. 1798, *ibid.,* 821–828.
6. 26 April, *ibid.,* 1556–1557.

7. 27 April, *ibid.*, 1559.
8. Williams to Pickering, 31 May 1798, Dudley W. Knox, ed., *Naval Documents Related to the Quasi-war between the United States and France*, 7v. (Washington, 1935–1938), I, 97.
9. Higginson to Pickering, 6 June 1798, *ibid.*, I, 106–107.
10. Robert Greenhalgh Albion, "The first days of the Navy department," *Military Affairs*, XII (Spring, 1948), 1–11. Hereafter cited: Albion, "First days."
11. R. J. Purcell, "James McHenry," *Dictionary of American Biography*.
12. Williamson to McHenry, 27 Jan. 1796, Bernard C. Steiner, *The Life and Correspondence of James McHenry* (Cleveland, 1907), 164–165. Hereafter cited: Steiner, *McHenry*.
13. *Ibid.*, 181, 185n., 290n.–291n.
14. Harper to Hamilton, 27 April 1798, Hamilton papers, Library of Congress.
15. Wolcott, Jr., to Hamilton, 10 Oct. 1798, George Gibbs, *Memoirs of the Administrations of Washington and John Adams*, 2v. (New York, 1846), II, 101.
16. Wolcott, Jr., to John Adams, 13 Aug. 1798, *ibid.*, II, 106.
17. Hamilton to Sedgwick, 29 Aug. 1798, Hamilton, *Works*, X, 318.
18. Hamilton to Washington, 29 July 1798, *ibid.*, X, 302.
19. Hamilton to McHenry, 16 Sept. 1799, *ibid.*, VII, 126.
20. Sedgwick to King, 26 July 1799, Rufus King, *The Life and Correspondence of Rufus King*, ed. C. R. King, 6v. (New York, 1894–1900), III, 69–70.
21. 5 Cong., 2 Sess., 2 July 1798, *Annals*, 2078.
22. Albion, "First days," XII, 2; McHenry's request was dated 8 March 1798 in Steiner, *McHenry*, 302; *ASP: Naval Affairs*, I, 33–34.
23. 8 March, *Annals*, 1246.
24. *Ibid.*
25. *Ibid.*, 1248.
26. 2, 3 April, *ibid.*, 534–535.
27. 16 April, *ibid.*, 541–542.
28. 25 April, *ibid.*, 1545–1552.
29. *Ibid.*, 1552–1553. Perhaps Livingston's low estimate of shipbuilders was influenced by the behavior of Clement Humphreys in administering a public beating to Benjamin Franklin Bache, the vitriolic editor of the Philadelphia *Aurora* in April 1797; Clement Humphreys was the son of naval constructor Joshua Humphreys. J. B. McMaster, *A History of the People of the United States*, 5v. (New York, 1883–1913), II, 323.
30. *Ibid.*, 1547–1548.
31. *Ibid.*, 1549.
32. *Ibid.*, 1548–1549.
33. 25, 26 April, *ibid.*, 1553–1554.
34. *Ibid.*, 3725.
35. *Ibid.*, 1553–1554.
36. *Ibid.*, 3743.
37. Charles Oscar Paullin, "Early Naval Administration under the Constitution," *Proceedings of the United States Naval Institute*, XXXII (1906), 1014–1016. (Hereafter cited: Paullin, "Early Naval Administration"); Philadelphia *Gazette of the United States*, 4 May 1798.
38. New York *Commercial Advertiser*, 26 May 1798.
39. Ames to Pickering, 4 June 1798, Fisher Ames, *Works*, ed. Seth Ames, 2v. (Boston, 1854), I, 229.
40. Paullin, "Early Naval Administration," XXXII, 1014–1016.
41. Albion, "First days," XII, 3.
42. New York *Commercial Advertiser*, 25 June 1798.
43. Gardner Weld Allen, *Our Naval War with France* (Boston, 1909), 54.
44. Hindman to McHenry, 13 June 1798, Steiner, *McHenry*, 303.
45. Albion, "First days," XII, 1.

XII

A Navy for Offense

May–July 1798

In the later days of March and through the month of April 1798 the naval legislation of the Congress was intended to provide a defense of the coast of the United States and its nearby waters. The increase of naval power in those weeks was the response of the Congress to the "X. Y. Z. Affair," and the Congress was encouraged to move ahead by its own feelings and by the outcry which came from the principal seaports. However, it appears to have underestimated the strength of the national revulsion against France. In the early weeks of May the true temper of the country became plain and the navy-minded Members discovered they could go even farther in building a navy.

An important cause of the increase of popular anger was the publication in April of material sent to President John Adams from Paris on 27 January by the Commissioners. These papers occupied forty-one columns in the *Annals of the Congress*. The most infuriating part was a French order, approved as law on 18 January, which proscribed all British property from the seas and barred from any French port every vessel which on its present voyage touched at any British port.[1] But even before this the fury had been steadily growing.[2] The peak which was reached in May seems not to have been the effect of events of that month but was the climax of a delayed build-up of public feeling, delayed because of the slowness of the communications of the time.[3]

Public indignation was written into addresses composed and approved by public meetings in various parts of the country, and sent to the President. Abigail Adams, the President's wife, appeared to think the most important of these were the ones which came from the merchants of the principal cities.[4] The President must have spent most of his time in May, June, and July 1798 writing answers to the addresses,[5] and the tone of his answers undoubtedly helped to whip up the excitement. A selected thirty-two were published in John Adams's *Works,* of which six made specific references to the need for naval protection of American commerce. A widely quoted one was his reply to the address of the young men of Boston (22 May), "To arms, then, my young friends,—to arms, especially by sea." He also assured the students of Harvard, "your country will have armies and navies in which you may secure your own honor." [6]

The opposition feared the effect of Adam's fiery statements. Vice President Thomas Jefferson thought them designed to help the passage of legislation which was opposed by the Republicans. Even Timothy Pickering, after he became an arch-enemy of Adams, credited the national spirit of resistance more to John Adams than to any other one man.[7] James Madison thought Adams's remarks showed a shockingly monarchical bent.[8] And the Boston *Chronicle* satirized the youth of Boston who claimed they wished to defend their country. The youth of Boston had said they numbered 1500 but the frigate *Constitution* was lying in Boston harbor only half manned.[9]

Alexander Hamilton, practicing law and Federalist politics in New York, did what he could to direct the popular emotion. He gave to the press a series of letters entitled "The Stand," signed "Titus Manlius," beginning 30 March. These letters identified the Jeffersonian Republicans with subversion.[10] Letter number six, which appeared late in April, called for the establishment of foundries and arsenals, the creation of "a respectable naval force," permission to arm merchant ships with power to capture or sink their attackers, using the infant Navy to convoy and to capture all privateers within twenty leagues of the coast. This, he said, would be called war. It would be war, of a limited kind. How long would it last? For the duration of the latest French decrees.[11]

Other leaders poured gasoline on the flames. Fisher Ames, the former leader of the Federalists in the House of Representatives, pleaded with his successor in the House: it was "too late to preach peace" and to say war was not wanted. The United States must have a defensive war, whether it was declared or not, or else must submit to the French.[12] On 10 May Speaker Jonathan Dayton of New Jersey announced to the House of Representatives a startling bit of news—the French armed forces were being prepared for the invasion of the United States and not for an attack on the British Isles. This intelligence was "confirmed" by the Federalist organ, the Philadelphia *Gazette of the United States,* on 9 June, the confirmation being based on "authentic information" from Europe.[13] "A Senator of the United States" burst into martial song in the same paper.

COLUMBIA'S CALL

* * *

Sons of Columbia, arise!
Your country calls, for war prepare;
Equip your fleet, to arms! to arms!
Protection
Give, liberty,
Your property,
Lives, and all, all that's dear.[14]

President Adams gave the indignation a theological base by the proclamation of a day of national fast, set for 9 May. On that day the administration press abstained from publication but not the hottest of opposition papers, Benjamin Franklin Bache's Philadelphia *Aurora,* which appeared as usual.[15] After reading a good many of the sermons preached on the national fast day, Bache commented on them by saying he could now see the reason for the proclamation; to give Federalist divines an occasion for political preaching; "rancorous fulminations and party invectives issued from most of the pulpits." [16]

Bache's *Aurora* tried hard to sweep back the rising tide of public anger, usually by the technique of publishing pseudonymous letters or statements which were contrary to the trend. "A Virginian . . . who has been in Congress" said the dilemma offered to the people was a choice of war with France or war with Britain. If true, it would be better to side with France because the road of the 1770s was still open, and the Royal Navy had been unable to keep the French out of America then.[17] A ballad in the guise of an ode, signed by "Jonathan Pindar," told of a farmer who went whaling at the coaxing of a sailor, and drowned. It ran to a hundred lines of which the last four were

Thus, if to gratify the Tar
Ye farmers, ye engage in War,
Thousands will surely find their graves,
Like honest PLOUGHSHARE in the waves.[18]

"Nestor" claimed the excitement was artificial and contrived with the aim to centralize the power of government. "A standing army, a navy, immense debt and extravagant taxes are admirable instruments to bow the neck to obedience." [19] The letter of "a Virginian to his Member of the Congress" said the naval defense of American commerce was impossible because both France and Britain despoiled it. Protection would require a navy equal to the navies of France and Britain combined.[20]

A congressional uproar was created when Federalist Representative Josiah Parker of Virginia gingerly presented a heated "petition" from some of his Republican constituents who were members of Captain Bernard Magnien's Company of Grenadiers of Portsmouth, Virginia. The militiamen opposed the use of a standing army and an "expensive" navy for defense because the militia could do the job dry-shod, and such regular and expensive establishment lent themselves to "domestic subjugation, slavery, and ruin." [21] Captain Magnien was accused of being "a foreigner from St. Domingo" [22] (what we would call a fifth-columnist), but his Congressman "cleared" him with a letter-to-the-editor identifying Magnien as a veteran of Rochambeau's army and "a respectable character." [23] The democratic leanings of this and other militia units reminded responsible public officials of the political tendencies of the American militia of the 1770s and—with Jacobinism abroad in the world—they shivered at the phantasm.[24]

On the other side of the political fence fears ran deeper, and with reason, for this was the season of the germination of the ugly and un-American Sedition Act. Jefferson's letters to his most intimate correspondents painted a somber picture of the boiling passions of the moment but usually closed on a note of hope for the survival of republicanism. While he sat at the head of the Senate, the ablest of the Virginians, one by one, rode home from Philadelphia to Virginia, or went over to the Federalists.[25] Albert Gallatin of Pennsylvania, the House Republican leader, like a modern Saint Sebastian, stood almost alone to receive the Federalist arrows.

The Republican attempts to sweep back the sea of popular wrath were useless, of course. Probably the Federalist work to stir up excitement was unnecessary, although it heightened the pitch. There is plenty of evidence of the reality of the popular sense of outrage, evidence of simultaneous acts of protest over a broad area—toasts at public dinners, private letters from all quarters, and public enthusiasm for the presidential family.[26] The newspaper advertisements reflected the new spirit. In April and May the following advertisements appeared in the Philadelphia *Gazette of the United States* for the first time: a military academy directed by a British ex-officer; military colors, flags, drums, gunpowder, cannon, muskets, pistols, cartridge papers, Steuben's infantry drill regulations and copies of the federal Militia Act for sale; a new private militia company, the "Federal Grenadiers"; copies of the "X. Y. Z. Papers" for sale; a book attacking ex-Minister James Monroe's apologia for his discountenanced mission to France.

During these feverish weeks the administration was at long last preparing to send some ships to sea. Secretary of War James McHenry had to draft the Captains' instructions and, as usual, turned to Hamilton for advice. He wrote on 12 May, saying he hoped to be able to send out one or two of the great frigates and a converted merchantman within a week. What should their instructions be? There would be no Secretary of the Navy in office in time to undertake this matter. McHenry's principal concern was to avoid the appearance of warlike provocation by the executive branch.[27] Hamilton replied he foresaw the necessity of congressional action. He was not certain the President could do more than convoy American merchants, repel force with force (but not to capture) "& stop hostilities in our waters, including a marine league from our coasts." Any more than this would be reprisals and would require the "sanction of that department which is to declare or make war." He thought the President should exercise "no doubtful authority." Since the House of Representatives differed on the question of the President's powers in such affairs, it might be well to send a message to the Congress stating the limits to which he was confident he had the power.[28]

On the same day as Hamilton's reply, Senator Uriah Tracy of Connecticut was writing to Hamilton of the congressional mood. He told of a bill to be introduced in the Senate to void the French treaties, to authorize the capture of French armed vessels within forty leagues of the coast, to authorize convoys, and to instruct merchant captains not to allow the French to search them. But, he said, "the idea was too strong for our Committee." Perhaps with "immense labor" they could "drive thro' the Senate a bill authorizing instructions to capture a cruiser that has unjustifiably taken one of our Vessels on our Coast.—" But the treaty business would have to be postponed until the American Commissioners left France. He did not "despair of the Common Wealth" but it was very difficult to get things done. The best men were timid and the worst men very active. Mutual trust among the Federalists was shaken.[29]

Tracy was a chronic croaker. On the next day the Senate's naval committee (of which he had spoken), headed by Benjamin Goodhue of Massachusetts, reported a bill to clear the coast of armed French intruders. It went through handily in five days. The preamble showed it was aimed specifically at the French. Republican attempts to delete the reference to the French, and to postpone action until the last possible news came from the Commissioners in Paris, were crushed in succession by identical votes of 7–16. The vote on passage was the same, 16–7.[30] All Senators from states north of the Chesapeake and south of Cape Fear voted aye. The Senators from Virginia, North Carolina, Kentucky, and Tennessee voted no. The only reflection of the matter in the press was a plaintive gloss on naval history in Bache's paper: British herring boats at Falmouth numbered three hundred before the war with France. Now they numbered but twenty. Of what value was a navy? [31]

While the Senate was preparing instructions for the United States Navy, the House was at work on a similar project. French privateers were at that moment reported to be prowling on the coast. On 22 May Samuel Sitgreaves of Pennsylvania offered four resolutions. (1) Armed merchants might attack and destroy any French cruiser which attacked them for search of seizure. (2) Public vessels might do the same to any Frenchman which insulted American merchant ships. (3) Either private or public ships might retake any captured American ship and take or destroy the captor. (4) The United States Navy might take any armed Frenchman "within _____ of the shore." [32] The Republicans delayed action with parliamentary technicalities for two days while Bache gloomily equated the resolution with a declaration of war,[33] but, after a very acrimonious debate, the resolutions were referred to the House Naval Committee, headed by Samuel Sewall of Massachusetts.[34]

Nothing more was heard of these resolutions because at that moment the Senate's Bill to clear the coast came down stairs and was seen to answer pretty much the same purpose. The significance of the House action was its proof that the majorities of both chambers were now in agreement on the necessity for offensive action against armed Frenchmen on the western waters of the North Atlantic Ocean.

The Senate's Bill was in the hands of the Sewall committee just two days. The committee recommended that it do pass and the fight was on.[35] As in so many of these parliamentary struggles the real issues were veneered with a factitiously statesmanlike debate. Ostensibly the heart of the matter was the question whether there was any further hope of negotiating with France. In fact, the Republicans opposed the bill because they regarded it as a pro-British stratagem, a practical alliance with monarchism against republicanism, while the Federalists for their part were burning to throw a naval force against the French privateers lurking in the coastal waters, as soon as possible. The Republicans insisted the British were as guilty of despoiling American shipping as the French were, to which the Federalists replied with quotations from insurance rates, which, they claimed, showed the risks from the French to be five times as great as from the British. The critical point in the debate was the presence of a French privateer in Delaware Bay at that very moment. When Republicans appeared to scout the report as a mere rumor, an affidavit of a merchant skipper was produced. This put the bill in the status of an emergency measure and they proceeded to pass it by a vote of 50–40.[36] "An Act more effectually to protect the commerce and coasts of the United States," approved 28 May 1798, began with a preamble citing the presence of armed French ships which were committing depredations on or near the coast. It authorized the President to use the United States Navy to "seize, take, and bring into port" French ships found "hovering" for that purpose, and also to retake any captive American ships.[37]

Bache mourned the toleration of British restrictions which injured American trade with countries paying hard money for American produce. French restrictions only injured the trade with countries which drained the United States of its hard cash.[38]

The sectional alignment on the bill was typical. New England supported it eleven to one, the middle states two to one. The Southern states opposed it four to one, and the members from Kentucky and Tennessee were unanimously opposed.[39]

Two days before the final passage in the House, Captain Richard Dale of the United States sloop-of-war *Ganges,* a converted merchantman, had dropped down the Delaware River, ready for sea, in shipshape and Bristol fashion. The newly enacted authority was promptly sent to him by pilot boat. The quasi-eternal work of preparing the frigates *United States, Constitution,* and *Constellation,* went on. The United States and France were now in a state of undeclared war, but only in the coastal waters of the United States.

About this time the Republicans began to be seriously weakened, either by the departure of members (for example, William B. Giles, who had been in every Congress thus far, resigned to enter the Virginia legislature) [40] or by their conversion to the causes promoted by the Federalists. Manning J. Dauer's valuable tables of the votes of these Congresses enables one to see the weakening of the Republican Party. Using Dauer's tables it can be calculated that the average total vote on roll-calls for the whole Congress declined from ninety-three in February 1798 to eighty-four in June. A study of the number of votes cast by state delegations shows the sharpest decline in the Virginia delegation which had supplied much of the brains and oratory to the Republican Party in the Congress. On five roll-calls in February Virginia cast eighty-four votes. On five roll-calls in June Virginia's total was only fifty-nine. North Carolina's totals in the same two months were forty-nine and forty-five respectively; Massachusetts's, sixty-nine and fifty-seven.[41] With Madison in retirement, with Josiah Parker a Federalist, with John Nicholas, Williams Giles and other Virginians at home, real strength had been lost to the Republicans. As a Federalist wrote to Rufus King in London, "Gallatin continues to clog the wheels of government, but he has not sufficient strength to stop its motion. Without him the party would be completely scattered . . ." [42] Fisher Ames knew the time had come for the Federalists to put their whole program into effect. The government was at its strongest, the opposition at its weakest. The Congress lagged behind the people. More force should be used against France, a more warlike use should be made of the ships. The French treaties should be abrogated, the President should have power to embargo the French West Indian trade, there should be a sedition bill, "more decision and dispatch." The Jacobins were few in number, but might rise again. Half-measures were weak measures and the country must wage full but undeclared war. The multitude could not be kept in suspense—give them action and shifting scenes.[43]

On 6 June Representative Dwight Foster of Massachusetts (who could not yet have learned Ames's views) anticipated this program in part by offering three resolutions. After a preamble stating the United States was no longer bound by treaties with France the resolutions went on to propose the nullity of the treaties, the desirability of authorizing the President to issue letters of marque and reprisal to American privateers, and the encouragement of the capture of French ships by offering a federal bounty based on the size and number of guns of any ship captured.[44] Bache's paper claimed to know the Federalists caucused on these resolutions at the City Tavern on the next day, where Sewall and Robert Goodloe Harper of South Carolina, among others, opposed the Foster resolutions as inexpedient "*at present.*" John Allen of Connecticut ("the most virulent" of Jacobin-smellers) [45] and Harrison Gray Otis of Massachusetts urged committing the country to a state of war before Elbridge Gerry, the Commissioner to France who had remained in Paris after his colleagues left, could "tie their hands by a damned treaty." The caucus decided to commit the resolutions in order to let them sleep. Bache thought the resolutions would have been approved except three members "had left the house to buy gingerbread." [46] Bache's account may not have been accurate (but it well illustrates the polemic journalism of the day).

On the eighth Foster called up his resolves and moved to refer them to Sewall's naval committee. A good part of the day was spent debating this motion to commit. Obviously the resolutions had embarrassed some of the Federalists who doubted either the constitutionality or the expedience of acting on a diplomatic question in this way. After acrimonious argument it was moved to postpone the motion to refer, but this lost, 41–42. Finally Josiah Parker, the chief Virginia Federalist, moved to postpone all consideration of the resolutions for two weeks, which was carried 44–40.[47] Foster's action had been a trick play. Once the resolutions were brought forward for discussion the Republican opposition must either agree with some pretty strongly worded statements or be put in the position of telling the French the United States would never retaliate. Parker, a recent convert to Federalism, took the Republicans off the hook with his two-week postponement.

Thomas Blount of North Carolina tried a riposte. He handed in a set of resolutions of his own, closely paraphasing Foster's language, declaring relations with Great Britain suspended and the Jay Treaty void. Harper outgeneraled him by calling for an immediate vote by roll-call. Since Blount probably knew they would not carry and wished them to be brought up only after Foster's resolutions were acted upon he grumpily withdrew them.[48]

For five or six years the Republicans had tried to pin the label "made in Britain" on Federalist policy.[49] Blount's attempt to embarrass the Federalists was a typical gambit in this long match, and occurred simultaneously with another move in the House by John Dawson of Virginia who presented a resolution asking the President to inform the Congress how well Great Britain had observed the neutral rights of the United States since the ratification of the Jay Treaty. It was beaten without debate on the same day on which Foster's and Blount's resolutions were disposed of. The vote on Dawson's motion was 38–47.[50]

Bache had been improvising on this theme through May. The British were regularly convoying American merchants bound westward[51] and Bache's shipping-news column once listed them as "the following vessels, that were pressed into the service of the British Government, under convoy of the schr. Fly."[52] He also remarked on Benedict Arnold who, like the Federalists, also wished to collaborate with Britain against France.[53]

The country had excellent grounds for complaint against Britain if anyone in the executive department had wished to do more than lodge conventional protests through diplomatic channels. A British Vice Admiralty Court in what is now Haiti condemned the majority of twenty-two American ships brought in by British privateers in March and April,[54] their value being estimated at more than a million dollars.[55] The British ship *Thetis* alternately convoyed and annoyed American shipping off the southern states. Of all the Federalists only Hamilton saw the political hazard of tolerating such conduct. He suggested to Secretary of State Timothy Pickering that a frigate might be sent "to Charleston, to protect effectually our commerce in that quarter, and, if necessary, control the *Thetis* . . . This conduct will unite and animate."[56] He was willing to risk that most improbable of all wars, a triangular conflict in which each nation fought the other two.[57] But most

Federalists shut their eyes to British improprieties and treaty-infractions.

The notion of two Federalist attitudes, one of anger toward France and one of friendship toward an equally guilty Britain, was deeply fixed in Republican minds. Madison saw the Federalist policy as a practical alliance with Britain to starve the French, which fully justified French suspicions of the Jay Treaty.[58] Monroe said the administration had done all it could to rouse France against the United States. Thus the country became a dependency of Great Britain under John Adams, "our present Viceroy." [59]

Meanwhile the Senate had been at work on a bill introduced by Goodhue's naval committee on 6 June which was intended to strengthen the public fleet by allowing the President "to accept of any armed vessel, offered for the use of the United States . . ." either as a gift or a loan. The Republicans tried unsuccessfully to fix the rate of interest on bonds exchanged for ships loaned, to write terms of reimbursement most favorable to the government, and to place an upper limit on the number of guns to be carried by any such ship. As it passed the Senate the bill provided for accepting up to twelve vessels of not less than twenty guns each. It passed in 14 June by a vote of 16–7.[60] Although Bache's *Aurora* had twice commended communities for privately suscribing funds to build ships for the public fleet [61] it greeted the passage of the Senate's gift-of-ships bill with attacks on the Navy as impossibly puny and as draining needed manpower from business and industry.[62]

This bill was not acted on by the House because the House wrote its own bill on the subject, incorporating the specific Republican points which had failed to convince the Senate: method of redemption of the bonds, the installments which were to be paid, the interest rate (a maximum of six per cent), and the time of redemption. All of these specific clauses were offered by Gallatin and accepted by Sewall. It passed without debate or roll-call on 25 June.[63] The House included in its bill a manpower section requested by Captain John Barry of *United States* via the Secretary of the Navy. The law allowed *United States* a complement of 364 men but she needed four hundred. No boys were provided in the earlier legislation, but a man-of-war also needed one boy for each gun. Secretary of the Navy Benjamin Stoddert recommended giving the President authority to fix the strength of the crews and to enlist boys. A special section was accordingly written into the bill to meet these needs.[64] The Senate accepted the House bill instead of its own, with only minor amendment.[65]

"An Act supplemental to the act, entitled, 'An Act to provide an additional armament for the further protection of the trade of the United States, and for other purposes,'" approved 30 June 1798, provided: (1) The President could accept ships from private persons, giving United States bonds in exchange, bearing interest not to exceed six per cent, redeemable at the pleasure of the Congress, up to a total of twelve ships. (2) The rates of the ships under this act and under the earlier legislation of this session should be ("as nearly as may be") six ships up to eighteen guns each, twelve ships from twenty to twenty-four guns each, and six of not less than thirty-two guns each. (3) The President might accept ships as gifts. Two other sections concerned the manning of the ships.[66]

These techniques worked. Even before final passage, subscription-funds were being raised in the chief seaports. From 13 to 30 June the New York *Commercial Advertiser* noticed fund raising campaigns in Philadelphia, New York City, New York (state-wide), Baltimore, Norfolk, Petersburg, Richmond, and Rhode Island (statewide).

In this month Philadelphia's fund reached $70,000 (of which $5000 was contributed by Senator William Bingham), Baltimore's total was $76,100, and New York City's $66,000.[67] A Boston meeting, early in July, produced pledges of $72,500 in thirty minutes, the largest contribution being that of William Philips, $10,000, with the promise of $20,000 if needed. Seventeen promised sums of $1500 or more, including Samuel Eliot's pledge of $4000. The sponsors felt certain of raising $120,000 and hoped to make it $150,000. It was hoped the General Court would vote $50,000 and allow the Governor to draw another $50,000 if needed.[68]

This movement was carefully stimulated by Secretary Stoddert who prodded the Philadelphians a bit and suggested that some federal money could be added to their fund "if required" to help it along.[69] He wrote the same to Boston, and he offered "The Public Timber" collected for shipbuilding in Baltimore to the fund-raisers there.[70]

All in all, the Navy acquired nine ships by the loan-certificate plan, seven ships were built or converted under the acts of 27 April and 30 June, and twenty smaller craft were acquired by these methods.[71] The bonds issued in exchange for loaned ships amounted to over seven hundred thousand dollars in 1799.[72]

The old question of arming the merchant ships remained unsettled, so far as Federalist sponsors of the idea were concerned. Minister Rufus King in London found the question of protecting ships westward-bound from Britain to America a vexing one, simply because there was no known policy for him to quote. He was pressed by the merchant skippers for permission to arm, a permission he could not give. All of them were subject to the obnoxious French decrees because they carried British goods. If they might sail together, armed, they would probably be safe from small French cruisers, and, even if they were taken would be no worse off than they were without having attempted to protect themselves. The British government was willing to convoy the trade, in large fleets, if asked. Insurance rates would be lower that way. Also, a convoy under naval protection was more secure than a group of self-defended ships because merchant ships, no matter how well armed, could not hope to resist French public ships.[73] Late in January King said he would soon have to decide whether to authorize sailing in British convoys "or to sail with the increased Risque of Capture and certainty of condemnation."[74] A few days later he told Secretary Pickering he had been informing the merchant captains they could accept British offers of protection "as Private individuals" without hurting the United States. He said he did not dare apply to the British government for such protection because the French would have learned of his application "in less than a week" and the position of the American Commissioners then in Paris would have been prejudiced.[75] On the British side of the question, it was planned to introduce a bill in the Parliament which would tax imports and exports 2½ per cent to defray the costs of convoying. Neutrals who did their own convoying would be exempted from the tax. If it were adopted, King thought it would be cheaper "as well as in other respects wiser" for the United States to do its own convoying.[76]

The Republicans were probably correct in their belief the country could not yet build a navy large enough to meet this need, but a typical informed merchant, George Cabot of Massachusetts, thought the merchants might be glad to club together "in forming little armaments for the protection of their vessels in a single voyage."[77] The arguments against the practice had already been well rehearsed in public. Throughout the spring there flowed in a steady stream of addresses opposing the project of arming private ships.[78]

Sewall's naval committee brought a bill into the House of Representatives on 8 June which provided specifically for the merchants to defend themselves against France alone by resisting and capturing any Frenchman which tried to search or which attacked an American ship. No clearance would be granted from an American port to a private armed vessel unless it was American-owned and was bonded to do no harm to the ships of any nation in "amity" with the United States. If prizes were taken half the proceeds should go to the owner of the captor, the other half to the officers and crew. No armed vessel would be allowed to carry contraband of war,[79] nor could cargo be carried to a place blockaded. Armed vessels were not to carry the public or private property of a belligerent nation. All arms were to be brought back to the United States at the end of the voyage. The ships were to be subject to any further regulations of the President.[80]

In Committee of the Whole much of the discussion concerned the international law of carrying the property of belligerents. It was a noticeably calmer debate than usual for those days; the rarefied atmosphere of an almost purely legal discussion apparently kept the members cool. An amendment to kill the prohibition against carrying belligerent property to blockaded places was carried with fifty-two ayes. The bill was also amended to allow armed Americans to recapture Americans in the hands of French privateers.[81]

The matter now being before the House of Representatives, Harper renewed a motion which had lost in Committee, to allow the armed merchants to "attack, take, or destroy, any vessel, sailing or acting as aforesaid, which may have made any such capture." To reject this amendment, he argued, meant the Congress would not allow the merchants to do what was most useful, "clearing the coast of those plundering marauders which infest it." Joshua Coit, irregular Connecticut Federalist, apparently expressed the majority view when, after debate had produced a visible split in the Federalist ranks, he remarked it was better to leave the defense of the coast to naval officers than to merchant captains. Harper's amendment was beaten, 28–47.[82] The hard core of the war-group can be seen here. Harper intended to allow private ships to hunt out and take French ships. The sectional alignment on that question was illuminating.

The vote on Harper's amendment showed he had pushed too far. He temporarily divided the war bloc from the navy bloc. The motion received only four votes south of the Potomac, including his own, and every New England delegation split evenly except the bastion of hyper-Federalism, Connecticut. The motion received majorities only in the Connecticut, New York, New Jersey, and Delaware delegations. This was an interesting neighborly juxtaposition—three of these states made considerable use of New York port (see p. 173).

On the next day, 13 June, the bill to arm the merchants passed the House without division.[83] Upstairs the Senate passed the bill by a vote of 16–3, with one amendment,[84] an allowance for salvage to be paid for re-captures from French privateers. After minor revision in the House this amendment became part of the bill.[85]

"An Act to authorize the defence of the merchant vessels of the United States against French depredations," approved 25 June 1798,

Vote on Motion to Allow Merchant Ships to Take Aggressive Action, 12 June 1798

	Ayes	*Noes*
New England:		
New Hampshire	1	1
Vermont	1	1
Massachusetts	6	6
Rhode Island	1	1
Connecticut	5	2
Total	14	11
Middle States:		
New York	4	2
New Jersey	4	0
Pennsylvania	2	6
Delaware	1	0
Maryland	1	4
Total	12	12
Southern States		
Virginia	1	12
North Carolina	0	7
South Carolina	1	3
Georgia	0	1
Total	1	23
Western States:		
Kentucky	0	1
Tennessee	0	0
Total	0	1
Grand Total	28	47

provided the following: (1) A merchant ship wholly owned in the United States might resist search and seizure by armed ships with French colors or which pretended to be French, and might capture the attacker, and retake any captive American ships. (2) The proceeds of such prizes were to be divided, half to the owners, half to those on board the captor. Prize cases could be heard in any United States court with admiralty jurisdiction. Salvage was to be paid at from one-eighth to one-half the value of recovered ships, at the discretion of the court. (3) A method of the clearance of outward-bound armed ships was provided. Friendly vessels were not to be attacked. All unexpended arms and ammunition taken out were to be returned to the United States. Special regulations of the President were to be obeyed. (4) A method for receiving any such regulations was provided, as was a procedure for reporting any "rencounter" on return. (5) The act was to be effective for a period of one year plus the duration of the following session of the Congress. (6) When the French quit annoying American trade the President would instruct the merchant-men to conduct themselves as in peacetime.[86]

This act was welcomed by the merchants. As Stephen Higginson, Boston merchant and United States Navy agent, wrote, "Our merchant ships are arming and some are waiting for commissions, which have been expected for some time . . . We shall soon be capable of exertion." [87] Before peace was restored more than a thousand merchants were armed, with from one to thirty-four guns each. Many performed deeds of real utility to the country.[88]

Another matter remained to be regularized—the proper disposition of any ships and men captured by the United States Navy. A bill for the purpose originated in the Senate's naval committee and went through both houses in eleven days, without much debate and with no significant roll-calls.[89] "An Act in addition to the act more effectually to protect the commerce and coasts of the United States," approved 28 June 1798, provided for the disposition of captures made by the Navy. Ships, equipment, and cargo (unless the cargo had been first captured from an American owner) might be condemned. American ships recaptured were subject to the payment of a salvage claim of one-eighth of their value. If a captured ship were equal to or stronger than the naval vessel which took it, all of its value went to the officers and crew, otherwise half the proceeds were to go to the officers and men and the other half to the Federal government. Captured officers and crews might be incarcerated.[90]

It was now late in June and the question of adjournment began to occupy some minds. Jefferson thought they might stay in continuous session.

> Their system is, professedly, to keep up an alarm. Tracy at the meeting of the joint committee for adjournment declared it necessary for Congress to stay together to keep up the inflammation of the publick mind; and Otis expressed a similar sentiment since . . . To separate Congress now, will be withdrawing the fire from under a boiling pot.[91]

To understand Jefferson's bitterness it is necessary to remember that the Naturalization Act had been passed a few days earlier and the first of the Alien Acts was then in progress through the Congress. Soon the second Alien Act would be passed and finally the hateful Sedition Act. Philadelphia had become an unpleasant place for a man of Jefferson's political philosophy and personal kindliness, a place where hatred was corrupting even the social life of the legislators gathered there. And physically it was becoming less comfortable day by day. The weather had turned hot and the streets stank. There was much dysentery. A minor throat inflammation was epidemic. Cases of yellow fever were reported.[92] The *Annals of the Congress* for 26 June contain the concise entry: "On request, the Vice President was excused from attendance in Senate for the remainder of the session." It is curious that the two next Presidents, both of whom were to make considerable use of the naval force then being born, had withdrawn to Virginia, repelled and disgusted by the tone of public life.

As June neared its close the navy-minded men could look on their work with satisfaction. The three great frigates were at last seaworthy. The fleet was being multiplied by the ingenious lend-gift system. The armed sea force was to be augmented by a privately armed merchant fleet. The Navy was ordered to clear the coastal waters of the United States. A few loose ends remained to be tied. In a fortnight the country would see the naval design neatly rounded off.

NOTES FROM PAGES 160 TO 175

1. 5 Cong., 2 Sess., 4 May 1798, *Annals of the Congress, 1789–1824*, ed. J. Gales and W. W. Seaton, 42v. (Washington, 1834–1856), 3369–3410. Hereafter cited: *Annals*. All references below are to the second session of the Fifth Congress. Dates are given where helpful to search.
2. For example of a public demonstration see Abigail Adams to Mary Cranch, 26 April 1798, *New Letters of Abigail Adams*, ed. Stewart Mitchell (Boston, 1947), 164–165. Hereafter cited: *New Letters*.
3. This conclusion is drawn from a study of the Philadelphia *Gazette of the United States*, 2–18 May 1798.
4. Abigail Adams to Mary Cranch, 22 April 1798, *New Letters*, 161.
5. A very large number of President Adams's replies appeared in the Philadelphia *Gazette of the United States* for these weeks.
6. John Adams, *Works*, ed. C. F. Adams, 10v. (Boston, 1850–1856), IX, 182–215.
7. Manning J. Dauer, *The Adams Federalists* (Baltimore, 1953), 159–161.
8. Madison to Jefferson, 20 May 1798, Madison papers, Library of Congress. Hereafter abbreviated: LC.
9. "A Young Man," Boston *Chronicle*, copied in Philadelphia *Aurora*, 14 June 1798.
10. On this point see especially, numbers five and seven, Alexander Hamilton, *Works*, ed. Henry Cabot Lodge, 12v. (New York, 1904), VI, 302, 312.
11. Philadelphia *Gazette of the United States*, 27 April 1798.
12. Ames to Otis, 23 April 1798, Fisher Ames, *Works*, ed. Seth Ames, 2v. (Boston, 1854), I, 225.
13. Dauer, *The Adams Federalists*, 150.
14. Philadelphia *Gazette of the United States*, 8 May 1798. The whole was sixty-nine lines.
15. Philadelphia *Aurora*, 9 May 1798.
16. *Ibid.*, 26 May 1798.
17. *Ibid.*, 7 May 1798.
18. *Ibid.*, 17 May 1798.
19. *Ibid.*, 22 May 1798.
20. *Ibid.*, 9 June 1798 (letter dated 20 May).
21. 15 May, *Annals*, 1707–1724.
22. Philadelphia *Gazette of the United States*, 16 May 1798.
23. *Ibid.*, copied in Philadelphia *Aurora*, 19 May 1798.
24. Eugene Perry Link, *Democratic-Republican Societies, 1790–1800* (New York, 1942), 178–184.
25. Jefferson to Madison, 26 April 1798, to Lewis, 9 May 1798, Jefferson papers, LC; to Martha Jefferson Randolph, 17 May 1798, Sarah N. Randolph, *The Domestic Life of Thomas Jefferson* (New York, 1871), 249.
26. For samples, see: toasts of the "Fancy Hill Fishing Company," Philadelphia *Gazette of the United States*, 4 May 1798; Lloyd to Washington, 6 June

1798, Washington papers, LC; Abigail Adams to Mary Cranch, 28 April 1798, *New Letters*, 167; Henrietta Liston to Jackson, 3 May 1798, Bradford Perkins, "A Diplomat's Wife in Philadelphia: Letters of Henrietta Liston, 1796–1800," *William and Mary Quarterly*, third series, XI (Oct. 1954), 616–617, Washington to Hamilton, 27 May 1798, George Washington, *Writings*, ed. John C. Fitzpatrick, 39v. (Washington, 1931–1944), XXXVI, 272.

27. McHenry to Hamilton, 12 May 1798, Hamilton papers, LC.
28. Hamilton to McHenry, 17 May 1798, *ibid.*
29. Tracy to Hamilton, 17 May 1798, *ibid.*
30. 18, 21, 22, 23 May, *Annals*, 559, 560, 561–562, 562–563.
31. Philadelphia *Aurora*, 22 May 1798.
32. 22 May, *Annals*, 1783.
33. 22, 23 May, *ibid.*, 1783, 1797–1812; Philadelphia *Aurora*, 23 May 1798.
34. 24 May, *ibid.*, 1812.
35. 23, 24, 25 May, *ibid.*, 1793, 1812, 1813.
36. 25–26 May, *ibid.*, 1813–1835.
37. *Ibid.*, 3733.
38. Philadelphia *Aurora*, 26 May 1798.
39. *Annals*, 1834–1835.
40. Irving Brant, *James Madison, Father of the Constitution* (Indianapolis, 1950), 463.
41. Dauer, *The Adams Federalists*, tables, 304–309.
42. Troup to King, 10 June 1798, Rufus King, *The Life and Correspondence of Rufus King*, ed. C. R. King, 6v. (New York, 1894–1900), II, 345. Hereafter cited: King, *Life and Correspondence*.
43. Ames to Pickering, 4 June 1798, Ames, *Works*, I, 226–228.
44. 6 June, *Annals*, 1870–1871.
45. Dauer, *The Adams Federalists*, 142.
46. Philadelphia *Aurora*, 15 June 1798. Bache had no praise for the French privateers. He referred to them as "a set of unprincipled fellows, of all nations, whose only object is plunder" and cited the privateer *Jean Bart*, commanded by an Irishman, with thirty Americans in the crew. *Ibid.*, 6 June 1798.
47. 8 June 1798, *Annals*, 1881–1892.
48. *Ibid.*, 1892.
49. Marshall Smelser, "Republicanism and the Menace of Monarchy, Plutocracy, and Anglophilia," in a forthcoming issue of the *Review of Politics*.
50. 7, 8 June, *Annals*, 1874, 1877.
51. For example, Philadelphia *Gazette of the United States*, 8 May 1798.
52. Philadelphia *Aurora*, 20 May 1798.
53. *Ibid.*, 19 May 1798.
54. *Ibid.*, 7 June 1798.
55. *Ibid.*, 8 June 1798.
56. Hamilton to Pickering, 7 June 1798, Hamilton, *Works*, X, 293.
57. Hamilton to Pickering, 8 June 1798, *ibid.*, X, 294.
58. Madison to Jefferson, 10 June 1798, Madison papers, LC.
59. Monroe to Jefferson, 16 June 1798, Jefferson papers, LC.
60. *Annals*, 572, 573, 575–576, 577, 578–579, 579–580.
61. Philadelphia *Aurora*, 1, 9 June 1798.
62. *Ibid.*, 15, 16 June 1798.
63. *Annals*, 1926, 1938, 2032–2034.
64. Stoddert to Sewall, 23 June 1798, Dudley W. Knox, ed., *Naval Documents Related to the Quasi-war between the United States and France*, 7v. (Washington, 1935–1938), I, 131, hereafter cited: Knox, *Quasi-war; Annals*, 2034, 3752.
65. 25–28 June, *ibid.*, 588, 590–592.
66. *Ibid.*, 3751–3752.
67. New York *Commercial Advertiser*, 13–30 June 1798.
68. Representative Isaac Parker of Massachusetts in Philadelphia *Porcupine's Gazette*, 5 July 1798.
69. Stoddert to Fitzsimons, 26 June 1798, Knox, *Quasi-war*, I, 143.
70. Stoddert to Sears, 6 July 1798, *ibid.*, I, 170; to Yellott, 6 July 1798, *ibid.*, I, 173.
71. Gardner Weld Allen, *Our Naval War with France* (Boston, 1909), 56.
72. George Gibbs, *Memoirs of the Administrations of Washington and John Adams*, 2v. (New York, 1846), II, 67. Hereafter cited: Gibbs, *Memoirs*.
73. King to Pickering, 14 Jan. 1798, King, *Life and Correspondence*, II, 271–272.
74. King to Pickering, 27 Jan. 1798, *ibid.*, II, 274–275.
75. King to Pickering, 7 Feb. 1798, *ibid.*, II, 280.
76. King to Pickering, 17 March 1798, *ibid.*, II, 290.
77. Cabot to Wolcott, 9 June 1798, Gibbs, *Memoirs*, II, 54.
78. Most of them found their way into print in Philadelphia *Aurora*.

79. 8 June, *Annals,* 1896.
80. 12 June, *ibid.,* 1899.
81. *Ibid.,* 1899–1915.
82. *Ibid.,* 1915–1916.
83. *Ibid.,* 1925.
84. 13, 15, 18–20 June, *ibid.,* 579, 580, 582–584.
85. 22 June, *ibid.,* 2032; 23 June, *ibid.,* 587.
86. *Ibid.,* 3747–3749.
87. Higginson to Wolcott, 9 July 1798, Gibbs, *Memoirs,* II, 70.
88. Robert Greenhalgh Albion and Jennie Barnes Pope, *Sea Lanes in Wartime; the American Experience, 1775–1942* (New York, 1942), 82.
89. 4–25 June, *Annals,* 580–582, 589, 590, 1973, 2034.
90. *Ibid.,* 3750–3751.
91. Jefferson to Madison, 21 June 1798, Jefferson papers, LC.
92. Abigail Adams to Mary Cranch, 23 June 1798, *New Letters,* 194.

XIII

Fitting Out, Shaking Down

As June came to its end a great deal had been accomplished in the way of fitting out and shaking down the new United States Navy. Manning, rigging, arming, the purchase and conversion of merchant ships—all proceeded as rapidly as possible. A small anti-privateer patrol was sent to sea, and was aided by the Treasury's cutters.

The officers of the frigates *United States, Constitution,* and *Constellation* were recruiting seamen during the spring. The standard of fitness was laid down by Secretary of War James McHenry: "healthy, robust and well organized Men," not "scorbutic or consumptively affected." [1] Stephen Higginson, well-to-do Boston Federalist who served as Navy Agent there, had some decided opinions on the standards for the selection of naval officers. He thought the smaller vessels being procured would be good training ships to produce officers for the large ships. The United States must not only form a Navy but

> we have to root out and counteract the ill habits contracted in our navy last war, when no proper characters were in the service, and no examples that will serve as models for an [*sic*] young man to follow. In my view, it is a primary object to select proper characters for the Navy; such as have right habits, principles and feelings; capable of being trained to proper discipline. Upon this depends the reputation and utility of our Navy; but no aid can be derived to this purpose from any character I ever knew in our Navy last war. A good man, who has been in the service, ought not to be neglected; it should give him a preference in promotion; but when you will recollect that bluster and noise, too often brought improper men into the service the last war . . . it should be a caution against an indiscriminate promotion.[2]

Alexander Hamilton had an additional criterion. When he sent in the name of an applicant for a naval commission he said the man had been well recommended. "It seems, however,—that he has been heretofore rather Democratic . . . I barely wish" that he be considered "fairly but carefully." [3] (In the Army, of which Hamilton was to be Major General and Inspector General, Hamilton approved the commissioning of Jeffersonian Republicans, but only in company grades and for the purpose of making converts to more correct political principles.)

During the spring months a note of urgency was added to naval preparations by the constant flow of reports of the activities of French privateers. Inbound merchantmen brought reports of sightings, seizures, and "chaces" with almost every tide.[4] These were emphasized in the Federalist press and even given some attention in the Republican papers. Editor and publisher Benjamin Franklin Bache of the Philadelphia *Aurora* noticed these insults very little, but did what he could to publicize the British seizures of American ships carrying French cargoes.[5]

Something of the atmosphere of those months can be recreated in the imagination by a selection of privateer reports from the contemporary newspapers. (The dates of publication are in parentheses.) The ship *Superb* was boarded by a French privateer (30 May). The sloop *Nancy,* bound to Philadelphia from the West Indies, on 30 May "ten miles within the [Delaware] Bay . . . was boarded by the French privateer" (2 June). A privateer was working the waters east of Long Island Sound from 8 to 21 May (2 June). A Rhode Islander said he was hailed by a privateer on 29 May "off Cape May" but the Frenchman went after another ship. The encounter was reported to the master of the Revenue Cutter *General Greene* who went in search (2 June). A few days earlier a French privateer "was at Cape May taking in water" (6 June). The brig *Prudent* was taken "about 10 leagues to the S. S. E. of the [Sandy] Hook" and burned. About three o'clock in the afternoon of the same day the despoiler was fired on by His Majesty's brig *Earl Moira.* After the Britisher had fired about twenty rounds the Frenchman escaped to the southward. The master of *Prudent* said he was told by the French captain "his orders were, in case any American armed vessel made resistance, to give them no quarter" (7 June). Captain Arnold of the ship *Federal George,* of Boston, at latitude north 39° 20′, longitude west 72° 30′, saw a French privateer take the ship *Eliza* bound from Lisbon to Alexandria (14 June). The ship *St. Tammany,* in ballast, was boarded after a twelve-hour chase by a privateer of twelve guns, Cape Henlopen bearing W. S. W., but was dismissed (17 June). A French privateer was sighted on 27 June ten miles south of Barnegat (2 July).[6] The intruders apparently thought the entrance to Delaware Bay would be their happiest hunting ground. These reports help one to understand the public anger of those weeks.

The reference to His Majesty's brig *Earl Moira* was significant.

British warships were arriving in American ports from time to time as escorts of groups of American merchant ships from the British Isles. After a while a squadron of these escorts accumulated at Norfolk, Virginia, under Admiral Vandeput. At the moment there was a good deal more British than American naval activity in American coastal waters.[7] This fact no doubt encouraged Republicans to think of the naval policy of the Federalist Party as merely an extension of British naval policy and therefore pro-monarchical and anti-republican. An American off Bermuda was told by the Captain of the British frigate *Hinde* that he had taken three French privateers off the American coast in May.[8] An unconfirmed report of early June said His Majesty's frigate *Thetis* had taken a Frenchman in Long Island Sound.[9] The New York *Argus,* a Republican paper, sneered at the Royal Naval vessels in American waters as "our faithful Guarda Costas," reflected on their villainy, and thought it was no great favor to be protected in American harbors by British ships of war.[10]

The only extended American naval operation before the end of June was the cruise of the United States sloop-of-war *Ganges,* under Captain Richard Dale, as an anti-privateer patrol between New York harbor and Cape Henry. *Ganges* had been the property of the Philadelphia mercantile firm of Willing and Francis, who advertised her for sale early in February after Captain John Green had brought her back from Bengal with two hundred tons of sugar, forty-five tons of pepper, and twenty-eight kinds of fabrics, including "Patna" handkerchiefs, and some "Bandannoes." [11] She was purchased for the United States in April and her command offered to Dale by Secretary McHenry; the conveyance was completed in May, at the same time as the government bought the ship *Hamburgh Packet,* which was later converted to naval service under the name *Delaware*.[12] Dale was commissioned in the Navy in 1794. When the construction program was cut back he took leave and went into the China trade. Now he accepted command of *Ganges*. The new captain had learned his aquatic trade under a master, for he was First Lieutenant of *Bon Homme Richard* when John Paul Jones literally fought her to her death in taking *Serapis*.[13] His orders at the moment were the purely defensive orders originally envisaged before the Congress took courage and decided the French privateers should be hunted down: he was to defend against armed vessels within "One Marine League" of the coast.[14] As soon as the bill to clear the coast was signed (28 May 1798) its substance was sent to Dale by President John Adams.[15]

But first Dale had to see to the conversion job, and he did it smartly. On 19 May she was reported to be armed with twenty nine-pounders, fully manned, and lying at anchor at Philadelphia, "having completed her preparations for sea." [16] Four days later Secretary McHenry ordered *United States* to have a boat ready the next morning to put him on board *Ganges*,[17] and his visit was recorded by the local journalists.

> Yesterday at 11 o'clock, the Secretary of War, accompanied by Capt. Barry, commander of the frigate United States, and captain Dale, commander of the ship of war the Ganges, went on board the latter ship, and delivered his orders to captain Dale. On the Secretary's leaving the ship, a salute was fired; immediately after which, she weighted anchor, to proceed to her cruising station.[18]

In the fourth year of the naval program of the United States a public ship was for the first time actually ready for service and proceeding to sea under orders.

On 27 May a New York merchant "passed the *Ganges* sloop of war at Reedy Point" [19] and she was seen in Delaware Bay two days later.[20] One of Dale's officers sent back a letter by the pilot's hand. They were going to look for a rumored privateer of sixteen guns, in company with the Revenue Cutter *General Greene*. He added, "we have just been examining our men and proving the guns, which answer our most sanguine expectations." [21] A Frenchman then in the Bay knew she was coming. He boarded an American merchant ship and "enquired particularly . . . if he knew anything of the *Ganges*." [22]

Dale passed the Capes of the Delaware on 30 May and beat out to sea against a fresh wind from the northeast, "with rain and thick weather." He hoped to surprise a privateer which might not expect the hunter to be out on such a day and might even be drawn as a duck is drawn to a decoy. But his arrival at sea was no surprise, for on the following day a French captain told the skipper of a pilot boat he had heard *Ganges* was out, as Dale wrote, and, "it was time for him to be off—Some *Dam rascal* has been giveing him information of my giting out." [23] Two days later Dale came up with a merchantman which had been abandoned in the haze by a privateer on sight of *Ganges;* Dale went in pursuit "under a heavy press of sail" but never even saw the fleet corsair.[24]

Pleasant rumors of striking successes by Dale twice excited the people of Philadelphia but afterward he told a pilot he had taken nothing.[25] An Accocmac county correspondent reported a naval engagement eight or ten miles off shore on 8 June, between "two large ships" but that was the only word of such an affair. Perhaps visiting Royal Navy ships were exercising their gun crews.[26] Secretary McHenry warned Dale of a twenty-gun privateer off the New England coast which had been "confidently" reported to him. Her master was quoted as saying five others of the same size were to follow her [27]—an obvious gasconade.

In this period Dale had one specific assignment beyond his anti-privateer patrol. The ship *Adriana* had arrived at New York from London and was bought for the public service on 3 May.[28] (Her captain, Frederick Lee, had a brush with English law in February. Exactly what happened one can not tell; Bache's *Aurora* said he was fined £10 "for having put pow[d]er in his hair without permission.") [29] *Adriana* was to sail fully laden from New York to Philadelphia, and Dale convoyed her safely down to the Delaware early in June.[30] This was the sort of work to be appreciated by the public. Noah Webster exulted, "In the arrival of one single vessel are the expenses of the *Ganges* reimbursed." [31] Republicans took what comfort they could by observing that *Adriana* brought in a sword for the Polish patriot, General Tadeusz Kosciuszko (then in Virginia), the gift of the Whig Club of England and valued at two hundred guineas.[32]

At the end of June Dale still had not caught an interloper. The new Secretary of the Navy, Benjamin Stoddert commiserated with him. Even though he had made no captures he had "frightened the French Cruisers from our Coasts . . ." [33] There was no doubt of the value of Dale's work as he regularly escorted merchantment into the Delaware River.[34] He had executed no great deed to arouse public applause but he had done a straightforward piece of necessary naval work in a manner to merit approval.

The frigate *United States,* under Captain Barry, completed her manning in May and received orders to get to sea. She lay at Newcastle, Delaware, as late as 25 June, awaiting "a few necessaries," and put out shortly after that.[35]

Captain Thomas Truxtun of the frigate *Constellation,* built at Baltimore, received his orders, dated 30 May, to cruise between Cape Henry and Florida.[36] He dropped slowly down the length of the Chesapeake, combining shakedown with recruiting as he went (fifty men from Alexandria, 120 from Norfolk), and lay at Hampton Roads on 21 June.[37]

The sloop-of-war *Delaware,* ex-*Hamburgh Packet,* was also being converted for the Navy. She was built at Philadelphia for the merchant service in 1794, and would seem a little tubby to modern eyes, being about ninety-five feet in length over-all, with a twenty-eight foot beam.[38] Nineteen days after the purchase was completed her guns were being proved,[39] and a few days after that she was ordered to receive her powder, shot, cartridges, and matches.[40] Manning and carpentry were almost complete nine days later, and she was armed with sixteen nine-pounders below and four six-pounders on the quarter deck.[41] But she had no Marines of her own and Secretary McHenry delicately asked the Army to propose to some infantrymen that they take a cruise in *Delaware,* with the pay of Marines, and a promise to be returned to the bosoms of their fellow dog-faces when the cruise was completed.[42] A few days after this, on 15 June, Captain Stephen Decatur, Sr., was ordered to take command of *Delaware,* complete the recruiting, and finish the fitting out.[43] At that time she lacked a few seamen and boys, but little else.[44] Decatur was given permission to keep his Delaware Bay pilot on board at thirty-five dollars a month, on the ground it would be a great convenience which would not cost much more than pilotage-fees by the job.[45] Finally, dated 26 June, came orders for Decatur to go to sea, join Dale if he were met with, cruise with him from Cape Henry to Long Island until 10 July, then to go south and put himself under command of Truxtun on his station.[46]

Up in Boston the Navy was having personality trouble. It was very difficult to enlist men to serve in the frigate *Constitution.* One of the naval contractors, who happened to be the nephew of Secretary of State Timothy Pickering, wrote to the Secretary the difficulty was

> owing considerably to the *unpopularity* of the Commander [Samuel Nicholson]; tho' no one alleges any thing against him that partakes of misconduct in any respect. He is poor—it is his only living. What can be done, I know not. It is to be regretted, that So fine a Ship should lie uselessly at her anchors.[47]

A week later this opinion was confirmed by Higginson, the Navy Agent there (it may be added the contractor and the Navy Agent were not on terms of mutual admiration so an anti-Nicholson cabal may be ruled out). Higginson described Captain Nicholson as "a rough blustering Tar merely," perhaps a coward. The Second Lieutenant was probably a drunkard. As for the Surgeon, "there is not a man in this Town who would trust the life of a dog in his hands" and the assistant Surgeon was the same kind of man "but not so highly finished." The First Lieutenant, Edward Preble, was a good man. He was absent and probably would not serve in the ship when he arrived and evaluated his fellow officers.[48] By 11 June about half of *Constitution*'s complement was enlisted, partly by vigorous recruiting in the "out posts" of Massachusetts.[49] Another ship was fitting in Boston, the ex-merchantmen *Herald,*[50] and service in her was more attractive to the young men of the Bay State than was that of *Constitution.*[51]

Thus by the end of June, the United States had instituted a patrol of its coastal waters, using *United States, Constellation, Ganges,* and

Delaware. *Adriana* and *Herald* were fitting out and converting. *Constitution* had everything but a crew. Soon a new fleet would be "in being" on the waters of the Ocean Sea.

NOTES FROM PAGES 178 TO 184

1. McHenry to Barry, 5 May 1798, U. S. Navy, Miscellaneous manuscripts, Library of Congress. Hereafter abbreviated: LC.
2. Higginson to Wolcott, 13 July 1798, George Gibbs, *Memoirs of the Administrations of Washington and John Adams*, 2v. (New York, 1846), II, 71–72.
3. Hamilton to McHenry, 1 June 1798, Bernard C. Steiner, *The Life and Correspondence of James McHenry* (Cleveland, 1907), 289.
4. For numerous of such reports see the New York *Commercial Advertiser* for June 1798.
5. See the Philadelphia *Aurora* for May 1798.
6. These reports are all from the New York *Commercial Advertiser* and the Philadelphia *Aurora.*
7. New York *Commercial Advertiser,* May–June 1798.
8. *Ibid.*, 8 June 1798.
9. *Ibid.*, 5 June 1798.
10. "A Small Merchant," New York *Argus,* March 1798.
11. Philadelphia *Gazette of the United States,* 8 Feb., 3 May 1798.
12. McHenry to Dale, 3 April 1798, Dudley W. Knox, ed., *Naval Documents Related to the Quasi-war between the United States and France,* 7v. (Washington, 1935–1938), I, 51, hereafter cited: Knox, *Quasi-war; ibid.*, I, 63–64; Philadelphia *Gazette of the United States,* 5 May 1798.
13. Edgar Stanton Maclay, *A History of the United States Navy from 1775 to 1894,* 2v. (New York, 1897), I, 160.
14. McHenry to Dale, 22 May 1798, Knox, *Quasi-war,* I, 77.
15. *Ibid.*, I, 88.
16. Philadelphia *Gazette of the United States,* 19 May 1798.
17. McHenry to senior officer present on board *United States,* 23 May 1798, U. S. Navy, Miscellaneous manuscripts, LC.
18. New York *Commercial Advertiser,* 26 May 1798.
19. *Ibid.*, 31 May 1798.
20. *Ibid.*, 1 June 1798.
21. *Ibid.*, 5 June 1798.
22. *Ibid.*, 2 June 1798.
23. Dale to Willings and Francis, 1 June 1798, Knox, *Quasi-war,* I, 101.
24. New York *Commercial Advertiser,* 2, 5 June 1798.
25. *Ibid.*, 8, 16, 18 June 1798.
26. *Ibid.*, 8 June 1798.
27. McHenry to Dale, 11 June 1798, Knox, *Quasi-war,* I, 110.
28. *Ibid.*, I, 62–63.
29. Philadelphia *Aurora,* 28 May 1798.
30. McHenry to Dale, 29 May 1798, Knox, *Quasi-war,* I, 91.
31. New York *Commercial Advertiser,* 11 June 1798.
32. Philadelphia *Aurora,* 18 June 1798.
33. Stoddert to Dale, 27 June 1798, Knox, *Quasi-war,* I, 145.
34. New York *Commercial Advertiser.*
35. McHenry to Barry, 8 May 1798, U.S. Navy, Miscellaneous manuscripts, LC; New York *Commercial Advertiser,* 31 May, 9, 13, 25 June 1798.
36. McHenry to Truxtun, 30 May 1798, Knox, *Quasi-war,* I, 92–93.
37. New York *Commercial Advertiser,* 16, 19, 21, 26 June 1798.
38. Knox, *Quasi-war,* I, 68.
39. McHenry to DaCosta, 24 May, to Harris, 25 May 1798, Knox, *Quasi-war,* I, 82.
40. McHenry to Harris, 1 June 1798, *ibid.*, I, 101.
41. New York *Commercial Advertiser,* 9 June 1798.
42. McHenry to Miller, 11 June 1798, Knox, *Quasi-war,* I, 110.
43. McHenry to Decatur, Sr., 15 June 1798, *ibid.*, I, 116–118.
44. New York *Commercial Advertiser,* 16 June 1798; Stoddert to Decatur, Sr., 21 June 1798, Knox, *Quasi-war,* I, 127.

45. Stoddert to Decatur, Sr., 22 June 1798, *ibid.*, I, 128.
46. Stoddert to Decatur, Sr., 26 June 1798, *ibid.*, I, 141–142.
47. Williams to Pickering, 31 May 1798, *ibid.*, I, 97.
48. Higginson to McHenry, 6 June 1798, *ibid.*, I, 106–107.
49. Higginson to McHenry, 11 June 1798, *ibid.*, I, 109.
50. Philadelphia *Aurora*, 7 June 1798.
51. Higginson to McHenry, 6 June 1798, Knox, *Quasi-war*, I, 106–107.

XIV

Naval Federalism at High Tide

The hot weather which had settled on Philadelphia late in June, persisted into July. On the second of July the temperature was 91°. The heat-wave stayed and worsened; Salem, Massacusetts, reported 99° on 11 July.[1] In a manner of speaking, the political heat-wave of 1798 well coincided with the weather, for the public excitement at the behavior of the French remained at a high pitch, and tended to increase rather than to abate. At this time and in this mood the final touches of this session of the Congress were put on the naval policy of the United States.

The press reflected the continuing feeling against France. When John Marshall, one of the three American Commissioners to France who had been spurned in the "X. Y. Z. Affair," returned to Philadelphia he was fêted at Oeller's Hotel at a dinner organized by Senators William Bingham and Jacob Read, and Representatives Samuel Sitgreaves, Harrison Gray Otis, and John Rutledge, Jr., all "regular" Federalists. The seventh of a long string of toasts drunk in the sweltering dining room was "the navy of the United States. May its infant efforts, like those of Hercules, be the presage of its future greatness." [2] The New York *Commercial Advertiser* (Noah Webster's daily) published "NEW VERSES —To an old Tune," in fourteen stanzas, of which the last was

> If we are firm, peace will return,
> Sweet peace, the very dandy;
> May they that flinch a single inch
> Ne'er taste the sugar candy.
> Yanky doodle (mind the tune)
> Yankee doodle dandy,
> If Frenchmen come with naked bum,
> We'll *spank* 'em hard and handy.[3]

By this time William Cobbett, the English born editor who called himself "Peter Porcupine," regularly published a column headed "Military

Intelligence," which retailed the social and military affairs of the Philadelphia volunteer militia units.[4] The "Old City Troop" of Horse had its usual Independence Day dinner. Again the published list of toasts. Number ten was: "The Navy of the United States; plane sailing to truth and virtue." [5] Practically all public dinners now toasted the Navy.

Stronger sentiments were being expressed editorially and in private. Noah Webster justified the existence of the Navy in his columns: France was so busy with Great Britain at the moment that the United States might be safe for one or two more seasons, but Britain was likely to be defeated. Then the last barrier, the Royal Navy, would be gone and France would dictate to the United States. This "suggests to us our interest, our duty and *our only means of safety*—a NAVY." Americans must learn to ignore talk about the "freedom of the seas" and fighting Great Britain "to *liberate the ocean from her tyranny*." Such talk was merely deception.

> We may regret the necessity of a navy—we may calculate the expense with the fractional exactness of a miser; but *we cannot have Commerce without protection*—our trade, our commercial wealth, will forever be exposed to lawless plunder, *without a navy*. We *must* have a navy, and we *must* have a military force, or we are not an independent nation.[6]

He returned to the subject a few days later with a quotation from the *Minerva* of Dedham, Massachusetts. The United States was much better fitted for naval power than was supposed. It had great trade. Great trade supported a navy. The country must resolve to be a great naval power. A few ships would stop the piracies of the coast and the "West Indian Algerines." The country should not trust any foreign protector.[7]

Ex-Senator George Cabot of Massachusetts, who had declined the office of Secretary of the Navy, wrote to his friend Rufus King, the United States Minister to Great Britain, and told of a group of armed merchants which sailed from Boston, carrying a total of 130 guns. The West Indian "pirates" would not be able to hurt the trade very much if this spirit continued to operate. The Navy was to be increased to forty or fifty ships "in the course of the year & surely we are capable of doing much more." Britain and every anti-French statesman should welcome the late news from America. With the European balance so even, the naval strength of the United States would be important. If the Americans had thrown their weight on the other side "G. B. must have yielded to so much discouragement" (here he was considering the naval mutinies and the troubles of the Bank of England). But, together, the British and the Americans "can command the ocean in opposition to all Europe, Russia alone excepted . . ." If the war lasted "several years" Britain and the United States could engross the trade of America and Africa, and of the best part of Europe and Asia. The French colonies would admit their traders from sheer necessity.[8]

Even apart from its interesting prophetic juxtaposition of the United States, Great Britain, and Russia, this was a very interesting letter, from one leading mind of Federalism to another. It frankly admitted American sea power was a make-weight for Britain and was to benefit the mercantile community—mostly Federalists, of course. On the floor of the Congress these were things only claimed by Republicans and always denied by Federalists. Alfred Thayer Mahan later saw the economics of the matter and observed that French commercial strategy had been very ill-advised. With French merchants hunted off the seas only American merchants remained to carry for France. Having alienated the Americans, France was to suffer more from the absence of the American merchant fleet than from the presence of the American public fleet.[9] In Philadelphia the British Minister, Robert Liston, saw the dawn of a new day and wrote to the Royal Navy commanders in the West Indies. The substance of his circular was: the United States is actually although not professedly at war with France; beware of angering our new ally.[10]

Benjamin Franklin Bache's Philadelphia *Aurora* still tried to discredit the naval policy. He undertook to answer Webster by asking, if the British could not defeat France how could the United States? Would it not be better to be friendly with France? A navy sufficient to defend American trade would cost ten times what the trade was worth. It would be better to abandon the sea; unlike Britain, the United States did not depend on it.[11] A few days later he published a letter which he claimed was from a Virginian in the Congress to his constituents: The warships voted by the Congress would be insufficient to do more than provoke the enemy. It would be better to spend the money for defense on land. Manning the fleet would pose a special problem. Laborers were making twenty-five to thirty dollars a month; the Navy proposed to pay fourteen dollars, but Great Britain pressed men at six dollars. How would the United States enlist seamen except by the intolerable method of impressment?[12] But the anti-naval voices were drowned out.

On the last day of June, in Committee of the Whole, the House of Representatives began to consider yet another bill for the protection of commerce. The principal effect of this new measure would be to "unleash" the Navy, to allow it to take armed French ships in any sea, not merely in the waters near the United States. It also proposed to allow the commissioning of American privateers. Peleg Sprague of New

Hampshire moved to throw off all restrictions by allowing the capture of all French ships, whether armed or unarmed. Enactment of this policy would have changed the nature of the quasi-war by completely abolishing its defensive character. This proposal lost 32–41.[13] The project for encouraging armed merchantmen to become privateer hunters, which had failed a few weeks earlier, had received twenty-eight votes. Now the proposal to allow attacks on all French vessels had the support of thirty-two. The "war party" had gained four votes.

Samuel Sewall of Massachusetts, chairman of the House's naval committee, made it clear the bill as written would allow privateers to take all property shipped from French ports, regardless of the nationality of the owner. It would apply, said Samuel Smith of Maryland, to wine shipped to Denmark, the property of a Dane in Bordeaux. This legal point aroused a storm in the Republican minority. Smith had made it plain the Federalists were trying to enact legislation solely to damage France, going far beyond the ostensible purpose of protecting American commerce.[14] On this note the Committee of the Whole rose for the week-end.

On Monday, 2 July, the debate raged around the question of privateering, which the opposition said was an avowedly belligerent measure, not one of self-defense. There was little French commerce on the seas and disappointed American privateersmen would be strongly tempted to prey on neutrals. The proposition was, claimed Samuel Smith, a preliminary test vote to determine whether a declaration of war would pass. The dilemma posed by the Federalists, to declare war or to pay tribute, was artificial. Negotiation was not yet impossible.

Federalists supported the privateering section of the bill by charges that the Republican speeches would weaken the country's will to defend itself. Robert Goodloe Harper of South Carolina said it was a legal question. Without such commissions the crews of American merchants would not be treated as prisoners of war but as pirates. At the moment "our merchants find a difficulty in obtaining crews." As to war, it was not in the power of the United States to decide it. "War is made upon us," he cried, and he called on the spirit of 1776 to guide the nation. W. C. C. Claiborne of Tennessee said Harper showed "the liveliness of . . . fancy; but he had declined the use of any arguments." Samuel Dana of Connecticut defended Harper by an attack on Claiborne: if Claiborne spoke so violently when favoring peace, "the most extravagant fancy could not easily imagine what must be the manifestation of his zeal when in favor of war."

The debate continued in this unrewarding fashion for some time until finally a motion to strike out the authority to commission privateers was lost, 38–41. A motion to give a bounty on captures, at so much for each gun of the captive, next lost 37–43. The Committee of the Whole rose and reported the bill to the House.[15]

In the House the motion to strike out the privateering section was renewed and lost again, this time by a vote of 39–43. The sectional balance was the same balance previously established on naval bills, except that New York's delegation divided evenly, and Pennsylvania's vote was six ayes and four noes. Sprague also renewed his motion to allow American ships to take all Frenchmen whether armed or unarmed. There being more members present than on the previous Saturday, he lost by a wider margin, the vote being 31–52. Sprague's was a pretty advanced measure, calling for naval war in every respect except a declaration. Therefore the roll-call showed the sectional strength of the war party.

	Ayes	*Noes*
New England:		
New Hampshire	4	0
Vermont	1	1
Massachusetts	7	4
Rhode Island	1	1
Connecticut	4	3
Total	17	9
Middle States:		
New York	3	4
New Jersey	1	2
Pennsylvania	5	5
Delaware	1	0
Maryland	2	5
Total	12	16
Southern States:		
Virginia	1	10
North Carolina	0	9
South Carolina	1	3
Georgia	0	2
Total	2	24
Western States:		
Kentucky	0	2
Tennessee	0	1
Total	0	3
Grand Total	31	52

The extremists had gone too far. The Chairman of the naval committee voted no, the Massachusetts phalanx was shaken, and stout Connecticut barely produced a majority for it. Pennsylvania split and New Jersey went over to the "Jacobins." As New England weakened, the middle states refused to go along, and the south stood firm and even picked up the vote of the North Carolina Federalist, William Barry Grove.[16]

It is possible to count fifteen members who had always voted "navy" but would not now vote to make all French vessels fair game. If eleven of them had stayed in their usual column the amendment would have carried. In a sense this was the closest to a "test vote" on full war which was had in the House. Very likely a vote on a declaration of war would have been much the same, unless the declaration had been requested by President John Adams.

The bill passed the House on 3 July, without a roll-call.[17] The Senate accepted it by a vote of 18–4, without amendment.[18] "An act further to protect the commerce of the United States," approved 9 July 1798, extended the field of naval operations to the seven seas. It had eight sections, as follow: (1) The United States Navy could take armed French ships anywhere. (2) Letters of marque and reprisal might be issued to privateers with the same powers, under regulations to be made by the President. (3) The paperwork necessary for ship owners to qualify for these commissions was detailed. (4) Privateers must post bonds to observe federal laws and treaties. (5) French ships and French property would become wholly the property of private captors. (6) Recaptured American ships must pay a salvage claim of from one-eighth to one-half the value of the property recovered. (7) A procedure for cashing-in on prizes was provided. (8) Captured crews might be incarcerated.[19] President Adams sent the naval order to capture in all seas on 10 July, by way of the Secretary of the Navy, Benjamin Stoddert.[20]

The Congress next proceeded to give the Marines a standing organization. Men called Marines had served in the Treasury Department's revenue cutters in the early 1790s. The Naval Act of 1794 had provided for Marine units in the frigates then authorized. These were Marine "quotas" and could not literally be called Marine "detachments" because there was no corps from which they were detached. A lieutenant of Marines was commissioned for *Constellation* on 16 March 1798, and one each for *Ganges* and *Constitution* on 5 May. The first known enlisted Marine of the United States Navy under the Federal government was enrolled on 7 May.[21]

The House naval committee recommended on 22 May the establishment of the United States Marine Corps. Chairman Sewall argued the advantage of having all Marines in one corps as part of the military establishment on the ground it would make for better order and economy than were possible when the men were scattered in "minute detachments." The Marines would be ashore occasionally, could be kept in better discipline, and could be used wherever needed.[22] He might have added that uniformity of regulation and tactical doctrine would be impossible so long as each unit was independently commanded by its ship-captain, nor would the service offer much attraction to young men seeking military advancement.

Sewall proposed the following resolution:

> *Resolved,* That, in addition to the present Military Establishment, there shall be raised a battalion, to be called the Marine Corps, to consist of a Major, and suitable commissioned and non-commissioned officers, five hundred privates, and the necessary musicians, including the marines now in service; and the marines which shall be employed in the armed vessels and galleys of the United States shall be detachments from this corps.[23]

The discussion of this resolution concerned the cost of the Corps and the function of the battalion commander. The sponsors claimed the only additional cost would be the Major's salary, and he would be very useful to superintend, hear complaints from his men, and recruit.[24] There was only slight objection but the bill which Sewall was instructed to write and which quickly passed the House slumbered until July. It then completed its passage of the Senate without contest.[25]

"An act for establishing and organizing a Marine Corps," approved 11 July 1798, provided a table of organization for 881 officers and men, fixed their pay and enlistments, and authorized the President to form them into detachments. These "detachments" might replace the "quotas" earlier assigned to the ships, at the discretion of the President. The Marines were to take the oath and obey the regulations of the Army and the Navy. Immunity from arrests for debts or violations of contracts was provided for the Marines, and also extended to soldiers and seamen. The President was free to use the Marines to garrison fortifications.[26]

The headquarters of the United States Marine Corps was established at Philadelphia under the "Major Commandant" on 23 August, and a camp was pitched near the city "a few days later," [27] probably to receive recruits.

On 3 July Harper made a push for an even larger armed force. He offered seven resolutions, most of them approving an enlargement of the Army, but the last two recommended the acquisition of up to ten more vessels of at least thirty-two guns each (which would be in the *Constellation* class), and "one or more dock yards." [28] The Philadelphia *Aurora* quoted Representative William Shepard of Massachusetts as saying Harper brought out resolutions as a sow did, a litter at a time. And, said editor Bache, like a sow, he often eats them, too. "The first question in the morning at Congress Hall is 'Do you know if Harper is likely to *farrow* today?' "[29] Apropos of Harper, Bache once said he was bellicose in the Congress because he wished to be a General. Late in July Major General Alexander Hamilton wrote to Lieutenant General George Washington a letter which showed Bache had made a shrewd hit.

> Mr. Harper, of the House of Representatives, is desirous of being in your family. He is a man of very *considerable talents* and has the temper of a soldier. The shade of his useful qualities is *vanity*, but I think the good much outweighs the ill. Pardon this liberty in a point so delicate.[30]

Whether Harper caused it can not be known, but the Congress, on the last day of the session, appropriated six hundred thousand dollars to build three ships of not less than thirty-two guns each.[31] Thus were revived the frigates originally authorized in 1794—*President, Congress,* and *Chesapeake*—on which work had been stopped after their keels were laid.[32] While this appropriation bill was still pending, Bache mocked the current popular slogan, "Millions for defence, but not a cent for tribute." Three years ago, he wrote, the Americans paid tribute to Algiers and gave the Dey a ship to punish them with if they did not behave according to Algerine standards. He said the total cost of the Barbary diplomacy had so far been $1,623,178.88, with annual tribute yet to be paid.[33] This was an indirect way of reminding what readers he may still have had that the quasi-war with France was to be financed in 1798 by two million dollars of property taxes and a five million dollar loan.[34]

Several bits of "housekeeping" legislation were enacted in this session to fill in the broad outlines of naval policy. An earlier act which limited the export of arms and ammunition, and encouraged their importation, was extended.[35] An act was passed for the relief of sick and disabled seamen.[36] The Department of the Navy was given an accountant, and a purchasing and disbursing procedure,[37] and departmental salaries were appropriated.[38]

In scrutinizing the Army appropriation the House made the surprising discovery that the Army, in the west, was becoming amphibious. The Quartermaster estimates of 1798 included money for the captain and crew of the sloop *Detroit,* repairs for the sloop, construction of a schooner and a packet boat then building at Detroit, the pay of the captains and crews of the boats a-building, four galleys under construction at Pittsburgh, the pay and subsistence of their 240 men, a shipyard and wharf at Pittsburgh, several "Kentucky boats," some keel boats, and money for the hire of private boats and boatmen. And the Army intended to devote an unspecified share of its money appropriated for materials, tools, freight payments, and hardware, to these amphibious purposes. Some of the Representatives were irked to learn of this frontier aquatic program since none of the building had been expressly authorized by Congress.[39] However, in June the Army appropriation act was written so as to include these items.[40] The fruit of the program was reported in the press when the galley *John Adams* was launched on 9 June at Pittsburgh: "A handsomer or tighter boat never stemmed the tide, or floated with the current—well built, well manned and well armed, she is able to protect the weak or humble the haughty." The galley *Senator Ross* was to be launched in about six weeks.[41]

The last large issue to occupy the attention of this session of the Congress was the revival of a question which had come up in the Committee of the Whole at the time when the bill to allow naval captures anywhere was under consideration. At that time it had been moved to give a bounty on captures of French ships, at so much for each gun of the ship taken. The motion had lost, 37–43, on 2 July.

The whole business had been anticipated by a Wilmington correspondent of the Philadelphia *Aurora* a fortnight earlier. He suspected Harrison Gray Otis, Representative from Massachusettes "perhaps . . . wants war because his kinsman and namesake at Newburyport, may go a privateering, and feather his relative's nests by taking French *guns,* for we understand here that a bounty is to be given for every gun which shall be taken."[42]

The matter was brought up in the Senate on 9 July, by Benjamin Goodhue's naval committee, which brought in a bill to encourage captures in that matter. On 11 July it passed, 16–4.[43] The bill applied to armed French vessels when brought into the United States by armed ships owned by United States citizens. The owner and the captain were to receive the bounty. It rated guns from two-pounders at fifty dollars to those above twelve-pounders at $250. There would be no payment until the condemnation was certified by the judge of the prize court, and the number and size of the guns stated in the certificate.[44]

When the bill came down stairs to the House, Carter B. Harrison of Virginia promptly moved to postpone it until the first Monday of November. He lost, 31–38. When the bill was called up the next day, 12 July, Nathaniel Macon of North Carolina moved to postpone it until the next session. He too last, this time by 32–37.[45] (A vote had switched —perhaps some member wished to go home.) It went swiftly through first and second reading. Then, on third reading, Joseph McDowell of North Carolina attacked it. He said it would open the door to frauds because ship owners would connive with their friends in the West Indies to throw vessels and arms in their way—"our Treasury would be drained to an extent which no man could at present foresee." The bill was useless and would not be financially profitable to any honest man. A call was made for the yeas and nays and it was killed on the spot, 34–36. Two regular Federalists voted no, George Dent of Maryland and Grove of North Carolina.[46] If they had stayed with their usual allies the bill would have passed.

At this point Sitgreaves arose and tried a new "ploy." He said there were thirteen members in town who were absent on that roll-call. He proposed to appoint a committee to bring in a slightly different bill in the hope attendance would be better. This propositon would not go down. Even some of those who favored the bill murmured at the idea because, they said, if the practice were adopted there would never be an end to any congressional business. On the next day Sitgreaves forced a vote on his plan but lost, 40–41.[47] And thus died the "bill to encourage captures."

To judge by the existing record of the debates, McDowell beat it single-handed. But Fisher Ames (far away in Dedham) said it was Harper's fault the bill failed to pass. It "was negatived by Harper's perverseness . . . H. is a fine fellow, but praise has half spoiled him, and made him sometimes cold and sometimes opposed towards right things originated by others." [48] Both Hamilton and Ames had testified to Harper's vanity. Let Gallatin now make it unanimous: He said Harper was "as great a bungler as ever I knew, very good hearted, and not deficient in talents, exclusively of that of speaking, which he certainly possesses to a high degree; but his vanity destroys him." [49] What Harper had done to hinder the passage of the bill remains a mystery. He voted for it but did not say anything significant in its support. Perhaps the silence of the chairman of the Ways and Means Committee was thought to be fatal.

Looking back, the value of the bill to encourage captures seems doubtful, but Ames was sure it was needed.

> It would have wakened the privateering spirit, cut out work for the active, warmed the frigid, and placed our safety beyond the dreaded stroke of French coaxing. I own my own hope is that we are beyond it. But as the trade of France affords no prizes, something was needed to give a spur, instead of the usual one. A bounty per gun was that spur. I am afraid of inertness, of languor, of the collapsing of the national spirit . . .[50]

The brilliant, hypochondriac Ames always found it difficult, if not impossible, to believe any other man's patriotism was the equal of his.

The last fortnight of the second session of the Fifth Congress, the first two weeks of July, had seen the naval policy of the young republic strengthened and made more vigorous. In eight days, from the sixth to the fourteenth, the Navy had been authorized to take French armed ships anywhere, privateering was legitimized, the Marines were molded into a Corps, and money was appropriated to double the number of the country's super-frigates. The only preconcerted naval measure with organized support which failed to pass was the bill to pay bounties for captured French ships according to the numbers of their guns, and this was not an essential of the program. A new Navy had been born and a naval war begun.

One more question remains to be examined: why the sea war with France remained undeclared. This peculiar state, between war and peace, was unwelcome both to the Republicans who wished peace and to a sect in the Federalist Party who wished to make it war outright. This Federalist faction is usually called the Hamiltonian Federalists but in this instance Hamilton was not one of them, nor was his successor and liege-man in the Treasury, Oliver Wolcott, Jr.

The extreme Federalist group had a trident policy: to make an alliance with Great Britain, to cooperate with Britain in a scheme to conquer South America, and to acquire Louisiana and the Floridas. Any practical step toward any of those goals would necessarily be based on a declaration of war with France.[51] As of 1 July Senator Theodore Sedgwick of Massachusetts thought to declare war would be the wisest policy. Some Federalists, he wrote, feared a declaration would allow the Republicans to divide the country into a peace party and a war party. He thought not. If there were to be no declaration people might still rely on the Republicans to prevent one; if there were a declaration the people would elect the men best qualified to direct a war. He told the United States Minister in London, Rufus King, the measure might come up in a few days. They did not wish to carry it in the Senate only to lose it in the House, so it would probably be tried in the House first. By his calculation every Federalist in the Senate except William Bingham of Pennsylvania would vote aye.[52] Manning J. Dauer believes these early days of July 1798 saw the closest approach in American history to a declaration of war without a prior request from the President.[53] On Independence Day Senator Lloyd of Maryland, the sponsor of the Sedition Bill, wrote to his old friend, George Washington:

> I fear Congress will close the session without a declaration of War, which I look upon as necessary to enable us to lay our hands on traitors, and as the best means that can be resorted to, to destroy the effect of the skill of the [French] Directory in their transactions with Mr. Gerry.[54]

What the gentleman from Maryland really wished, it is obvious, was to declare war on the Jeffersonian Republicans. As of 9 July Abigail Adams had about given up the Congress—it was too timid to declare war.[55] Apparently the crisis had come and passed, in the first nine days of July. What had happened?

It is certain the Federalists of the Congress had caucused on the subject. The date is not precisely known, but it was very likely in the first days of July. Manning J. Dauer believes it may have been immediately after 5 July,[56] but the tone of Lloyd's letter to Washington shows it might have been a day or two earlier. Bache's *Aurora,* on 14 July, said the "tories" caucused and found they lacked ten votes. Thomas Jefferson collected hearsay of the episode; one of his second-hand authorities said the war group fell five votes short. The British Minister Liston reported to the Foreign Office that the Federalists were "mortified" when, in caucus, their calculations showed they did not have the votes needed to carry a declaration.[57] And thus passed the best chance of the Federalists declaring war.

They failed because they did not have leadership of national stature in their movement. A declaration of war was not wanted by President Adams, nor by Hamilton, nor by Wolcott. Fisher Ames wanted it, but knew it was not politic—and anyway he was at home in Dedham. George Cabot wanted it but was too indolent to do more than write querulous letters bemoaning its lack. Without either Adams or Hamilton the movement was hopeless.

Adams took the result of the caucus as a confirmation of his policy of seeking "reconciliation without debasement."[58] Adams thought Hamilton wished war[59] but he was mistaken. Sometime between 24 January and 15 Febuary Hamilton had written to Secretary of War James McHenry giving his reasons against a formal declaration of war. There would be no profit in it—France had no trade to capture, no territory to conquer which the United States would wish to keep. Meanwhile "a mitigated hostility" left the door ajar for future negotiations.[60] (In November 1798, Hamilton's Philadelphia echo, Secretary Wolcott, gave the identical idea to the President,[61] *after* the President had made up his mind not to ask the Congress for war.) Independently the two front rank leaders of the Federalist Party had decided against a declararation of war.

Ames's view was a curious blend of military exaltation and practical politics. He wrote to Secretary of State Timothy Pickering: Although the United States could not declare war it could enact the effects of a declaration, one by one. "Wage war, and call it self-defence . . ." It must be done in a hurry "or we shall be lost." Britain could blockade the French ports while the United States cleared the French out of the North American and West Indian waters. "My faith is that we are born to high destinies." [62]

There was to be regret at the failure to declare war. For example, George Cabot mourned the decision not to try to declare war. A declaration would have clarified every man's duty and, he seemed to say, the Republicans could have been extinguished.[63] Sedgwick thought a declaration would have made the Sedition Act unnecessary. Without it "we might have hanged traitors and exported frenchmen." [64]

But all of this careful, and sometimes spiteful, calculation was irrelevant to the job of the United States Navy. Secretary of the Navy Benjamin Stoddert went into the matter as far as the Navy needed to go: "Congress will break up on Monday, without a declaration of war against France. We shall not on that acct. be the less at War, against their armed vessels." [65] Senior Captain Barry and the other officers commanding at sea had a simple doctrine to follow: ignore unarmed Frenchmen, take or sink armed Frenchmen.

NOTES FROM PAGES 186 TO 198

1. Philadelphia *Aurora*, 3, 11 July 1798.
2. New York *Commercial Advertiser*, 23 June 1798.
3. *Ibid.*, 29 June 1798.
4. Philadelphia *Porcupine's Gazette*, 3 July 1798.
5. *Ibid.*, 7, 9 July 1798.
6. New York *Commercial Advertiser*, 25 June 1798.
7. *Ibid.*, 28 June 1798.
8. Cabot to King, 2 July 1798, Rufus King, *The Life and Correspondence of Rufus King*, ed. C. R. King, 6v. (New York, 1894–1900), II, 354–355. Hereafter cited: King, *Life and Correspondence.*
9. Alfred Thayer Mahan, *The Influence of Sea Power upon the French Revolution and Empire* (Boston, 1894), 259.
10. Liston to Royal naval commanders on the West India station, 29 June 1798, U. S. Miscellany, Box 2, 1797–1816, Library of Congress. Hereafter abbreviated: LC.
11. Philadelphia *Aurora*, 28 June 1798.
12. *Ibid.*, 30 June 1798.
13. 5 Cong., 2 Sess., 30 June 1798, *Annals of the Congress, 1789–1824*, ed. J. Gales and W. W. Seaton, 42v. (Washington, 1834–1856), 2061–2062. Hereafter cited: *Annals*. All references below are to 5 Congress, 2 Session, 1798. Dates will be given where helpful to search.
14. *Ibid.*
15. 2 July, *ibid.*, 2067–2082.
16. *Ibid.*, 2082–2083.
17. *Ibid.*, 2083.
18. 3, 5, 6 July, *ibid.*, 597, 600–601.
19. *Ibid.*, 3754–3757.
20. Dudley W. Knox, ed., *Naval Documents Related to the Quasi-war between the United States and France*, 7v. (Washington, 1935–1938), I, 187. Hereafter cited: Knox, *Quasi-war.*
21. Clyde H. Metcalf, *A History of the United States Marine Corps* (New York, 1939), 28–31.
22. 22 May, *Annals*, 1784–1785.
23. *Ibid.*
24. 28 May, *ibid.*, 1835–1836.
25. *Ibid.*, 570, 571, 597, 600, 601, 1855, 2132.
26. *Ibid.*, 3774–3776.
27. Metcalf, *A History of the United States Marine Corps*, 28–31.
28. 3 July, *Annals*, 2084.
29. Philadelphia *Aurora*, 12 July 1798.

30. Hamilton to Washington, 29 July 1798, Alexander Hamilton, *Works*, ed. Henry Cabot Lodge, 12v. (New York, 1904), X, 303.
31. *Annals*, 3791.
32. James Russell Soley, "The Wars of the United States," in Justin Winsor, ed., *Narrative and Critical History of America*, 8v. (Boston, 1889), VII, 363.
33. "Theophrastus," and an editorial note thereon, Philadelphia *Aurora*, 11 July 1798.
34. James Schouler, *History of the United States of America under the Constitution*, rev. ed., 7v. (New York, 1894–1913), I, 415n.
35. *Annals*, 3721.
36. *Ibid.*, 3787–3789.
37. *Ibid.*, 3792–3793.
38. *Ibid.*, 3793.
39. 25 April, *ibid.*, 1542–1545.
40. *Ibid.*, 3736–3737.
41. New York *Commercial Advertiser*, 16 June 1798.
42. Philadelphia *Aurora*, 22 June 1798. The account from Wilmington was dated 16 June 1798.
43. *Annals*, 604, 605, 606–607.
44. Senate records, National archives.
45. *Annals*, 2173, 2176.
46. 11, 12, 13 July, *ibid.*, 2173, 2176, 2178.
47. *Ibid.*, 2180, 2181.
48. Ames to Gore, 28 July 1798, Fisher Ames, *Works*, ed. Seth Ames, 2v. (Boston, 1854), I, 236.
49. Gallatin to Hannah Gallatin, 19 December 1797, Henry Adams, *The Life of Albert Gallatin* (New York, 1943), 188.
50. Ames to Gore, 28 July 1798, Ames, *Works*, I, 236.
51. Manning J. Dauer, *The Adams Federalists* (Baltimore, 1953), 172.
52. Sedgwick to King, 1 July 1798, King, *Life and Correspondence*, II, 352–353.
53. Dauer, *The Adams Federalists*, 169–170.
54. Lloyd to Washington, 4 July 1798, Washington papers, LC.
55. Abigail Adams to Mary Cranch, 9 July 1798, Abigail Adams, *New Letters, 1788–1801*, ed. Stewart Mitchell (Boston, 1947), 201.
56. Dauer, *The Adams Federalists*, 225.
57. Thomas Jefferson, "The Anas," 10, 13 Jan., 24 March 1800, *Writings*, ed. A. A. Lipscomb, 19v. (Washington, 1903–1904), I, 430, 431, 436; Dauer, *The Adams Federalists*, 170.
58. Stoddert to Adams, n.d., John Adams, *Works*, ed. Charles Francis Adams, 10v. (Boston, 1850–1856), IX, 305n.
59. *Ibid.*, IX, 306.
60. Hamilton to McHenry, n.d., Bernard C. Steiner, *The Life and Correspondence of James McHenry* (Cleveland, 1907), 292.
61. Wolcott to John Adams, Nov. 1798, George Gibbs, *Memoirs of the Administrations of Washington and John Adams*, 2v. (New York, 1846), II, 169. Hereafter cited: Gibbs, *Memoirs*.
62. Ames to Pickering, 10 July 1798, Ames, *Works*, I, 233–235.
63. Cabot to Wolcott, 25 Oct. 1798, Gibbs, *Memoirs*, II, 109.
64. Sedgwick to King, 20 Jan. 1799, King, *Life and Correspondence*, II, 515.
65. Stoddert to Barry, 13 July 1798, U. S. Navy, Miscellaneous manuscripts, LC.

XV

Reflections and Conclusions

In the Federalist Period naval policy was made in the Congress. The Congresses of the 1790s, although they received and occasionally heeded advice from outside, actually originated policy. Only the most technical details, such as the exact dimensions of ships and the precise tables of organization, were left to the executive. The policy which was enacted was the policy of the congressional Federalists.

The Federalists had to overcome much resistance to the idea of having any navy at all. Except for the feeling of national outrage which arose after the "X. Y. Z. Affair" the founding of a true navy might have been postponed for years. The United States owes its independence to the friendship of France in the 1770s and 1780s, and owes the Navy, which has preserved that independence, to the enmity of France in the 1790s. The Federalists must be applauded for their foresight in bringing forth a new naval power in the world. However, in cataloging their very real talents and virtues one must omit *savoir faire* and charity. The head says their naval policy was the correct one, but the heart secretly admires many of the effective strokes of the anti-naval bloc. The Federalists thought of themselves as the wise and the good, and they nominated themselves as superior persons, yet they behaved on the floor of the Congress with almost incredible arrogance and insolence. The Republicans had nominated themselves as the defenders of the common man, yet they were the gentlemen of the day. The debates in the Congress present a paradoxical contrast of the snobs and climbers of an "aristocratic" party baiting gentlemen of poise and assured social position with accusations of leveling, class war, and revolutionary subversion.[1] Nevertheless, it must be remembered, the Federalist Party founded the Navy and did it against strenuous opposition.

It is a temptation to believe the excitement over the "X. Y. Z. Affair" was factitious and contrived in order to promote a feeling of rage which would help to get naval legislation passed (among other motives) but the contemporary newspapers, private letters, public oratory, and congressional debates do not support the hypothesis. There were too many simultaneous addresses from towns and cities all over the country. Of course, a collection of these indignant statements is not the same as a scientific poll. They were written, no doubt, mostly by the local Federalist bigwigs, but their tone makes it certain the authors were genuinely outraged, and the opposing addresses and petitions were relatively much fewer. A feeling of the righteous wrath of moral indignation is apparently always necessary before the American people accomplish a national military purpose, and the anger over the "X. Y. Z. Affair" changed the large Federalist minorities of 1797 to the small majorities of 1798, in congressional roll-calls on what was pretty much the same schedule of legislation.

The Federalists had to work hard and skillfully in the Congress to get their plan enacted in its details. Albert Gallatin of Pennsylvania, the House Republican leader, twice made a complaint which illuminated Federalist congressional tactics. He criticized the Federalists for bringing in their bills one by one. It would have saved much time and breath, he claimed, if they had let the House see the program whole. (This was a challenge to the Federalists to attempt to pass a declaration of war.) It emphasizes for us the narrow majorities by which the Federalists were putting their bills across. It now seems must unlikely they could have carried a declaration of war. By presenting the Federalist mosaic fragment by fragment they could continue to protest their love of peace and at the same time squeeze their bills through as an unrelated series.

This method allowed them to keep their fingers on the public pulse. The series of bills might be considered a series of experiments to see how far they could push the House toward war. If they went too far, as they did in the bill to encourage captures, they would only lose the specific bill in issue.

The Federalists themselves were not united in favor of war. There were two groups, those for a-navy-with-war, and those for a-navy-without-war. The former were the most vigorous in the Congress and they carefully led the peaceful-navy bloc along as far as they could. But when the peace-Federalists had gone so far, they would go no farther. Naval war was had, but it was undeclared, and the gate was always ajar for negotiators to enter the scene.[2]

To fierce Jeffersonians a navy born of the session which also produced the impolitic Alien Acts and the despicable Sedition Act was a navy conceived in sin. In a republic, an army or a navy is an object of national pride or it does not exist. (In a monarchy, it can be an object of personal pride.) A good many of the Jeffersonian Republicans had little national pride. They were provincial-isolationists hoping for a happy future for a "little America." Neither a regular army or a regular navy could make an appeal to them. Their only contribution to the naval thought of the age was their continuous support, beginning in the first Congresses, of a system of passive defense which would use galleys, floating batteries, and shore defenses. This was a dubious, almost comical legacy, which makes a strange contrast to the greatness of the civil heritage they embodied for us in the flaming paragraphs of the Declaration of Independence and in the Bill of Rights. The Jeffersonian Republicans were "natural-born" civilians.

The Republicans said the Federalist naval policy was pro-British. It was. When Benjamin Franklin Bache's Philadelphia *Aurora* claimed the purpose of the Navy was to protect Anglo-American trade he was not giving the whole truth, but he had part of it. There seems no doubt the Federalists had decided to put the nation at the side of Britain. Both France and Britain seized any American ship which was acting in violation of their decrees (and some other ships, too). Great Britain prohibited Franco-American trade and the United States Navy was not instructed to do anything about British captures. But the British had a treaty with the United States, and kept up diplomatic relations. French excesses drove the Americans to choose amity with Britain and enmity with France.

Today the "X. Y. Z. Affair" perhaps seems an insufficient ground for war, and more of an episode of operetta villainy. However the positions of France and Britain, in relation to the United States, were basically different. France had publicly humiliated the sensitive young American republic, and diplomatic relations did not exist. Britain had shrewdly driven a very hard bargain with the Americans in the Jay Treaty, but it was drafted as an agreement between equals, and the British offered the possibility of the redress of grievances in her courts and in mixed commissions. There was no way to converse with the French except with the mouths of guns. Secretaries of State have always found it very hard to hold the attention of the American people long enough to explain the details of foreign deadlocks. Slogans do the job quickly, whether they read "Fifty-four forty or fight," "Containment," "Too proud to fight," "All out or get out," or, as in 1798, "Millions for defence but not one cent for tribute."

Even though the war was not declared as such, it was only a micron from real war. United States men-of-war were prohibited from seizing or sinking unarmed Frenchmen, but there were very few unarmed Frenchmen afloat—only little inter-island traders, canal boats, and shoal-draft coasters.

A close scrutiny of these years shows who were the fathers of the United States Navy. There was President George Washington who kept a construction program going from 1794 to 1797. President John Adams asked for a navy in 1797 and got it in 1798. Alexander Hamilton wrote numerous influential essays and letters on naval policy. Benjamin Stoddert, the first Secretary of the Navy, snipped and knotted the ravelings left to him by his untidy administrative forerunner. In the Congress the phalanx of navy-minded men was too large to be enrolled here, but William Loughton Smith of South Carolina carried the burden in the Third and Fourth Congresses, fighting for the naval measures to the last ditch in every case. Josiah Parker of Virginia, Samuel Smith of Maryland, and John Swanwick of Pennsylvania, were quondam Republicans in the House without whose aid Federalist naval proposals might have been treated even more roughly. Among the Federalists, Jeremiah Wadsworth of Connecticut, Fisher Ames, George Cabot, and Theodore Sedgwick of Massachusetts, and William Vans Murray of Maryland, contended energetically to create an American naval power.

Editors John Fenno (the Philadelphia *Gazette of the United States*) and Noah Webster (the New York *Minerva,* and, *Commercial Advertiser*) missed no opportunities to promote the naval interest of the country.

In the Fifth Congress Senator Benjamin Goodhue and Representative Samuel Sewall, both of Massachusetts, were chairmen of their chambers' respective naval committees, and Sewall, or some anonymous adviser, was singularly sharp at gauging in advance just how much the opposition could be made to accept. Robert Goodloe Harper of South Carolina, chairman of the House Ways and Means Committee, showed great zeal (but less skill) in promoting the creation of the Navy.

The names above make up a minimum list of those who can realistically be called the founders of the Navy. They number eighteen—fifteen Federalists and three somewhat irregular Republicans. That ratio illustrates the point that the Republican Party could take no credit for the happy outcome of this episode of the American political struggle. The founding of the United States Navy was a political act, even a partisan act, the work of the Federalist Party.

NOTES FROM PAGES 200 TO 203

1. Matthew Lyon, "the Beast of Vermont," was an exception to the general rule of Republican congressional civility, but the Federalists exerted themselves to provoke him to vulgar speech and violence. And Lyon, although defended by the Republicans, was not personally popular with them. He often failed to get a second for a motion or to get assistance on his calls for recording the yeas and nays

(which required that one-fifth of the members present agree to the request). Outside of Congress Hall, notably among editors, the Republicans seem to have been neither more nor less intemperate and abusive than their Federalist opponents.

2. The composition of the Federalist Party has been very well explained in Manning J. Dauer, *The Adams Federalists* (Baltimore, 1953), a book which is essential to our understanding of the politics of the 1790s.

Epilogue

The schooner *Croyable,* carrying a French letter of marque and reprisal, sailed north from the French islands in June, bound for the happy looting grounds off the coast of the United States. She was an old but fast little ship, originally built for the slave trade, rather too lightly framed to be a perfect man-of-war. Some of her later victims thought she was Baltimore built but they were mistaken.[1] She was pierced for eighteen guns on one deck but carried only twelve.[2] In her crew were sixty-odd Frenchmen, an American, an Englishman, and an English-speaking seaman of undetermined nationality.[3] Her captain was thought by some to be an Englishman [4] but actually he was a Spaniard. It was her First Lieutenant who was the Englishman, and he was said to be a deserter from the Royal Navy, wanted first for murder and now for treason.[5]

Somewhere east of Hatteras *Croyable* came upon and seized the ship *Alex Brown* of Newburyport, bound from Charleston, South Carolina, to Oporto. That was on 13 June. Two days later she took *Leander* of New York, on a passage to Havana. "Soon afterward" she fell in with two schooners sailing from Saint Croix to Massachusetts. These and "several others" were plundered and dismissed. Working north, she arrived off Delaware Bay early in July. There she took the ship *Liberty,* Captain Vredenburgh, from Philadelphia for Liverpool,[6] carrying, among other things, official dispatches from the Secretary of State to the American Minister in London. *Alex Brown, Leander, Liberty,* and perhaps others unknown to us, were sent back to the West Indies with prize crews.[7]

At ten in the morning on Friday, 6 July, *Croyable* met the ship *Alexander Hamilton,* bound out of New York for the Bahamas, off Egg Harbor, New Jersey (which would place her about six miles south or south-south-west of present-day Atlantic City). The American ship was detained four hours for search. The visitors took eighty-four bottles of wine, thirty dollars in cash, a ham, a case of razors, an "elegant embroidered fan," several pounds of prunes, and a box of candy "belonging to the British Consul at Baltimore." [8]

But *Croyable* had a rendevous with history. Up the Delaware River, at Philadelphia, the United States sloop-of-war *Delaware,* née *Hamburgh Packet,* commanded by Captain Stephen Decatur, Sr., cast off her lines on 2 July and moved down the river by easy stages.[9] Two days later she was at Newcastle, Delaware, having picked up her surgeon, Dr. Samuel Anderson, who made a pier-head jump at one of her anchorages.[10] On Thursday, 5 July, at eight in the morning, she weighed anchor and steered for the ocean.[11] Decatur gained the open sea on the sixth.

His first encounter was with the humiliated *Alexander Hamilton* on the seventh. The merchant captain, probably unshaven, smarting under the loss of his culinary trifles, his razors, elegant fan, and petty cash, hailed Decatur and gave him the story and a probable course to steer. The wind was from the south, by west, a fresh breeze, and the sky was cloudy. As well as one can calculate without precise fixes, this gave Decatur a broad reach and *Delaware* probably romped along at her maximum speed.

Off Egg Harbor *Delaware's* look-out spied four schooners. Probably the marauder was one of them. But which one? Decatur tried a *ruse de guerre* which worked. He changed course and stood off the land as if he were an alarmed merchant trying to avoid an encounter. *Croyable*'s captain rose to the lure and put out in chase. When closer, he saw to his dismay, that *Delaware* was an armed ship, and incorrectly guessed she was one of His Britannic Majesty's sloops-of-war which had outfoxed him. He turned and beat toward Delaware Bay where he would be safe from British attack in the territorial waters of the United States. It was no use. Decatur cut him off, fired one gun, and happily saw the Frenchman strike his colors.[12]

Delaware and *Croyable* sailed in company up the Delaware River, making very good time. Justifiably pleased with his work, Decatur left his ship and his prize at Newcastle and went overland to Philadelphia to deliver the tidings. The vessels went up to Fort Mifflin, the quarantine station.[13] The news was well received. The bells of the city were rung, not, as Editor William Cobbett put it, for a twelve-gun ship and "70 lousy Carmagnoles" but for the "beginning of the good work." [14] Grumpy Benjamin Franklin Bache wrote in his Philadelphia *Aurora* that the celebration was the merriment "of great numbers of the opulent mercantile interest of this flourishing city assembled at the Coffee house to reciprocate their congratulations on the occasion—*the taking of a French schooner* after a desperate action of one gun." [15] But Bache's jeer rang hollow. As for the administration's feeling, Secretary of the Navy Benjamin Stoddert promptly bought *Croyable* into the Navy (and named her *Retaliation*) after she had been surveyed by the naval constructor Joshua Humphreys. In Stoddert's mind her speed out-weighed the disadvantages of her age and lightness.[16]

The press soon had the story of the capture and the dialogue which occurred at the meeting of the two opposing captains. *Croyable*'s Spanish master was astonished to learn *Delaware* was a United States ship.

"I know of no war between the two republics," he said to Decatur.

"The French have been making war on us for a long time," replied his captor. "Now we find it necessary to take care of ourselves."

Just then the United States flag was broken out in place of the tricolor at the schooner's main peak. The privateer captain stared gloomily across the water to his former ship. "I wish she had sunk."

"She would have been," said Decatur, "if you had stood on board and fought her." [17]

This was the first capture by the United States Navy under the Federal government. Rarely does real life close a scene with such a grand curtain-line.

NOTES FROM PAGES 205 TO 207

1. Philadelphia *Porcupine's Gazette,* 9 July 1798.
2. Humphreys to Stoddert, 14 July 1798, Dudley W. Knox, ed., *Naval Documents Related to the Quasi-war between the United States and France,* 7v. (Washington, 1935–1938), I, 208–209; Philadelphia *Porcupine's Gazette,* 9 July 1798. The naval documents hereafter cited: Knox, *Quasi-war.*
3. Philadelphia *Aurora,* 14 July 1798; Philadelphia *Porcupine's Gazette,* 13 July 1798; Troup to King, 10 July 1798, Rufus King, *The Life and Correspondence of Rufus King,* ed. C. R. King, 6v. (New York, 1894–1900), II, 363.
4. Philadelphia *Porcupine's Gazette,* 10 July 1798.
5. Kitchin to Decatur, Sr., 12 July 1798, Knox, *Quasi-war,* I, 177.
6. *Ibid.*
7. Pickering to King, 9 July 1798, *ibid.*, I, 175; Boston *Columbian Centinel,* 14 July 1798, *ibid.*, I, 176. Captive *Liberty* was liberated by H. M. S. *Lynx* when intercepted with her prize crew on board.
8. Affidavit of the captain of *Alexander Hamilton,* and two others, 12 July 1798, *ibid.*, I, 178.
9. Stoddert to Truxtun, 2 July 1798, *ibid.*, I, 158.
10. Stoddert to Anderson, 2 July 1798, *ibid.*, I, 160.
11. John Mullowney, journal on board the frigate *United States,* 5 July 1798, *ibid.*, I, 169.
12. *Ibid.*, I, 174; Philadelphia *Porcupine's Gazette,* 9 July 1798, relying on Claypoole's Philadelphia *Daily Advertiser;* Philadelphia *Aurora,* 10 July 1798.
13. Pickering to King, 9 July 1798, Knox, *Quasi-war,* I, 175; Boston *Columbian Centinel, ibid.*, I, 175–176.
14. Philadelphia *Porcupine's Gazette,* 9 July 1798.
15. Philadelphia *Aurora,* 10 July 1798.
16. Stoddert to McHenry, 9 July 1798, Knox, *Quasi-war,* I, 183, Humphreys to Stoddert, 14 July 1798, *ibid.*, I, 208–209.
17. Boston *Columbian Centinel,* 8 Aug. 1798, in *ibid.*, I, 176. I have converted the report to direct discourse.

APPENDIX A

Naval Considerations in the Location of the National Capital

The story of the compromise of 1790 by which the site of the District of Columbia was chosen has been well and often told. ("You southerners vote for our bill to have the federal government pay the state debts and we'll vote to put the capital in the south.") But the fact that naval considerations figured in the First Congress debates on the subject is not so well known.

Before the present location was selected, the merits of Trenton, Germantown, Baltimore, and of some undesignated spot on the banks of the Susquehanna River were debated. Proposals to settle at Germantown, Baltimore, and on the Susquehanna were actually approved by one or the other chamber before the final choice of the Potomac Valley was made.[1]

In the course of congressional argument, which occupied parts of the first two sessions of the First Congress (September 1789, and July 1790) the question of naval defensibility came up several times. One of the first to speak on it was Representative Fisher Ames of Massachusetts, perhaps the ablest of the Federalists who served in the House. He thought the capital must be on or near the coast because, "Being more liable to invasion, Government should be near to protect it." But he rejected the Potomac Valley suggestion— "The Potomac is, in some degree, exposed to two dangers; by sea, and from the mountains. Large vessels can go to Georgetown. The events of the late war have proved that there is foundation for this apprehension." He favored putting the capital somewhere on the Susquehanna, "safe from the dangers of invasion by sea." [2]

Representative Thomas Hartley of Pennsylvania also supported a Susquehanna site. Since access by water was urged as a necessity he said "as to its convenience to the navigation of the Atlantic ocean, the distance is nothing more than to afford safety from any hostile attempt," [3] and John Lawrence of New York rose to say that he agreed.[4]

As the days passed, the Susquehanna location lost support and its movers went over to the defensive. Unable to convince their colleagues that their river was navigable they began to argue that a waterway was not essential.[5] When Marylanders suggested that some spot on the lower reaches of the Susquehanna, within the boundaries of the Old Line State, would be a better choice, Hartley scorned the notion—"a place exposed to the depredation of hostile nations." [6]

In the Senate the admirers of Germantown were strong enough to pass a bill, ten to nine (Vice President Adams cast a tiebreaking vote), designating that suburb of Philadelphia as the capital.[7] They could not recommend Philadelphia itself, partly because it contained a third of the wealth and population of Pennsylvania and they could not afford to give it away.[8] The Germantown choice was defended in the House, unsuccessfully, by Connecticut's Roger Sherman who, in listing its advantages, pointed to "good buildings, and convenience for arsenals and ship yards." [9] At this point William Smith of South Carolina charged Sherman with inconsistency. He had been a Susquehanna man before and had praised the river site because it was inaccessible to sea-going vessels. Sherman admitted he "had said the Susquehanna was safe from vessels of war" but it was not his idea of a good reason for choosing. He had addressed the argument to members who thought access from the sea was undesirable. He, Sherman, feared no invasion, indeed he expected no war for years to come.[10]

No decision was reached during the first session of the First Congress, but the matter came up again in the second session. A motion for Baltimore passed in the House by three votes. Some weeks later, Richard Bland Lee, a Virginian and a Potomac supporter, worked to undo that decision by arguing that Baltimore was just as far south as any likely Potomac site—hence not thereby more desirable to northerners—"besides being exposed by its frontier position on the sea." [11] He was followed by James Madison who said all the advantages of Baltimore were equally to be had on the Potomac, and the Potomac had some advantages unknown to Baltimore. "In respect to security from invasion, I aver the Potomac has the advantage also." [12]

An anonymous poet in the *Gazette of the United States* had tired of the naval debate months before Madison's unprophetic speech. He recorded his ennui in

THE RURAL RETREAT

O, WHAT a charming thing and pretty,
To have a noble Federal City!
Surpassing in a few years to come,

All that history says of Rome;
That ancient seat of arts and wars,
The mother of eternal jars!
Not near old oceans' margin built,
Where blood by hogsheads may be spilt;
Where ships which vomit smoke and fire,
May force the people to retire;
May set a scampering our patricians,
Cursing all maritime positions.
Besides, all sea port towns, we know,
The floods of horrid vice o'erflow [13]
. . .

It is a curious irony that Madison was later Commander-in-Chief of the armed forces of the United States when the British were repulsed at Baltimore but succeeded in occupying Washington-on-the-Potomac. Of course the naval argument was not decisive in the selection of the site of the District of Columbia, but one can not help wondering whether anyone ever reminded President Madison—after the defense of Fort McHenry and the battle of Bladensburg—of his earlier strategic theorizing.

NOTES FROM PAGES 209 TO 211

1. Irving Brant, *James Madison, Father of the Constitution* (Indianapolis, 1950), 276–281, 312–316; Edward Channing, *A History of the United States* (New York, 1932–1936), IV, 74–79.
2. 1 Cong., 1 Sess., *Annals of the Congress, 1789–1824,* ed. J. Gales and W. W. Seaton (Washington, 1834–1856), I, 868, 872, 873. Hereafter cited: *Annals.* The First Congress is covered in two volumes, hence the roman numerals.
3. *Ibid.*, I, 837.
4. *Ibid.*, I, 846.
5. *Ibid.*, I, 897.
6. *Ibid.*, I, 898.
7. *Ibid.*, I, 924.
8. William Maclay, *Journal,* ed. E. S. Maclay (New York, 1890), 274.
9. 1 Cong., 1 Sess., *Annals*, I, 924.
10. *Ibid.*, I, 924–925.
11. 1 Cong., 2 Sess., *ibid.*, II, 1662.
12. *Ibid.*, II, 1665.
13. *Gazette of the United States,* 12 September 1789. It goes on for about fifty more lines, getting steadily worse.

APPENDIX B

Hamilton's Naval Contribution to the President's Message to the Congress 7 December 1796

Below are reproduced Alexander Hamilton's undated memorandum to President George Washington, written between 15 November and 7 December 1796, and the President's remarks on the same subject in his Message at the opening of the second session of the Fourth Congress, 7 December. The Hamilton memorandum is in the Hamilton papers, Library of Congress. The President's message is collated from 4 Cong., 1 Sess., *Annals of the Congress*, 1593–1594, and *The Writings of George Washington*, ed. J. C. Fitzpatrick, 39v. (Washington, 1931–1944), XXXV, 314.

In the Hamilton text parentheses enclose words which were scratched out by the writer. The asterisk leads to a sentence which was written on the margin of the manuscript for insertion at that point.

Hamilton:

A systematic plan for the creation of a moderate navy appears to me recommended by weighty considerations—(A nation which carries on) A [*sic*] active external Commerce (ought not to leave it to the mercy) demands a naval power to protect it— * It is a truth which (our) our Experience has confirmed that the most equitable and sincere neutrality is not sufficient to exempt a State from the depredations of other nations at war with each other. It is essential to induce them to respect that neutrality that there shall be an organized force ready to (repel agg) vindicate the national flag—This may even prevent the necessity of going into war by discouraging from those insults and infractions of right which sometimes (illegible letters) proceed to an extreme that leave [*sic*] no alternative—The U States abound in Materials—Their Commerce fast increasing (in proporti) must proportionately augment

* Our relative situation likewise for obvious reasons would render a moderate force very influential more so perhaps than a much greater in the hands of any other power.

the number of their seamen and give us rapidly the means of a naval power respectable if not great—It is submitted as well deserving consideration whether it will not be prudent immediately and gradually to provide and lay up magazines of Ship Timber and to build & equip annually one or more ships of force as the developpment [*sic*] of resources shall render convenient & practicable—so that a future War, of Europe if we escape the present storm may not find our Commerce in the defenseless situation in which the present found it.

Washington:

To an active external Commerce, the protection of a Naval force is indispensable: this is manifest with regard to Wars in which a State is itself a party. But besides this, it is in our own experience, that the most sincere Neutrality is not a sufficient guard against the depredations of Nations at War. To secure respect to a Neutral Flag, requires a Naval force, organized, and ready to vindicate it, from insult or aggression. This may even prevent the necessity of going to War, by discouraging belligerent Powers from committing such violations of the rights of the Neutral party, as may first or last, leave no other option. From the best information I have been able to obtain, it would seem as if our trade to the Mediterranean, without a protecting force, will always be insecure; and our Citizens exposed to the calamities from which numbers of them have but just been relieved.

These considerations invite the United States to look to the means, and to set about the gradual creation of a Navy. The increasing progress of their Navigation, promises them, at no distant period, the requisite supply of Seamen; and their means in other respects, favour the undertaking. It is an encouragement, likewise, that their particular situation, will give weight and influence to a moderate Naval force in their hands. Will it not then be adviseable to begin without delay, to provide, and lay up the materials for the building and equipping of Ships of War; and to proceed in the Work by degrees, in proportion as our resources shall render it practicable without inconvenience; so that a future War of Europe, may not find our Commerce in the same unprotected state, in which it was found by the present.

The only thing in the President's text that is not in the Hamilton manuscript is the specific reference to the Mediterranean trade.

BIBLIOGRAPHICAL NOTE

Complete bibliographical data has been given in the notes at the first citation of any source, and has been repeated at the first citation in each succeeding chapter. However a brief commentary on a selected list of the most valuable materials may be useful.

The papers of Alexander Hamilton, in the Library of Congress (hereafter abbreviated, LC) contain a remarkable series of letters on naval policy by Hamilton and some addressed to him on the same subject. Jefferson's papers, LC, have some constructive letters up to about 1791, and thereafter are useful in illuminating the growing distrust of the Federalist policies, including the naval policy. His papers and those of James Madison and James Monroe, both LC, where they mention naval policy, are interwoven like basket-weave, and can hardly be studied separately. The papers of James McHenry, LC, are of course full of naval matters from 1796 to 1798, when he was at once Secretary of War and untitled commissioner of marine affairs. William Loughton Smith's papers, LC, are scanty but the few relevant papers of this navy-champion should not be ignored. The papers of George Washington, LC, are a treasury of all kinds of historical data owing as much to the large collection of letters to Washington from all quarters, as to Washington's own writings.

In the National Archives three collections are especially useful. The Senate papers and the papers of the House of Representatives, in the Legislative records, are necessary to a study of the life, growth (and death) of bills in progress through the two houses. The collection of Naval records in the National archives includes "Out-letters on naval affairs, 1790–1798," of the War Department before there was a Department of the Navy; these deal mostly with construction problems but are valuable as showing the mass of detail with which McHenry tried to cope.

There are some useful naval papers in United States miscellany, Box 2, 1797–1806, Division of Manuscripts, LC, and in the same place there is a richer collection entitled United States Navy, Miscellaneous manuscripts, 1775–1804.

Among the published public papers there are the *American State Papers*, 38v. (Washington, 1832–1861), Classes I, *Foreign Relations*, and VI, *Naval Affairs*, of which volume I of each class has the relevant reports of the executive to the Congress. The richest of all sources is the *Annals of the Congress, 1789–1824*, 42v. (Washington, 1834–1856) which reports the proceedings and speeches of the two chambers (with a few annoying *lacunae*). Charles W. Goldsborough, *The United States Naval Chronicle* (Washington, 1824), is a kind of historical scrap-book constructed by the energetic use of scissors and paste-pot, but the able compiler, who was for many years Chief clerk of the Navy Department, knew what was significant and has a few documents not easily available elsewhere. When Commodore Dudley W. Knox, U.S.N. (Ret.), headed the Office of Naval History he instituted and edited two magnificent series of naval documents which will be exploited by scholars for generations to come: *Naval Documents Related to the Quasi-war between the United States and France*, 7v. (Washington, 1935–1938), and, *Naval Documents Related to the United States Wars with the Barbary Powers,* 6v. and supp. (Washington, 1939–1945). Volume I of each of these generously conceived collections is essential to this study. One may be permitted to hope his successors will continue this sort of work. The oldest of the really useful collections of public documents is *State Papers and Publick Documents of the United States,* especially volume X, *Confidential State Papers* (Boston, 1819) which is convenient for the study of the diplomatic background of early naval history.

The published private papers of contemporary leaders are numerous and invaluable. Abigail Adams, *New Letters, 1778–1801,* ed. Steward Mitchell (Boston, 1947) gives the correspondence of the President's wife with Mary Cranch and is quite useful to the imaginary re-creation of the emotional atmosphere which shrouded the nation's political peak. Henry Adams, *The Life of Albert Gallatin* (New York, 1943) includes lavish swatches of Gallatin's correspondence and some penetrating observations on contemporary politics by Adams himself. The letterbooks of John Adams are in series II of the microfilm "publication" now in process under the auspices of the Adams Manuscript Trust and the Massachusetts Historical Society. They bring to light matters which have been hidden for over a century and a half. Later reels will be even more valuable, but until some scholar with a passion for anonymous drudgery gives us a calendar of the whole we will never be sure we have uncovered all possibly significant facts hidden in this vast national monument. The *Works of John Adams,* ed. Charles Francis Adams, 10v. (Boston, 1850–1856), are still very useful and have editorial notes which sometimes provoke the exploration of unsuspected avenues. The *Writings of John Quincy Adams,* ed. W. C. Ford, 7v. (New York, 1913–1917), help us to understand how the Federalists arrived at their official view of the foreign policy of the French Republic.

Fisher Ames, *Works,* ed. Seth Ames, 2v. (Boston, 1854), records the thoughts and feelings of one of the ablest of Federalists, and a strong navy-man. The letters to and from Oliver Wolcott, Jr., Secretary of the Treasury during the time of the birth of the Navy, are presented in George Gibbs, *Memoirs of the Administrations of Washington and John Adams,* 2v. (New York, 1846). Alexander Hamilton, *Works,* ed. Henry Cabot Lodge, 12v. (New York, 1904), has a selection of the correspondence for those who can not get to Washington to see the manuscripts, and is the most convenient collection of Hamilton's published polemic prose. Thomas Jefferson's works have been often published but never completely. Until the editors directed by Julian Boyd at Princeton complete their work on the Jefferson papers, the best printed collection will remain the *Writings,* ed. A. A. Lipscomb and others, 20v. (Washington, 1903–1904). Rufus King, *The Life and Correspondence of Rufus King,* ed. C. R. King, 6v. (New York, 1894–1900), is mostly letters to and from King, and very well edited. William Maclay, *Journal,* ed. E. S. Maclay (New York, 1890), records the acid thoughts of the only member of the first sessions of the Senate who is known to have attempted a complete record; in spite of defects, it is an absolutely necessary work. James Madison, *Writings,* ed. Gaillard Hunt, 9v. (New York, 1900–1910), and James Monroe, *Writings,* ed. S. M. Hamilton, 7v. (New York, 1898–1903), round out the published record of the members of the Virginia triumvirate who rarely made a decision without consultation. So far the most satisfactory published collection of important personal papers is the *Writings* of George Washington, ed. John C. Fitzpatrick, 39v. (Washington, 1931–1944), which obviates the necessity of consulting his work in manuscript, but it does not contain the even larger mass of materials addressed to Washington and which survive in the Washington papers, LC.

Although the newspapers of the 1790s cared little for objectivity, the two families of papers, Federalist and Republican, must be consulted. Within the families, they bear a monotonous resemblance to each other. Among the leading Federalist papers were the Philadelphia *Gazette of the United States,* the New York *Minerva,* later, *Commercial Advertiser* (Noah Webster's paper), the Boston *Columbian Centinel,* and the Philadelphia *Porcupine's Gazette* (William Cobbett's). The chief Republican organs were the Philadelphia *National Gazette* (Philip Freneau's), the Philadelphia *Aurora,* the New York *Argus,* and the Boston *Chronicle.* Other papers drew on them heavily and, therefore, are mostly derivative.

The controversies over the ratification of the Constitution (which include naval argument, of course) have been collected by Paul Leicester Ford, *Pamphlets on the Constitution of the United States* (Brooklyn, 1888), and *Essays on the Constitution of the United States* (Brooklyn, 1892), and in Jonathan Elliot, *The Debates in the Several State Conventions on the Adoption of the Federal Constitution*, 4v. (Washington, 1836). Probably the best edition of the classic letters of Alexander Hamilton, James Madison, and John Jay, is *The Fœderalist*, ed. Henry B. Dawson (New York, 1863). An important lesser known pamphlet is James Madison, *Political Observations* (Philadelphia, 1795), which, among other targets, attacks Federalist naval policy.

There are too many works of synthesis of the researches on the Federalist period to attempt a complete list, but some deserve special mention. There are two books which have been indispensable to this study. Manning J. Dauer, *The Adams Federalists* (Baltimore, 1953), explains the composition of the Federalist Party and, in tabular form, gives the voting records of the Congress on key issues; this information is invaluable to anyone attempting to delimit the several congressional factions. Harold and Margaret Sprout, *The Rise of American Naval Power, 1776–1918*, rev. ed. (Princeton, 1946), have fifteen pages on the subject of this book; they were the footing on which this structure was erected.

Gardner Weld Allen's two well-known works, *Our Navy and the Barbary Corsairs* (Boston, 1905), and *Our Naval War with France* (Boston, 1909), are still very useful. James Fenimore Cooper, *History of the Navy of the United States of America*, 2v. (Philadelphia, 1839), is more detached and critical than the works of his contemporaries on the same subject. Stanley Lane-Poole, *The Story of the Barbary Corsairs* (New York, 1890), explains why Europe tolerated Mediterranean piracy and how the Christian captives were treated. Edgar Stanton Maclay, *A History of the United States Navy from 1775 to 1893*, 2v. (New York, 1894), may be read with profit. There are other important secondary works for this study which are so well known to students of the early national period that they may be dismissed with the mention of the authors' surnames: Bassett, Brant, Channing, Darling, Link, Mahan, Malone, and Schachner. The omission here of other "classic" authors is not invidious.

A number of monographs have been very useful. Robert Greenhalgh Albion, "The first days of the Navy department," *Military Affairs*, XII (Spring 1948), 1–11, is provocative, although brief. Henry Jones Ford's "Timothy Pickering," in volume two of Samuel Flagg Bemis, ed., *The American Secretaries of State and Their Diplomacy*, 10v. (New York, 1927–1929), was useful, as was Bemis's *Jay's Treaty, a Study in Commerce and Diplomacy* (New York, 1923). R. V. Harlow well explains legislative practices in *The History of Legislative Methods in the Period before 1825* (New Haven, 1917). Howard Irving Chapelle, *The History of the American Sailing Navy; the Ships and Their Development* (New York, 1949), combines naval architecture and historical method in a most authoritative way. Ira N. Hollis, *The Frigate Constitution* (Boston, 1931), has some information on the contemporary tactical theories. R. W. Irwin, *The Diplomatic Relations of the United States with the Barbary Powers* (Chapel Hill, 1931), probably tells its story about as well as it ever will be told in the absence of any corpus of Arabic texts on the subject. Charles Oscar Paullin, "Early Naval Administration under the Constitution," *Proceedings*, United States Naval Institute, XXXII (1906), is a very durable and instructive essay. Franklin Delano Roosevelt, "Our First Frigates, Some Unpublished Facts about Their Construction," *Transactions*, Society of Naval Architects and Marine Engineers, XII (1914), 139–155, digests the War Department's ship-construction correspondence of the 1790s. James Morton Smith, *Freedom's Fetters, the Alien and Sedition Laws and American Civil Liberties* (Ithaca, 1956), gives the best available picture of the frenzy of public life during the months when the first national naval policy was being put into effect; on its own subject Smith's book is *the* definitive work. Bernard C. Steiner, *The Life and Correspondence of James McHenry* (Cleveland, 1907), is a solid, dispassionate study of the career of the last Secretary of War who was also required to manage naval affairs.

The writer may be permitted to notice some obvious gaps in our naval literature.

Operations and naval heroes have been and are being well studied. Policy and civilian leadership have been almost ignored, except for Mahan's treatises on grand strategy and the Sprouts's work. The field of American naval history would be much enriched by the production of studies of the thought and careers of the influential "navy-minded" Senators and Representatives. It might not be too much to hope for a collection of essays on the Secretaries of the Navy to match Bemis's ten-volume anthology of essays on the Secretaries of State. The naval theorizing of several Presidents suggests itself as another fruitful field of research; Washington's "naval genius" when an Army officer has been analyzed by Commodore Knox, but the next three Presidents all used the Navy in combat and a study of their thinking would probably be very rewarding.

Index